Swamp Ponderings

(THE BOOK)

By

R. P. Wildes

Order this book online at www.trafford.com
or email orders@trafford.com

Most Trafford titles are also available at major online book retailers.

Note for Librarians: A cataloguing record for this book is available from Library
and Archives Canada at www.collectionscanada.ca/amicus/index-e.html

Printed in Victoria, BC, Canada.

ISBN: 978-1-4251-8119-2 (sc)

ISBN: 978-1-4251-8120-8 (dj)

ISBN: 978-1-4251-8121-5 (e-book)

*Our mission is to efficiently provide the world's finest, most comprehensive book publishing
service, enabling every author to experience success. To find out how to publish your book, your
way, and have it available worldwide, visit us online at www.trafford.com*

Trafford rev. 11/04/2009

www.trafford.com

North America & international
toll-free: 1 888 232 4444 (USA & Canada)
phone: 250 383 6864 ♦ fax: 812 355 4082

SPECIAL DEDICATION

I would like to dedicate this book of *ponderings* to the special people in my life who made it all possible.

To my parents who loved me (no matter what) and raised me in a Christian home…who put up with the mischievous antics of an inquisitive lad…who corrected what they could in me so I wouldn't end up a hoodlum on skid row…who never stopped believing that God had something special in mind for me.

To my brother and sister who loved to play their little tricks on me…who bore the brunt of my joking around, and my home-styled experimentation…yet, loved me and defended me when it was called for.

To Brother Dave who was, and is, my spiritual mentor…who has remained a good example of Christian love and leadership…who, for many years, felt really bad about the *Shark's Tooth Island* incident, until I admitted it was all my fault!

To all my Sunday School teachers who prepared good lessons, then tolerated my interruptions through them…who were faithful to their called tasks and taught me many of the great truths of faith.

To all the "other" Church Folk who loved me, prayed for me, and, perhaps, even feared me; yet, helped me see that God's Family is made up of redeemed sinners saved by grace who bear one another's burdens.

To all my Grade School Teachers, elementary through high school, who thought they may have failed in trying to teach this ole swamp-marsh boy much needed knowledge…who took special interest in me, and continually nudged me towards learning more; and, to the patient Principals who supported their capable teachers' efforts…who took their turn in my instruction and correction…and, who hid that electric paddling machine <u>very</u> <u>well</u>!

To my Children who were raised by a quirky, somewhat strange; yet, hopefully, loving father…who allowed me to learn parenting skills as we went along…who were willing participants in many of my adult adventures and celebrations of life. To Robbie (the oldest, and prefers 'Rob' or 'Robert') who was born with a purple head shaped like a football, but rounded out later…who has, at times, tested the limits of my patience; but, whose heart is big enough to love his family and give the shirt off his back to help a friend. To Ansley who was the first born of twins making her the 'middle child"…who likes to talk straight to the matter of things…who practiced hard at being a bit more practical than the others…who loves being with her dad, and who, in her own way, loves her brother and sister more than she will admit. To Jessica, the second-born twin making her the youngest child, by default…who was our birth surprise shocking the doctor who exclaimed, "I think there is another one in there!"… who is not afraid to try challenging things…who loves being with her dad and enjoys being a loving part of this strange, yet fun-loving family.

To their spouses who didn't know, for sure, what in the world they were getting into when they married into this family…who, in spite of it all, still love their spouses and me…and, who have helped produce some beautiful grandchildren.

To my Grandchildren (in order of their appearance: Katiana, Emily, Rachel and Victoria) who have brought me great joy…who makes my heart melt with each smile, wink , giggle or laugh…who call me "Grandpa" with a loving desire to play.

To my extended family (the Wildes and the Lewis clans) who still claim me as part of their own...who love me without restrictions...who shared in many of my adventures and lived to tell about it!

To my Colleagues in God's _called_ Christian ministry...who know what it is like to minister in the Lord's name to <u>everyone</u> (even those that most would write off!)...who may not care for the hours, but love their ministry assignment enough to hang with it...who spend hours in preparation for two sermons and a Bible study each week... who are '_on call_' 24/7 for their flock's spiritual welfare... who try to balance the needs of ministry and the needs of family, without going crazy...who have befriended me, and put up with my countless swamp and marsh stories...who are not super-human; but, are super gifted by a super God...who shall always remain my spiritual brothers and sisters whom I love and respect, deeply.

All these wonderful people, and countless more, have made these stories possible. I thank and honor them all. Yet, there is One above <u>all</u> that I must thank and give honor to: my Lord and Savior, Jesus Christ...who offered His life in my place on a cross, and died for my sin...who redeemed me by His shed blood...who loved and delivered me through my circumstances, time and time again...who arose from the tomb victorious over the grave and will, one day, return for His Church...including me!

Thanks to all, and thanks to you for sharing in these _ponderings_.

R.P. Wildes,

The Swamp Ponderer

CONTENTS

ILLUSTRATIONS

(All illustrations were drawn by my children: Robert Wildes, Ansley Collins and Jessica Boland)

PREFACE

What is this book about? Oh, about 300 pages!

Oh! You mean, why should you read this book? Maybe, because it is about you...and me...and someone you know!

Swamp Ponderings was born out of the adventures and celebrations of life that could have happened to any of us. It is a true-to-life, humorous, swamp-styled compilation of ponderings of an inquisitive, mischievous, loving boy who grew up along the Georgia coast and the Okefenokee Swamp. It is a bit biographical, a bit enlightening...But, mostly, it is a collection of humorous stories that illustrate some great spiritual truths.

Swamp Ponderings is amusing to read. But, watch out! Occasionally, a _revelation_ of some kind will sneak up on you! Think of a _pondering_ as a modern-day swamp parable with a twist of humor.

This is <u>not</u> a theological treatise. It is a user-friendly account of how faith can inspire and sustain us through all of life's adventures.

Swamp Ponderings is a book you will enjoy reading. You may even want to share it with other _ponderers_ like yourself.

So, get ready to have fun celebrating life and rediscovering someone you know; maybe, even yourself!

Bro. Ron

About the author

The author, R.P. Wildes, was born in a car on the way to the hospital in Folkston, Georgia, and has been on the go ever since!

He was raised in St. Marys, a small coastal Georgia town. He grew up among the beauty of the historic "marshes of Glynn", majestic "Washington Oaks", and the colorful flora of the Okefenokee Swamp.

His formal education includes degrees from Camden County High School, Shorter College, Southeastern Baptist Theological Seminary and doctoral studies at Luther Rice Seminary.

He has been a pastor of Southern Baptist churches for over twenty years; and, has served as the Director of Associational Missions for the past sixteen years. He is a pastor, administrator, counselor, mentor, encourager, writer, Christian humorist, good friend, and a loving father to three wonderful kids, who amazingly turned out alright! Oh! And, he is a proud grandfather!

He has spoken in churches, civic clubs, social gatherings; and, on high school and college campuses in many of the southeastern States. His sermons, humorous stories and *scriptlets (a humorous story that illustrates a Scriptural truth)* are welcomed and enjoyed by all ages.

Many have called him a 'citified' swamp boy who sees and experiences life through a keen sense of humor. Local readers have enjoyed his writings for years, and have encouraged him to write more! His ponderings and 'scriptlets' have encouraged and inspired others, offering an excuse to smile, or even laugh, at ourselves.

If you wish to contact him, he would welcome your e-mails. You can send your comments, suggestions or requests, to t.turtle2@juno.com.

AUNT FRANKIE

Do you have kinfolk, or people that were presented to you as kinfolk, that no one could ever remember *how* they became kin? If you don't, then that makes my family a little more unique. I had kinfolk like that. The fact was, once you got into our family it was hard to get out! You could be born in, married in or drafted in as family! In order to get out, you had to *really* want to get out! A divorce, death or remarriage wasn't a free ticket out of our family circle. Once you became an aunt, uncle or cousin, you were always an aunt, uncle or cousin…for life!

Aunt Frankie was one of those who were, *somehow*, kin to us; but, no one could remember how. Of course, as a child, it really didn't matter to me *how* they were kin. When folks were presented to me as "aunts" or "uncles", by my loving parents, or grandparents, they were immediately accepted as such, without question. As long as I can remember Aunt Frankie was always my 'Aunt' Frankie. I never questioned it, otherwise.

She lived with 'Uncle' Johnny. I didn't question that, either! No one knew, for sure, if they had ever *really* married. This caused some "whisperings" and "snickerings" at family gatherings; but, I wasn't old enough for it to matter to me. Until the day the Lord took them to their eternal home, I loved them as my aunt and uncle.

Aunt Frankie was an unusually loving person. This surprised most folks, since her expression was often a stone cold poker face. Any family photo would show you what I mean.

She always had dark hair, 'brittled' by hairspray. No matter how old she got, her hair remained the same. No one ever caught her coloring her hair; and, Uncle Johnny never talked about it. In fact, he would never say anything to the contrary, or to embarrass Aunt Frankie. He, basically, said nothing at all! This caused some uncles to refer to him as a 'whimp'! Uncle Johnny, however, said it was due to love and respect.

To hear him say that, then look at her, you would have to agree that love was, indeed, blind. Aunt Frankie was <u>not</u> a beauty queen. Not in the least! She wasn't cute as a baby, nor as a child! Neither had she blossomed in her youth, then wilted later in life!

She was a short, stocky woman, and often referred to as being "homely". More bold relatives called her "ugly as homemade sin"! Now, I'm not sure how ugly "homemade sin" is; but, it must have been pretty darn ugly!

Her skin was darkened, dried and wrinkled from ages of farming in the hot sun. Ever since her childhood, she had always been known as a "snuffer". I don't remember a time that she didn't have a wad of snuff in her mouth, which always leaked down the corner of her mouth and onto her chin!

In fact, she bore a permanent brown stain from the corner of her mouth that streaked down her wrinkled chin a shade darker than her skin. It was caused by continuous snuff-juice leakage. Otherwise, she was always neat and clean; but, no amount of cleaning could ever remove the permanently discolored, brown streak!

Her teeth were, also, stained brown. They, often, had little patches of snuff on them. When she wasn't having a picture made, she smiled a lot. When someone brought out a camera, she stopped smiling and put on her "poker face".

When she spoke up close to you, or breathed on you, the smell of damp snuff was strong and hard to take. It was, almost sickening, at times. But, no one ever mentioned it to her.

What Aunt Frankie lacked in looks, she made up for it in love and kindness. Her opened arms of love, and kind spirit made her a very loveable person. The problem in loving Aunt Frankie was that she always wanted to plant a big kiss on your forehead or cheek.

Expressing family love was a common trait among the Wildes and Lewis clans. There is no doubt in my mind, that we are the better for it. All that hugging and kissing brought us closer together as a family. As loving as we were as a family, to stand there, and let Aunt Frankie hug and kiss you with snuff streaming down her cheek, was extremely difficult to do! It was, definitely, a true test of family love and acceptance.

I have to be honest. Not all my cousins could take it! Some of them ran when they saw her coming towards them with her arms opened wide. At times, it was obvious that it hurt her feelings; but, she never mentioned it; and, she never stopped trying to give out her love.

Maybe, that's why I stood there, held my breath and took it. She, always, gave out her love so freely. It was kind of sad that I was the only one who, continually, stood still to receive it. It got to where she seemed to seek me out for a loving greeting, which I willingly gave her. Some may have called it an act of courage; but, I'd rather look at it like Uncle Johnny did, as an act of love and respect.

In every other way, Aunt Frankie was a loveable, fun-filled character. She was <u>always</u> concerned about how you were doing, and all that had happened, since last time she had seen you. I took it as genuine interest. Some took it as an attempt to load up for gossip.

I didn't care. I was always willing to spill my guts in exchange for some of her homemade brownies or gingerbread! They were so good when baked fresh. I can still taste them melting in my mouth!

Although she was not a trained nurse, if you ever had an injury, or a "boo-boo", around her, she was quick to the rescue with some old timey, often homemade, remedy. She *believed* in castor oil and milk of magnesia! They were cure-alls for <u>many</u> ailments. She, also, used

<u>Stanley's</u> salve and mustard packs for rashes, burns and scrapes. There were times, after receiving some of her doctoring, that you felt like a garden salad; but, she never lost a patient!

Once, while fishing off of a bridge in Florida, her baited hook caught me in the head while she was casting it out. Her line was weighted down with a heavy sinker to keep the tidal currents from carrying it off. That made casting the line more difficult; of course, that didn't matter to her. She was always up for the challenges of fishing. With all her strength, she reared back, and let it fly.

In this case, her flight path was obstructed by my head! Her cast was so forceful that, when it caught the back of my head, it nearly took me into the river with it! When her rod and reel was forced out of her hands, she realized something was amiss! She became gravely concerned when she realized what had happened. She, even, forgot about her fishing rod, and left it dangling.

She, quickly, sprang into action attending to my aid. The shrimp-baited hook was imbedded deep into my scalp. Aunt Frankie took full charge of the rescue efforts. She, carefully, inspected the wound. Then, after making her assessments, she, carefully, pulled the hook out!

She cleaned the wound, as best she could. Salt water from the river was used to wash it out. Concerned about infection from the baited hook, she put a wad of her wet, gooey, dark brown snuff over the wound! Then, she wrapped her sweaty scarf around my head to hold it in place.

She insisted that I keep it just the way she had it! For the following few hours, she watched me like a hawk! She wouldn't let me touch it, and headed off any attempt to remove it. She said the wad of snuff would draw out any poisons or infections. I felt dirty and "icky" the rest of the day...but, it never got infected!

When you met Aunt Frankie and Uncle Johnny, you could see their unique nature and warm hearts. They, always, tried to make <u>you</u> feel special. Beyond the snuff breath, and brown drippings, they were a joy to be around.

Once asked how he could stand to kiss Aunt Frankie, with her snuff juice oozing out, Uncle Johnny responded with a smile, "Her kisses are sweeter than snuff." 'Nuff' said about that!

As I ponder it, now, I would have to say that you've got to love someone, *more than just a bunch*, to kiss them with a mouth full of snuff! If you stop and think about it, though, the Lord loves us even more than that!

The acts of sin we commit make us more filthy than snuff! Sin is like an eternal dirt that cannot be washed away with soap! Nor do good works cleanse it away! In fact, sin makes us appear worse than snuff drippings to a holy God! Yet, God loved us, so much, that He sent His Son to take our sin stains away! Now, that's pretty good Love!

Our kisses and hugs among family and friends are, usually, reserved for those we count as special. God counts us as special and has kissed us with His mercy and grace! Even while we were dirty! And, He wants us to do the same to others! For some of us that's pretty hard; because, our love is, too, conditional.

The Lord's love, mercy and grace are undeserved treasures. He loves us, warts and all! He proved that love by sending His Son, Jesus, to redeem us (John 3:16). Then, Jesus said, "Love one another as I have loved you" (John 15:12, NKJV). My guess is, God means for us to love each other…bumps, warts, snuff and all!

I wonder how well we are following His commands!

My cousins ran from Aunt Frankie's affections, and missed a warm all-embracing hug. It was a hug that expressed immeasurable love and acceptance. Because of their prudishness, they missed a true blessing. Be careful not to miss yours…And, may God bless you for it!

"Aunt Frankie was a snuffer-lover!"

Blowing Up The Commode

Finally, the first day of *real* school had arrived! I had been looking forward to this day for quite some time. I was anxious to begin the first grade! You see, kindergarten hadn't worked out for me. But, now, I was a year older. I had matured a lot since my failed attempt at kindergarten. I was much wiser, than I used to be. At least, that's what everyone had hoped!

I knew that going to *real* school was a more grown up thing to do; and, I felt pretty good about it. I was ready for it!

I had already pre-registered with my mom and dad. We had walked through the school and familiarized ourselves with the layout. I knew exactly where my classroom was located; where the lunch room was; and, which part of the school yard was designated as our play area. When mom drove me to school that first day, and opened the car door I knew, exactly, where to go. In her cautioning parental tone, she told me to go straight to my class, and *nowhere* else! That's <u>exactly</u> what I did! This was an exciting day for me, and I did not intend to ruin it!

Not everyone felt the same way as I did about school starting up. My best friend, Buttons, hated this day. He cried like a whipped pup when his mom tried to pry him out of their family car. He had a supersonic grip on the car seat, and wouldn't let go! I never realized Buttons was so strong! It took two teachers, and the principal, assisting his mom to force him out of the car!

He did not go quietly! He was kicking and screaming all the way as they carried him into the school building. Unlike me, he *had* gone to kindergarten! If that's what it had done to him, I was glad I was asked to leave!

I felt sorry for Buttons; but, it wasn't going to ruin *my* day. It was still going to be a grand day for me! I, soon, discovered that there were others who felt the same way. I met some other kids who were ready for it, just like me.

The first day of school was special. You couldn't help but notice that everyone was sporting brand new school clothes. It was quite a sight to see. Boys walked around like robots in their stiff new jeans. Girls pranced around in their new dresses, and dangled pretty ribbons in their hair.

Even *I* was showing off my new stiff jeans and a new <u>red</u> plaid shirt. (Mom had given up on lighter colors!) I wore my new <u>Keds</u> tennis shoes, which allowed me to jump higher and run faster than those who didn't have them. At least, that's what the commercial said!

Mom had even splurged and bought me a <u>Roy Rogers</u> book satchel. Some of the kids showed off their new lunch boxes; but, my <u>Roy Rogers</u> book satchel doubled as a lunch box, too! My sandwiches might have come out flat and my chips broken; but, the flavor of the food was never compromised. What can I say…my mom thought I was very special. In fact, I felt special!

Unfortunately, my first grade teacher was Mrs. Nemcheck. I say "unfortunately"; because, she had taught my sister six years before, and my brother three years before. Now she had me! She had, already, heard about my kindergarten experience. This made her <u>very</u> 'anxious' to see me.

It was her assignment to teach the "dummo" class made up of those who didn't go to kindergarten…or, who didn't complete it. I guess, for some reason, this hardened her as a teacher; because, she seldom ever smiled. She was very strict and held to the "letter of the law"! Her law, of course!

She was, already, convinced who the "trouble-makers" were; and, I seemed to be high on her list! Those on her list were assumed guilty before, ever actually, doing anything! Every question we asked, every statement we made was assumed to be a mask for some underlying, sinister plot. Of course, at times that was true; but, not all the time!

Whenever something *did* happen, she rounded up her usual suspects, and questioned us first. It put us under a lot of stress and strain. I began to wonder what my brother and sister had done to make her so suspicious!

I know this may be hard to believe; but, I <u>wasn't</u> *the top* nasty guy on her list! That was reserved for Russell. He was considered the <u>worst</u> one of all. In all fairness to the suspicions of Mrs. Nemcheck, Russell had *<u>earned</u>* his placement on her naughty list. She had failed him twice, already, due to bad grades and bad behavior.

That made him older and bigger than the rest of us. He, easily, intimidated others, forcing them to share their snacks and lunches with him. You know…I cannot recall him ever, actually, bringing a sack lunch to school! Yet, he <u>always</u> had plenty to eat!

Russell was in a constant state of readiness…he was, always, ready for a fight, or a 'scrap'! His attitude made him, easily, labeled as a "fight-for-nothing" kid. He would fight anyone at the drop of a hat! He seemed to stay angry most of the time, and took it out on weaker students. He didn't seem to care *who* he hurt, nor how! Whenever Mrs. Nemcheck needed an example of "bad examples", she, always, used Russell!

Russell lived in a duplex project housing located at the end of my street. When my cousin first moved to St. Marys, he lived in one of those duplexes. Right next door to Russell! When I visited my cousin, I would run into Russell. The summer before the beginning of school, we all played together quite well. The "bully" didn't come out in him, until school started.

Our most favorite thing to play was "Army". We used Russell's plastic Army men.   He had 'zillions' of them! Not only that; but, he had all the army stuff to go with them! We loved to set up the plastic men that had been preformed into various attack positions. We lined up the tanks, jeeps and cannons in attack formation; then, we would shoot them down with BB guns.

Our mortar and cannon fire was very realistic, too. We used live firecrackers, M-80's and cherry bombs! It was very realistic...and, really, a lot of fun!

As I have mentioned, outside of school, Russell wasn't, too, bad! His father, Ed, seemed a little odd, though. To me he seemed, almost... spooky! You see, Ed had been a demolition specialist in the *real* Army. It seems that he came to love his specialty too much. They said he didn't know when to stop blowing up things! After some therapy, the Army asked him to leave.

In his civilian life, no one wanted to hire him. His suspicious past haunted him. No matter how hard he tried, he couldn't seem to get his Army days out of his system. He, still, liked to blow things up! He kept all kinds of explosives around his house, and in his storage shed. He stockpiled a bunch of fire-crackers, cherry bombs, M-80's and 'other' *good* stuff.

He loved to bunch them together to make larger charges. He used them to blow up ant beds, pine cone piles and tree stumps. If you needed something blown up (legally), Ed was the one to call!

When our mortar and cannon rounds were depleted, Russell would put the 'five-finger discount' on some of his dad's stash. It made playing "Army" a little dangerous...and, a lot more fun!

Mrs. Nemcheck knew of Ed's "*problem*". He had been involved in a 'Fourth of July' incident that included Mrs. Nemcheck. (Some homemade rockets had burnt holes in her hanging laundry...and, melted some shingles on her house!) After that incident, she never trusted Ed, nor Russell. She <u>never</u> had <u>anything</u> good to say about them. Not <u>ever</u>!

In her teaching wisdom, she felt it was best to isolate Russell, from the other children. Anyone who tried to befriend Russell was warned to "stay away". If that didn't work, she would send home notes with noncompliant children who came, too, close to Russell, encouraging the parents to "talk" to their child about this "matter".

Anyone who failed to heed her warnings was put on Mrs. Nemcheck's '*suspicion list*'. In truth, I think most of the boys in her class, eventually, made her *suspicion list*, anyway!

At recess it was difficult for her to keep her eyes on us, all the time. When she didn't feel like watching us, she sat all the boys under an old pine tree and forbade us to move. It wasn't because we had done anything wrong. She just didn't want us to <u>*do*</u> anything wrong while she took a break!

Her actions were a mystery to us. We couldn't understand why she treated us this way. We felt it was, extremely, unfair to grant us a recess; then, deny us the privilege to use it. Not having much choice in the matter, however, we gathered into small groups under the shade that the old pine afforded us. We used the time under the pine to ponder.

We discussed many of the awesome mysteries of our universe: *Why* do girls giggle so much?…*Why* were some girls harder to talk to than others?…*Why* do "red bugs" like tree moss so much?…*How do* chiggers end up in the most embarrassing places to scratch?…Did the principal *really* have a paddling machine hidden somewhere on campus?…These were, but a few of the important mysteries addressed under the pines.

The pondering that got the most attention was: Why *were* the first grade restrooms located in the back of our classroom?? Every other grade got to leave their classroom and walk down the hall to the restrooms. *We* only got to walk to the back of the class! Somehow, this seemed unfair to us…extremely unfair!

Several suggestions were made as to how we could remedy the situation; but, they were, mostly, temporary solutions. We needed something more permanent! Something that couldn't be fixed in a day...or, a week...maybe, even longer!

One day as we watched Russell's dad blow up stumps, an idea popped into our childish minds: Why not blow up the commode!? Yea! That would do it! That would take some time to fix! It seemed like a good idea, at the time!

There was no doubt that Russell's dad had plenty of stuff to use for such a plan. If we were successful, it would, certainly, take a long time to repair. While repairs were being made, they would *have* to let us go to the restroom down the hall...I mean, the big guy's restroom would be our only option! Right! It seemed to be the perfect solution.

The more we talked about it, the more an organized plan began to take shape. The 'plan' was, mainly, Russell's idea that included a major role for me. It was a simple plan. Those, always seemed to work the best!

Russell was to "borrow" some of his dad's devices. At an opportune moment, he would place the devices into the commode tank located in the classroom restroom. *My role* was to light the fuse with the matches he would provide. It was not a perfect plan...at least not for me!

I went along with the 'plan' thinking he wouldn't *really* do it. Our "what if" talks continued for quite a while. Each time we talked about it, the 'plan' bothered me and excited him! For us to get the best benefit from our covert operation, it would need to be done on a Monday or Tuesday. That would allow us a few days to stroll the hallways, before they could fix the damaged toilet.

To my shock and surprise, one day Russell decided that the time had come to put the 'plan' in motion. The plan almost fell apart, however, when Russell's dad caught him trying to smuggle one of the devices out of their house. Ed demanded information; and, Russell sang like a canary.

Russell expected the worse. Ed angrily responded, "Don't you know these devices could hurt somebody real bad…Take this one, instead!"

He gave Russell a bundle of cherry bombs taped together, with a long synchronized fuse. Ed said it should crack the tank enough to ensure its shut down; but, he didn't think it would hurt anyone. At least, not badly!

When Russell got to school that day he was wearing a big grin and a bulging winter leather bombardier jacket. Mrs. Nemcheck questioned Russell about the jacket right away, since it was warm outside. He told her in a gruffly mumbling voice, "Been sick."

With all of her previous suspicions and precautions, it was hard to believe that for some reason this answer seemed to appease her. Class went on as usual. Mrs. Nemcheck never questioned Russell about his jacket, again. Every now and then, Russell would turn towards me. Grinning from ear to ear, he would point to the bulge in his jacket. I knew that meant our plan was in motion; but, I was having second thoughts. I was still in a state of shock from him, actually, bringing the stuff to school!

At recess he showed me the bundle, and gave me the matches. I began to hedge a bit. My resolve weakened. My thoughts of severe punishment, almost, made me relent. Seeing my weakness, he trumped my doubts with the ever powerful *ace* card, "*Are you a sissy?*"

No one wanted to be labeled a sissy. Not even *girls* wanted to be called a *sissy*! No one had ever, successfully, called _me_ one, before! It was something that I could not allow…not in our marshy-swamp culture. The label would be hard to shake. Reluctantly, I, finally, agreed to do my part, just as we had planned.

When we returned to class, it took a while for Russell to build up his own courage. He was fidgety, and sweated most of the day. He was, obviously, nervous, and a bit scared; but, he wouldn't admit it. Not to mention he was burning up in his winter jacket. Finally, he raised his hand to be excused to the restroom.

As strict as Mrs. Nemcheck was with her *rules*, she _never_ denied anyone restroom privileges. We had heard that there had been some kind of an 'incident' in the past that, nearly, got her into trouble. Since then, and since the restrooms were in back of the classroom, she didn't restrict anyone on restroom privileges. Russell was, therefore, excused without any questioning.

My desk was right in front of the restroom door. As Russell passed on his way to the restroom, he gave me a little thump and a wink. It wasn't long before he emerged from the restroom with his jacket off.

His shirt was drenched in sweat! He was, obviously, relieved; and, obviously, missing a bulge! The next move was mine!

This plan was bothering <u>me</u> a lot more than it did Russell. I was concerned about my parents' response…about Mrs. Nemcheck's response…even about my church friends' response! I mean, what would Brother Dave think?

None of these things mattered to Russell! But, they did to me! These concerns caused me to delay my actions. I could see that Russell was getting angry. His "I'm gonna kill you" look, as well as, his frowns of disappointment ate at me. Slowly, I raised my hand to be excused. Without any hesitation, permission was granted.

My movement was sluggish. I felt a bit nauseous. My many doubts grew bigger, and bigger, with each reluctant step. Worries invaded my thoughts, and seemed to be more than I could fathom; <u>but</u>, I knew I couldn't back down, not now!

Once I was in the restroom, it dawned on me why this plan seemed so lame. *I* was going to be the last one in the restroom before the explosion! My stake in this ill-advised plan had just gotten higher! What could I do? How could I save face in this situation? I couldn't *wimp* out. I would be labeled a "sissy". I would never be able to live that label down!

Whatever I was going to do had to done, quickly. Mrs. Nemcheck only allowed a certain amount of time in the restroom, before she came to check on you. My time was running out! I had to think of something in a hurry!

Suddenly, a solution came to me. The 'answer' was right outside the restroom door! That's where Lonnie sat. Right next to my desk! Lonnie was a distant friend of mine who was a human computer; but, had <u>no</u> swamp sense about him. I thought that I would tell him that he left '*something*' in the restroom. He was always forgetting stuff, anyway. He would, most likely, think that, maybe, he *had* forgotten something! All he needed to do was to go in; look around; see nothing; and then, come out. That would make *him* the last one in!

Don't get me wrong. Lonnie was not a "dufuss". He was brilliant… very, very book smart. He could add quicker and spell better than anyone in our class. He could read instructions, and know exactly what to do. 'Book smarts' was something he had plenty of! It was the common sense stuff that, often, eluded him.

He would forget to tie his shoes…or to put on socks. He would have his shirt on backwards, or his underwear inside out…don't ask! He had been sheltered by his parents, who were both brainiacs. They had homeschooled him in a day when that was frowned upon. His parents had cut off his contact from most other kids. Only, a select few were allowed to come to his house to play with him, or interact with him. His parents insisted that all their children turn out to be brainos, like they had turned out to be.

Now that he was allowed to come to public school, he tried to fit in; but, too often, he stood out. Since he had not gone to kindergarten, he was placed in the "dummo" class. A few of us felt it was our duty to tutor him on being 'swamp savvy'. At this point, however, I was hoping he had forgotten all that we had taught him!

With an exit plan in mind, I opened up the tank to complete my mission. Boy! The bundle was a sight to see! The bright red cherry bombs looked impressively huge under the water in the tank. The grey coiled fuse was excessively long, allowing plenty of time for the "Lonnie dodge" to take place. Still, I was a bit nervous and shaky.

I struck the first match and sent it flying into the air as it ignited. The next match stayed in my shaky hand. It ignited, perfectly. I stared at it burning, until it fizzled out! The third match was lit, carefully. I held it for a moment, then touched the fuse. The touch, instantly, fired the fuse. Hurriedly, I replaced the tank lid and laid the matches on the floor. It was, now, time to put the "Lonnie dodge" into play.

Without any question, nor any hesitation, Lonnie accepted my bogus information. He raised his hand to be excused. Russell looked puzzled. He didn't understand what I was doing. He just knew this was not part of his plan. I gave him the "OK" sign, which seemed to defuse his suspicious anger.

Everything was in place and going according to the revised plan. However, we, both, became very concerned when Lonnie stayed in the restroom…much longer than expected. My idea was a quick look around, then out! Lonnie's idea was a genuine trip to the potty. He *really* needed to go!

Who knew he would turn out to be a "take your time" sitter. Not knowing the situation, he stayed and stayed! I had forgotten that, in the past, Mrs. Nemcheck had, often, knocked on the restroom door to hurry Lonnie along. I kept saying (under my breath), "Come out! Come out!" But, he never did!

Finally, the cherry bombs blew! It was a loud and intense explosion. It sounded like both barrels of a shotgun had been fired! It was followed by screams of terror, from inside the restroom, and out!

Water began to gush from under the door. Stunned students didn't know whether to laugh, or cry. Mrs. Nemcheck ran to the restroom. The rest of us were hot on her heels. She flung the door open to reveal poor, little Lonnie sunk down into the toilet seat with his petite sockless feet sticking up into the air.

He had been _on_ the toilet seat when it blew! He was, now, stuck *in* the toilet seat screaming and crying!

Mrs. Nemcheck, quickly, took charge of Lonnie. While she cared for him, we inspected the damage. Thank Goodness, Lonnie had not been hurt!...At least, not physically!

The whole backside of the tank was cracked, or blown away! The front side had little cracks, but no holes. If the bundle had been paced differently, it would have blown out the front; and, Lonnie, no doubt, *would* have been hurt! With Lonnie in her arms, and toilet water gushing everywhere, Mrs. Nemcheck closed her eyes and exclaimed, "*Russell!*"

I didn't see Russell, anymore, after that. I heard he failed first grade, again -- somewhere else! Lonnie was moved from the "dummo" class to the "braino" class, which is where he should have been all along. Russell took the blame. He never mentioned any accomplices. That was the "school yard code". You never told on someone else. Still, those of us who had befriended Russell were rounded up, and paddled, just in case we *might* have been guilty!

Believe me! I took my licks willingly; and, almost asked for more! What mattered most to me was that Lonnie was alive! The "Lonnie dodge" didn't turn out like I had planned. Russell may not have cared; but, I didn't want anyone to get hurt. Not even almost hurt!

Volunteer 'room mothers' were called upon to escort us to the restroom down the hall, until ours was fixed. Getting permission to "*go*" became more difficult. This created a problem for some who couldn't hold *it* very long! When you did go, the door had to remain cracked, which was not always good idea for the rest of us!

Trying to impress my older friend turned out to be bogus! He never cared about me, nor about what was right or wrong. I did; but, I had allowed myself to forget.

I felt guilty and ashamed. I, eventually, told Mrs. Nemcheck that I had helped Russell. She thanked me for confirming her suspicions. She paddled me, again; and, gave me extra work to do. As far as I know, she never told my parents. I never understood why!

In the months that followed, one of my Sunday School lessons was on a verse in the Apostle Paul's letter to the Corinthian Church. *"Do not be deceived: Bad company corrupts good morals"* (1 Corinthians 15:33, NKJV).

Boy! That hit hard! I knew the plan was wrong. I chose to overlook it.

I wanted to be accepted by my new 'friend'. It is so easy to get caught up in stuff like that. It takes faith and courage to walk away…to refuse to go along…to do the right thing!

This was an important lesson; but, because of my stubbornness, it took a few other lessons for it to, finally, sink in. How about you?

"When it blew, Lonnie screamed bloody murder!"

Bulldog And Hazel

Bulldog and Hazel were very unique and special people. They were the classic "unlikely" pair. They definitely proved the saying that "opposites attract". They were not *the* "odd couple"; but, they were *an odd coupling*. Some might say they were proof that 'love conquers all'.

Bulldog could get scrappy at times. His talk was rough and always straight forward. He pulled no punches. If he had a "beef" with you, he would let you know it in a heartbeat! He would leave no doubt about where he stood on any issue. There were rumors…about him getting physical with someone who had crossed him, once. Though I never saw any such thing, he made you believe it *could* have happened. He was, definitely, someone you did not want to test, or push, too, far.

He was called "Bulldog" long before I ever met him. One good look at him might suggest how the name came about…and, why it stuck over the years. He was a short, stocky, bald man built hard and tough. His hands were small, and callused by hard work. His arms were muscular and tight. His legs were powerfully built and bowed a bit, like a bulldog's legs. Of course, no one mentioned it in his presence.

When he walked, he was, always, leaning forward, like he was ready to pounce on anyone who got in his way. He, constantly, frowned, which gave him an uncanny resemblance to an angry English bulldog.

He, often, gave the impression that he was staring you down when he looked straight at you. His dark, piercing eyes seemed to shoot right through you! Most people stayed out of his way, and never made eye contact, including me!

Though he, rarely, smiled in public, I did find him chuckling once; but, it was by accident! He told me never to tell anyone…You are the first ones I've told!

He didn't take crud from anyone; nor, did he grieve anyone who didn't have an issue with him. If you were to look up the phrase "junkyard dog" in a dictionary, you might see his picture associated with the term!

Mrs. May, a close, friendly neighbor, and a saintly lady at our church, suggested that he wasn't really a "junkyard dog"…"he ate them for breakfast!"

When he got angry, he really got angry! He didn't waste energy just being upset. He went straight through to being angry! It was not a pleasant sight to see! His eyes would glare in his rage. It was said that when he spat in anger, it would kill the grass!…Well, that's what 'they' said! When he got like that, there wasn't much you could do, but stay out of range! The only one who could tame the beast was his wife, Hazel.

Hazel was even shorter than Bulldog! She was a bit stocky; but, not really fat. She walked with a limp from having childhood polio. Her slightly gray hair and inviting eyes made her someone you just had to hug whenever you saw her. She was one of the sweetest ladies you could ever meet.

She spoke softly, never much above a whisper. Her voice, always, sounded a bit raspy, like she always had a cold. When she would say something to you, you might miss it, if you weren't careful; but, Bulldog heard every word. His ear was tuned to her voice like a honing device. Whatever she said, that was it! No matter what!

Hazel made friends easily. Bulldog made it hard to keep them! She was always willing to help someone in need. When she applied her graces to others, she became a genuine source of comfort to them; and, they appreciated her for it. It was easy to know Hazel up close and personal. I talked to her often at church. Bulldog, who, rarely, came to church, was the kind of person you wanted to know from a distance -- the further the better!

My first *real* job outside my home was at the St. Marys Hardware Store. Hazel was, already, employed there. Working with her was easy. She liked to make things fun. Her little jokes were, always, cute. She was very approachable and easy to like. This allowed me the opportunity to get to know Hazel even better.

She ran the gift shop and small appliance area. Wayne, one of my high school buddies, and I ran the hardware area. We were, constantly, trying to come up with 'special' deals for our customers; and, she was, constantly, trying to keep us from giving the store away!

She made work a pleasure. She made learning easy. She taught me many things about retail and gift shopping; and, I eagerly learned from her. Why, she even taught me how to gift wrap. I used to wrap gifts like you would market-wrap a piece of fish! She taught me a better way. She, even, taught me how to make bows and tie ribbons. Of course, *that* was something we kept among ourselves.

When rowdy customers came into the store, she would run interference for us. After they left, she would, quietly, have a nervous 'hissy fit' behind the coke machine in the storage area. Drinking an ice cold coke, usually, helped to calm her down, and made everything alright.

When I would see Bulldog and Hazel together, the coupling seemed so strange to me. They were so very different; yet, somehow, they were united together…and, very tightly bonded. I, often, wondered how they ever got together.

One slow, rainy day at work, I asked Hazel how this match came about. She paused…looked down at the tile floor, and slowly circled her small, petite foot across its surface. I thought I might have asked the wrong question. I, quickly, apologized for asking, and started towards the coke machine.

She stopped me. She assured me it was alright to ask. It, obviously, wasn't the first time she had been asked that question. In fact, she acknowledged that she had been asked this same question many times by family and friends. She thought for a moment as she smiled. Looking up from the tile floor, she said, "I see things in Bulldog that no one else sees."

'Nuff' said! I was willing to stop there! I didn't need to know more; but, she went on…as if she needed to explain. She said that there were 'better things' in him than most people could see. She saw things that were not evident on the surface. Beyond the rough, bulldog-like exterior was a good man who loved her deeply. From *her* view, she couldn't help *but* love him.

Her sincere answer surprised me. I wondered, at first, if we were talking about the same man. I, however, accepted every word without comment, nor debate. She, obviously, *did* see something in Bulldog that no one else could see!

After our discussion, I began to look at Bulldog in a different way. I tried to see him through Hazel's eyes. It was difficult not to just see the man on the surface; because, *sometimes*, he was the man on the surface! I kept looking, trying to see more through her eyes. The more I tried to see, the more I could see.

I could see that Bulldog had streaks of kindness. He *did* smile and chuckle…a lot more than I had realized. He was firm and corrective with us teens and children, but never harsh, nor mean. I saw a man with a surprising sense of humor that was hidden by his stern expressions and directness. I saw a man who valued honesty and integrity, and a man who would let you know if you were a person of either. I came to appreciate the Bulldog I was seeing through Hazel's eyes.

Learning to see through the eyes of others has helped me understand how God expects us to look at others through *His* eyes. That's why

He expects us to love our enemies…to bless those who curse us…do good to those who hate us and pray for those who spitefully use us and persecute us (Matthew 5:44-48). These things are impossible to do through the eyes of the flesh, or our self-centered eyes. It is only possible when God's spirit enables us to see through <u>His</u> eyes. When we do, we can love what, and who, He sees…even the most unlovable people among us!

His love towards us is an unmerited love (*agape*), which is much better than the world's conditional love. The love that God inspires, "bears all things, believes all things, hopes all things, endures all things" and never fails (1 Corinthians 13: 7,8 NKJV).

When we have loved the 'Hazels' in this world and have been loved back, we have done well. When we love the 'Bulldogs', too, we are perfecting God's love in us. Not every encounter will be pleasant. There will be many experiences filled with awkward moments; but, it **will** be worth the effort.

You may be a Hazel. You may be a Bulldog. Isn't it refreshing to know that no matter which you may be you can *still* be loved!

Hug a Hazel today. Extend a hand to a Bulldog; and, may God bless you for it!

What Would I Do

For One Little Kiss From You?

I would climb the highest mountain,

Drink from a poison fountain,

Cross the ocean, dangerous and deep,

Hold my finger in a dike's leak,

Make you a house of fresh cut lumber,

Wake an entire city from its midnight slumber,

Go exploring in the darkest jungle,

In search of diamonds in their biggest bundles,

Wrestle a lion with my bare hand,

Challenge Zorro to a last stand.

All this, and more, would I do

For just one little kiss from you!

R.P. Wildes

(1969)

Coastal Family Christmas

Christmas always brings back memories of family gatherings and turkey dinners gone by. Most of these memories are good, happy ones.

Our family tribe traveled near and far just to have dinner with Granny and Grandpa, and open a few presents. It was an enjoyable time to see cousins and relatives you didn't, normally, get to see that often. It was, also, a time to re-establish love-hate relationships and put an end to old family rumors....or start new ones!

Some cousins got prettier year to year, which made you proud to be kin to them. Some got funnier and goofier. Some got uglier and meaner. But, it was good to see them all.

Grandpa was known for doing things differently than anyone expected. One year he wanted to try a goose instead of turkey for the family meal. After we all tasted it, he and I feasted on the goose. The others fried some fish. After that, Granny never let Grandpa choose the meats for Christmas.

One year, a well-intending neighbor gave him a couple of wild wood ducks to try. Granny, promptly, refused to cook them!...at least, not for our Christmas meal. A distant relative from up north, however, volunteered to cook them in a pan of dressing after they arrived for the Christmas gathering. That relative, often, went against the grain on family matters. Her offer was <u>not</u> well received. She *did* cook them amid glaring eyes! Grandpa, my brother and I ended up eating the ducks, later. They were very good!

These coastal Christmases were special times. A coastal Christmas meant <u>no</u> snow. Sometimes, we had ice storms, which left <u>everything</u> encrusted within a layer of ice, which was quite a beautiful sight! The ice sparkled like diamond crystals in the morning sun! Ice came often, but <u>never</u> snow!

Each year, a wide variety of Christmas decorations would cover the marshes and swamp avenues of our fair city. The bright seasonal lights burned all night long, revealing very creative scenes. You might see a manger scene next to a surfing Santa, or baby Jesus next to Rudolf with sun glasses! Or, a baby Jesus with sun glasses riding Rudolf!

Families, sometimes, acted out their own live nativity scene, and carolers went house to house singing Christmas songs. They were always welcomed. The carolers would sing until their voices gave out, or the bitter cold drove them inside. It was a good time, and a good place for families to gather.

Our family, like many others, sang Christmas carols, played games, and opened presents. We rejoiced in the company, more than the things we gave, or received. It was more about catching up on relationships, than gloating over possessions.

It didn't matter who got what! We, often, swapped gifts around after opening them, anyway. What mattered was we got to play together. Sometimes, we didn't get to keep our gifts very long… like the slingshot I got one time. After Grandpa got two ricochets and one direct shot to the buttocks, the slingshot, mysteriously, and completely, disappeared!

Even that didn't matter; because, it was a chance to see Granny and Grandpa. It was a chance for them to hug and kiss all of us grandkids.

It was a time that we enjoyed; and, all too often, took for granted. We thought all Christmases would be this way!

It is, now, a time cherished, but gone for many!   Gone; but, not forgotten!

In recalling these wonderful times, I have come to realize that a real, true experience of Christmas can be seen in these old-time family gatherings. You see, a *true* Christmas is about re-establishing and embracing our relationship to our Heavenly Father. It is more about catching up on all the ways *He* has blessed us, and how *we* should honor Him, than worrying about what He hasn't done, yet. Christmas gives us a chance to revisit **His** love for us, demonstrated in the birth of His only Son. *He* was given, as a Gift, to be the Savior of all who would believe in Him.

Christmas is a time for us to share in *His* spiritual hugs and kisses that can only be felt by faith within the believer's heart. And, it is a time to rejoice as *He* expresses *His* continued love for us all. No one is left out of *His* expressions of love!

Christmas is not a time to gloat over possessions; because, Jesus forsook the riches of Heaven to be born in a lowly manger. It seems poor in earthly terms; but, it is rich in Heavenly terms.

The genuineness of Christmas helps us to understand that the joy of the season comes from the *love* expressed, His and ours, which is still being disbursed today.

If we know we are loved, and we love back, joy results from that love exchange. "*For God so loved the world that He gave His only begotten Son, that whosoever believes in Him should not perish but have everlasting life...*" (John 3:16, NKJV).

"*Then the angels said to them, 'Do not be afraid, for behold, I bring you good tidings of great joy which will be to all people. For unto you is born this day, in the city of David, a Savior, who is Christ the Lord...Glory to God in the highest, and on earth peace, good will toward men!*'" (Luke 2:10-14, NKJV).

So, when we gather for our family Christmases this year, let us enjoy the fellowship, the fun and the food; but, don't forget the true source of our joy, which is Jesus Christ, the Savior of the world! He is the greatest love gift we could ever receive from our Heavenly Father, who still loves us and desires fellowship with us.

Merry Christmas!

Cousin Millard Gets Published

Cousin Millard was a kind and gentle man who lived in the deep, dark areas of the Okefenokee Swamp. He lived there all of his seventy-three years. He never went to public school, and never took a correspondence course. He taught himself to read and write. He was a man who loved learning. He tried to learn something new every day, from any source he could find...anything he could make sense of, or understand.

He kept, pretty much, to himself. It was his custom to never venture far from his swamp home. When he, absolutely, had to, he would make an appearance in Folkston. It was the nearest small town to the swamp. He would get what he needed, then return home.

For someone who never ventured far from the swamp, he seemed to be endowed with a great deal of acquired knowledge and wisdom on many subjects. When asked how he knew so much, he would simply say that he learned it by "watching" the radio, and by reading this and that.

Cousin Millard was pretty confident that he had a good grasp of general knowledge. Most people around him, obviously, agreed. Whenever someone in the swamp wanted to know something, they would ask Cousin Millard. If he didn't have an answer, he would get one (or 'reason' one up!). His answers, always, seemed to satisfy the questioning minds of his inquisitors. There appeared to be no limits to the breadth and depth of his knowledge. From agriculture to "modern" science his answers, and opinions, sounded like reasonable responses.

Though he never claimed to be a doctor, he was, also, known for his knowledge of several "remedies" for whatever ailed you. He came to be revered as a good "fixer upper". If his old time-tested remedies didn't work, he would come up with new ones. His success in helping with minor ailments was, unbelievably, good. His return patronage proved that!

Anytime anyone needed a cure, relief from pain, or a health question answered, they would seek him out, knowing he would try to do something to help. He seemed to really care about folks, and really wanted to do all he could to help. His reputation was well established. Pretty much, everyone in the swamp community respected this obliging servant. His knowledge and wisdom was very impressive.

The most impressed, above all others, was Little Elrod. He respected Cousin Millard a lot, and loved to learn from him. Elrod was constantly at his foot heals, lapping up every word, observing every action. He was, always, ready to learn something new. He, especially, liked to learn about Cousin Millard's remedies.

Elrod didn't even have to be made to go to school. He loved it, too! Little Elrod would learn what he could from school teachers, then come home to learn more from Cousin Millard. That boy read books and "watched" the radio like nobody's business. Then, one day, Elrod discovered television. He got to be a good student of that, too! He was very smart from all his learning, and won several scholastic awards.

One day Elrod informed Cousin Millard that he was going to medical school. No one could have been more proud of Elrod than Cousin Millard. They, both, felt that Elrod would have the upper hand on other students; because, he had read so much, already. Not to mention all that he had learned from his mentor.

When he applied to his medical school, he asked for advanced placement testing, to see if he could skip some of the lesser courses. He wanted to hurry up and start healing people as fast as he could. They gave him some "pre-testing" material to go over, then set a date for his advance testing.

One of the testing materials included a list of words that Elrod would have to define. He wanted to do his very best; so, he tried to contact Cousin Millard for assistance. It was hard to contact Cousin Millard by phone. He had one, just not in the house! He was convinced that it would draw lightning; so, he had it installed on a telephone pole near the road in front of his house.

To make matters worse, his hearing wasn't what it used to be. Everyone nearby would hear the phone ring before he would. Either, some kind soul would answer it for him, or someone would have to go get him.

After much difficulty, Elrod, finally, made contact with Cousin Millard. As always, Cousin Millard was more than happy to help. When Elrod gave him the list over the phone, Cousin Millard told him he would need a little time; and, then he'd get back to him.

Knowing that this was important to Elrod, Cousin Millard wanted to ponder over these words to offer his best answers. After a few days of hard pondering, he mailed Elrod his results. Elrod, had been schooled a good bit by that time. As he looked over his list of defined words, he realized that some of the answers didn't fit right. He decided it might be best to ask one of his professors to go over the list.

The professor was amazed at what he saw. Grinning from ear to ear, he asked Elrod if he could publish them in one of his papers. He, reluctantly, gave permission. When Cousin Millard found out that _he_ was going to be published, he couldn't help but smile, real big. He felt quite accomplished and important.

The professor published the paper for his colleagues only. They seemed to enjoy reading the paper, immensely, including the list of Cousin Millard's definitions. The following is a partial list of defined words by this learned swamp master:

Artery - the study of fine drawings, paintings and statues.

Barium - the next thing you do after someone dies.

Colic - a sheep dog (kind of like Lassie).

Coma - the little dot with a tail on it that comes right after "Dear Somebody".

Congenital - being friendly to people and always polite.

Dilate - to live a long time.

G. I. Series - baseball games between teams of soldiers.

Hangnail - a nail to hang stuff on like a picture or horseshoe above the door.

Minor Operation - coal digging company.

Morbid - getting more than one offer, or bid on something you intend to build.

Nitrate - the rate for nighttime…different from the day rate.

Node - having knowledge of, when you just *node* something!

Organic - a church musician, or the person who works on the organ.

Out Patient - a person who has fainted in the doctor's office, probably from looking at the bill.

Post Operative - someone who delivers mail, or who works in the post office for the Post Master.

Protein - being in favor of young people and youthful things.

Secretion - hiding something, or keeping something secret from others.

Tablet - a smaller version of a table.

Tumor - an extra pair of whatever.

Urine - the opposite of you're out!

Varicose Veins - self-explanatory, veins that are very close together.

Benign - what you are after you be eight!

For a long time, Cousin Millard boasted about his being 'published'. It meant something special to him, and Elrod would not have it any other way. Elrod realized, however, that, from then on, *this* school would require help of a different kind. He still loved Cousin Millard; but, Elrod learned that, no matter how well intentioned someone may be, a college degree demanded college answers. 'Reasoning' up answers wasn't going to help him.

In some ways many of us are like Cousin Millard: making up answers to questions we know very little, or nothing, about! Sometimes, it works out OK; but, sometimes, it doesn't. For instance, questions about our faith seem to scare us most of all. The odd thing is, it should be something we know the most about! It scares us to death when someone asks us: "What do you believe?"; "Why do you believe?"; or, "What do some of these 'church' words mean?".

We get so nervous that we clam up, or start to stutter. We don't, necessarily, give 'wrong' answers; we just don't give any! We try to avoid the subject all together, which could be a worse thing to do, especially, if someone is really seeking an answer.

The challenge to us is to *"be ready in season and out of season"* (2 Tim. 4:2, NKJV), in order to give an account for our faith. The way to be ready is to *"study to present yourself approved of God, a worker who does not need to be ashamed, rightly dividing the word of truth"* (2 Timothy 2:15, NKJV).

Don't be like *some* we who just make something up, then want to blame the Holy Spirit for embarrassing results. You don't have to do that! Just make sure your words are <u>your</u> personal words of faith, and are true to your personal experience. Then, the answer you give will have meaning, purpose and depth to the one asking.

Cousin Millard meant well; but, Elrod found out that he had to do some studying, too. In order to be ready for any questions of faith, why don't we all do a little more studying? Hey! It couldn't hurt!

"Cousin Millard, tell me more!"

Dancing On The Graves

"*POW!*" The explosion was deafening! Men jumped. Women screamed. A few, almost, fainted! Then, the swarm of yellow jackets attacked with a vengeance. People were swatting, slapping, jumping, rolling…, almost like everyone was dancing on the graves!

The pastor was not immune! He was doing his own little dodge dance bumping into the pall bearers. He, almost, tipped over the casket! He tried to use his Bible as a shield, as if he was holding off little bloodsucking critters from Dracula's pit!

The funeral was completely disrupted! The casket had to be set down in order for the pall bearers to defend themselves against the marauding yellow jackets. Everything had to be put on hold, until the aggravated assault subsided. It all seemed to be <u>my</u> fault…Well, it *was* my fault!

I had been carrying that cherry bomb in my pocket, ever since the fourth of July. I was waiting for just the right moment to use it. After the yellow jackets popped me three times on my legs, as we walked in the funeral procession, I, *really*, believed, *now* was the time!

Piercing pain, and a sense of vengeance, was the only thing my little mind could think about. My eight years of life experience had convinced me that it was my 'duty' to do some serious harm to those pesty, biting critters.

It was by Divine chance that I happened to notice their, perfectly, rounded nesting hole in the ground. I could see where some of them were flying in and out of the hole in the ground. I *knew* what I had to do. I was convinced that my actions would benefit all mankind…and, offer some payback for myself.

A discarded cigarette, still glowing, provided the necessary ignition device. My cherry bomb was prepped, and ready. I had no doubt that it was still as potent as the day I put it in my pocket for safe keeping. I felt sure it still packed a powerful punch. I mean, it had only been in storage in my pocket for three months! Would it be appropriate to use it, now??…*Certainly*, the Lord would understand my actions.

Without regard to my own personal safety, and disregarding the purpose of our gathering, I approached the nesting entry. I will be the first to admit, that getting close to the nesting place was done with a great deal of fear and trembling. With a well-worn cherry bomb in one hand, and a glowing cigarette butt in the other, I put my plan of revenge into action. In one swift motion, I lit the cherry bomb and stuffed it into the yellow jacket hole.

The explosion came quickly! Much quicker than I had anticipated! It was, exceptionally, loud! Much louder than I had remembered. It caught the mourning multitude completely off guard. The result was disastrous! Dirt and yellow jackets flew everywhere!

The plan that seemed, so perfect, in my mind, now, revealed far-reaching consequences that I had not anticipated. I guess I had chosen not to think about the aftermath. I just wanted to get some vengeance on those biting critters. My act of selfish wrath, however, was, now, hurting all of us! What I, vainly, intended for good turned out to be quite bad in the eyes of many…well, everyone!

I guess, it should have remained between the yellow jackets and myself. Now, clueless, innocent people were being painfully affected. It was obvious, my vengeance had been blind. My actions were selfish. My mercenary decision was poisoned by the suppressed desire to do mischief. I was, suddenly, gripped with a question I could not answer: "What part of this was, actually, for the benefit of others?"

All eyes were, now, focused upon me! I stood there, shaking, still holding the cigarette butt in my trembling hand. Their whelp-covered faces glowed red with anger. Their watery eyes were swollen nearly shut. Exploded hairdos and wigs out of place were terrifying to look at! I wanted to crawl into that yellow jacket hole, and die! I believe if there had been another opened grave, they may have decided to use it…with me!

Instead, I was forced to face those I had offended. The swelling and blistered crowd slowly turned into an encircling mob. They inched closer, and closer to me. There was nowhere to run! Nowhere to hide! My meaningless, nonsensical explanations fell on dilated, deafened ears!

I fell to my knees in submission to whatever fate awaited me. I was guilty. There was no getting around it. I knew it! They knew it! There was nothing else to say!

The angry mob kept pressing towards me. They only stopped for the grieving widow to make her way to the center. Her move seemed to make sense. No one questioned her rights to "first dibbs"!

When the angry mob fell in behind her, she fell to her knees facing me. I could not look upon her face. Sighing, heavily, she spoke through swollen, bubbling lips, "B-blob told me to let Ronnie be Ronnie. Don't restrain him in any way…Now, I know why! He loved watching you do what you do. Never knowing what you may do next made him laugh, even when he was sick. Thank you for making his last words to me more meaningful."

She leaned over, drooling a bit from a stinger on her upper lip, and gave me a slurping kiss on my forehead. Then, she, painfully, tried to smile. She forgave me!

Everyone was stunned! So was I! All my reasonings were bogus. My tearful sobbing and inadequate explanations had been confusing and unclear. But, my apology was accepted!

For the first time in my short life, I realized the meaning of love, mercy and grace. This suffering widow had demonstrated all three. She had a clear, unquestioned right to retaliate. She chose mercy and grace, as an alternative. She had a wide opened door to hate me; yet, she chose to love me, instead. When she made those choices, the mob mysteriously, and reluctantly, changed back into a civil crowd!

I have, often, pondered upon this experience. I have come to realize that some of our actions are just as outrageous to a holy God, as my vengeance taken out on a nest of yellow jackets at a funeral! We never seem to get it through our heads that our actions never affect *only* ourselves. Whatever we do touches the lives of others in some way. It doesn't matter if we intend it to, or not. What is so amazing is to realize that, even in the midst of our making of wrongful decisions, God *still* loves us. He doesn't like the wrongful things we do; but, He does not cancel His love for us.

When we are covered in guilt and shame, He is ready to hear our confession, with mercy and grace. Not our excuses! It is so wonderful to know that, "*If we confess our sins, He is faithful and just to forgive our sins and cleanse all our unrighteousness…*" (I John 1:9, NKJV).

No doubt you have had a similar experience…Well, not exactly the same! But, you have been in a situation where God had every right to do worse things in response to your actions; yet, instead, He chose to respond in love, mercy and grace. That is really awesome! Isn't it!

My Heart's Repose

Take the sun from the morning,

And I will still have bright Son-shine.

Take away the moon and the stars from the night

And there will still be a glow in the darkened sky.

Take away the robins singing in perfect harmony,

And I will still hear symphonies from my heart.

But, take away Your love, mercy and grace,

And there will be nothing!

R.P. Wildes

(1969)

DEAD SKUNK IN
THE MIDDLE OF THE
ROAD

Have you ever done something that you swore you would never do, again!? Then, when you did it, again, you got angry, and swore you would never do it, again...*again*! But, <u>then</u>, you did it *again*!!

Well, I did! You're right! I should have known better! I should have learned from the first time. I don't know what happened. Something came over me, and I did it, anyhow. Yep! You're right. I ended up regretting it!

You see, I had this friend...Well, kind of a social friend...Well, sort of a...just an acquaintance, really. Let's just say, he was fun to be with, sometimes...like in public gatherings! But, there were certain places I did <u>not</u> want to go with him; and, circumstances I did <u>*not*</u> want to share.

I met him at the Baptist Student Union while attending Shorter College. He was the B. S. U. Choir director, and his name was David. In that capacity he was fine...more than fine. He was a great music leader. He got great results from the all-student choir. It was being with him socially, that didn't really appeal to me. I had come to accept the fact that we were going to be good friends in the B.S.U.; but, not in our free time. We would be friends from a distance…a safe distance!

The first violation of this resolve was a hunting trip that went wrong…terribly wrong! After that incident, I vowed I would never go off with him again on a hunting, fishing, hiking, or any kind of outing. He was, too, careless with…<u>everything</u>!

He was *so* careful with details in musical programs; but, he was *so* careless with details everywhere else. This fact always haunted him, wherever he went. This was not something that only I noticed. It was very noticeable, and was the reason why, hardly, anyone wanted to venture out with him.

Every time he mentioned an outing, everybody ran! They, immediately, thought of excuses. Some fell victim to the dreaded *sudden illness syndrome,* an imaginary illness that you plan to have at opportune moments in order to get out of doing things. Others, suddenly, remembered they *had* to go home for the weekend. Some just said, "I'll think about it"; then, mysteriously disappeared!

If you weren't careful, you would start to feel sorry for him, and give in. Your act of Christian compassion, charity…,or pity, would make you easy prey. If you ever gave in, you would pay for it, later. Believe me! There were very few exceptions.

One day, David was feeling <u>*really*</u> low. His grades were slumping, his girl friend had dumped him; and, no one seemed to care. As a result, he dipped into depression. That's when his grades, really, took a nose dive! He, definitely, needed someone to be a friend…to help him take his mind off his troubles. I just didn't want it to be me!

I suggested several <u>other</u> people; but, every one of them had, already, made excuses. Feeling more compassionate than, perhaps, I should have, I agreed to go fishing with him.

I did insist, however, on two conditions. One, we were to use artificial bait, only! I had, already, heard about his frantic slinging of pieces of worm bait off his fingers, and into the faces of others. (He couldn't stand the gooey messy stuff when you tried to place the worm on the hook!)

The second condition was that we leave when _I_ said so. No flimsy excuses for delaying departure; no wining about having to leave; and, no guilt trips about my decision! These were nonnegotiable conditions. To my surprise, he agreed to all my conditions. Under that agreement, I agreed to go.

My first thoughts were of compassion. It was the 'right' thing to do! Deep down, there were other feelings about my decision. I had a bad feeling about it.

We agreed to leave early in the morning. Every good fisherman knows that you've got to get there before the fish wake up! That way, they don't realize you are there to catch them! So, just as we planned, we were in his dad's boat, in the water, before sunrise.

We used a quiet electric motor to sneak into the desired fishing hole. From there, we paddled, ever-so-softly, to get into the perfect fishing position. "D" said he knew where all the good fishing spots were located. His dad had taught him. He promised this first spot to be among the very best.

By the time the sun peeked out above the horizon, we were in place and ready to cast our lines. Everything was up for grabs! Bass, crappie, red breast... _anything_ that felt like biting was our target!

We began making our casts...then reeling it in. Cast...and reel in. Cast and reel in...again...and again...and again. Nothing was biting. There was nothing...not a strike, not a bump, not even a snag!

As any good fisherman would do, we changed lures, then cast some more. We repeated this over and over. The fish, evidently, didn't like our fake cuisine. Maybe, they weren't home. Maybe, they were snobbish! Maybe, they heard us coming! In any event, they were not taking our bait!

By midmorning, we decided that this hole had, already, been fished out. So, we pulled up the anchor moved to another spot. Each new "proven" fishing hole produced the same result. None of his favorite holes brought forth *anything*…not a catch…nor a strike…not, even, a nibble!

We were on a large lake, which seemed to have countless fishing hole possibilities. Could all of the fish have taken a vacation at the same time! How could such a beautiful lake have, virtually, no fish population! We couldn't answer that question; but, we knew this for a fact: we tried every hole, using every one of our lures with the same result!

Of course, it could have been us! In fact, I am sure it was us! At every spot, where we set up to fish, David would start talking about his shipwrecked love life. I responded, every now and then; but, mainly, I just let him talk. I kept fishing.

I guess the fish overheard his woes and became, too, depressed to eat! Or else, they decided to vacate the depressingly gloomy area. By late afternoon, the fish and I, both, had had enough! I told him it was time to go.

He, almost, forgot his promise; but, then he corrected his himself, and pulled up the anchor. He, wisely, headed towards the landing without any additional words, nor wining opposition. I was proud of his self-control.

We hadn't realized it; but, in all our shuffling about, we had ended up on the other side of the lake across from the landing. We had to run the small electric motor against the wind to get back to his car and trailer. The little motor strained to push us toward our landing base. It weakened quickly against the wind, too quickly! It ran low on power; because, he had forgotten to charge it up.

We decided that since we were through fishing for the day, we could fire up the gasoline engine, not having to worry about disturbing fish beds. Besides, we could make better time with the stronger outboard motor.

That's when he informed me that he had forgotten to get gas for the motor. Another important detail had slipped his mind! Another part of the whole picture had been overlooked. To me, these were important details that should have been attended to, anytime you plan to go fishing. Yet, they went ignored!

After the battery 'gave up the ghost', we pulled out some oars, and starting paddling. The oars were long, fat and cumbersome to use. His dad had told him to get the "paddles" for the boat; but, he didn't know the difference between paddles and oars.

Oars work a lot better if you have *oarlocks* (U-shaped oar holders) on your boat. If you don't, which we didn't, they are very hard to use as paddles. We ended up breaking our backs 'paddling' with oars against the wind!

Night was beginning to catch up to us. We were, still, halfway across the lake striving against the wind. When the electric motor *was* running, he had decided to go straight across the middle of the lake towards our landing place. After all, everyone knows the shortest distance between two points *is* a straight line…right?

After the battery went dead, he was, still, convinced that this would be our best route. He saw no problem with us paddling, using our oars, across the center of the lake, even if the wind was contrary.

I had wanted to follow the shoreline along the edge of the lake. With darkness approaching, I wanted to be near land. At least, then, we could get out of the water and call for help, if the need should arise. Since this was the "pre-cell phone" era, we couldn't call for help from the middle of the lake!

By the time we reached the true mid-point of the lake, our arms were about to 'fall off'! We were, totally, exhausted! We *had* to stop for a rest. But, each time we rested, the wind would blow us backward, moving us further away from our desired destination.

We were forced to 'paddle' with those bulky oars. We had to paddle harder and longer than our tired arms could stand! After much travail, and many words spoken under my breath, we, finally, reached water shallow enough to get out and push the boat the rest of the way. I wanted to pinch David's head off! But, I was, too, tired to try!

It was late…well past "dark-thirty" when we loaded up the boat. I was wore out and starving. We had caught, absolutely, nothing. My ears were burning from listening to David's burdened woes. All I wanted to do was to get home.

Once again, I was, silently, promising never to venture out with this guy…never….ever again! My earnest plea was: "Why, Lord? Why am I here? Why didn't I heed my fears?"

We loaded our gear without saying very much. In fact, hardly a word was spoken. We got into his car, and drove off. The silence was heavy. Neither of us chanced a word!

He, finally, broke the silence with, "Well, I guess we'll get 'em next time." I felt as though I needed to do something…I *wanted* to 'beat the snot' out of him, right then and there; but, I refrained. Instead, I just grunted.

As we traveled towards his parent's house to drop off the boat and trailer, the car ahead of us appeared to swerve. It was attempting to avoid something in the road. It appeared to be a critter of some kind. After swerving, twice, it hit the critter dead on! The car made no attempt to stop. Instead, it sped off quickly.

By now, it was dark. In fact, it was so dark we couldn't tell what kind of critter the swerving vehicle had struck. When we arrived at the spot where the critter was struck, we, immediately, recognized the smell. There was no doubt! It was a dead skunk in the middle of the road!

We passed by quickly, trying to avoid the horrible stench. We were just about clear when David confessed he had never seen a real skunk. At least, not up close. Without any discussion, he decided to turn around to get a closer look.

I warned him that the smell of a skunk had a lasting nature to it. It is not something that will dissipate quickly, nor easily! I pleaded with him not to go back. I reminded him of his promised conditions. He thought they only applied on the water. In any event, he had complied enough for the day! He insisted on taking a quick look.

He drove his car right beside the skunk. It laid in the middle of the road, apparently, dead. He, slowly, drove up next to it, and opened his car door to get a better look. The moment he had his door fully extended, the '*dead*' skunk shot a stream of spray into the car!

It was all over both of us! The smell was horrendous! Our eyes burned from the fumes. I thought I had smelled a skunk before; but, <u>none</u> had *ever* smelled as bad as this!

We drove away coughing and gagging. We rolled all the windows down, gasping for fresh air! Our eyes were watering, heavily. David could, hardly, see the road. Fortunately, we were not far from his parent's house. As we drove up into his parent's drive, his mother came out, onto their front porch. We stopped and ran out of the care towards their house. She stopped us dead in our tracks! She said she could smell us a mile away, and wouldn't let us get any closer to the front porch.

Though David tried, she vowed he was <u>not</u> going into their house. Shooing us with her broom, she insisted that we go around to the backyard. She met us there with some hard lye soap and salt. We had to scrub down using both!

We washed and washed. We washed so hard, our skin was, nearly, peeling off! After several layers of skin having been scrubbed off, the smell seemed to have been getting lighter…at least to us it seemed that way. She insisted, however, it was still, too, strong for her approval. David's dad yelled from inside the house, "You got to burn or bury your clothes!"

These were the only clothes I had brought with me! I pointed this out to his mom! It didn't matter. The clothes had to go! I pointed out that David's clothes were, too, small for me. I mean, I had to wear something!

The best they could offer was his mom's full apron, or a towel. I chose them, both! When I returned to the campus, everyone got a good hoot and holler!

What can I say…I brought it upon myself! Right? I didn't listen to my own warning, and I paid the price. Well, don't snoot, too, much at me! Isn't that the way some of us are when it comes to listening to the Lord's warnings?

We <u>know</u> we should listen; but, somehow, we think we can get around it. When we ignore the Lord, we pay a terrible price! It is *always* best to listen to the Lord. He is *always* leading us towards the things that are best for us. If we trust and follow Him, we might just avoid some of the dead skunks in the middle of the road!

FAMILY NIGHT OUT

Friday night was our family night out! As a child, and through my teen years, our extended family got together to "eat out" on every Friday night. With an, occasional, exception, the family group was, mostly, made up of mom's brothers and sisters who lived within driving distance.

We would all meet at a designated restaurant to enjoy each other's company, and eat some great food! Most restaurants were happy to see us. Some seemed to have wished they had closed their doors!

We, always, had a large group; so, the business we offered was good. However, the noise level of our fellowship could get high. We tried to keep a lid on it; but, it was hard when you having so much fun! We were having a great time being together, telling stories, airing family gossip and filling up on delicious vittles.

Seafood was the main choice of the clan. Living along the coast, and near the Okefenokee Swamp, meant that there were several fine seafood restaurants offering fresh seafood and other critters of all kinds.

The Sandbar and The Pier restaurants in Fernandina Beach, Florida, had some great seafood. The Deck and The Forks in Brunswick, Georgia, served great seafood and steaks, as well. If steak was the *main* choice, The Western Sizzlin' and The Al Hombre in Jacksonville, Florida, served some of the best.

There were other great places to eat; but, not all of them could accommodate the large number our family brought to the table. I'm not sure *who* decided where to go; but, we all ended up at the same place. Some had to travel great distances, and got there just in time to place their orders! Every attempt was made to make it a, truly, well-organized, well-attended and very much appreciated family fun time.

I, even, got to eat my first lobster at one of these gatherings. The Pier restaurant was said to have some of the best Florida lobsters in the area. Just because *they had* it, didn't mean *I* could have it! It was, still, hard for *me* to *get* it! You see, mom and dad paid our family bill. That meant I had to get *their* permission to order it. I had to beg and plead for a taste of lobster for a long time, before I was allowed to order the gourmet crustaceous critter. My parents just didn't think I was ready for it. (In reality, they weren't ready to pay for it!)

To make matters worse, mom wouldn't eat lobster. She wouldn't *even* try it! She said it was one of three foods that looked back at you when served on a plate. To look at it, looking back at her made her skin crawl! Besides, she was *sure* I wouldn't like it.

My persistence, finally, prevailed! After a good bit of pleading, they, finally, gave in to my request. I got to try it for the first time on a Friday family night out.

I was so excited! I could, hardly, wait for it to be served. Mom and dad watched, intently, as I put the first bite into my mouth…It was great! Just as I, always, thought it would be! I had every intention to eat it all up; but, I wasn't sure what parts I was supposed to eat! They had served it with the tail meat hanging outside the shell, but still attached at the tail end. I supposed that the tiny legs had meat in them, as well. It was tedious; but, I managed to get the little bits out! I left the head alone.

My last bite was *that* portion still attached to the tail. I wanted it! I had to have it! I was not going to leave any tiny bit of the lobster meat behind! I was determined to get it all! Getting it to turn loose, however, proved to be very difficult!!

I tried to pry it loose with my fork; but, I bent my fork as the meat held on. Determined to get that last bite, I pried harder, and harder using my knife and fork to get extra leverage. Suddenly, you heard a "thunk". It, finally, came loose! When it did, it flung high into the air. Like a seafaring missile, it flew across the restaurant dining room.

Much to my surprise, and everybody else's shock, it targeted a non-family patron, who was sitting, quietly, with his own family. Without any prior warning, it hit him square on his forehead, in between slurps of oyster stew. The man froze still in his eating motion. Then, as if it were being viewed in slow motion, it slid down his forehead, and into his stew!

Everyone in the restaurant witnessed what happened, except the man! Unfortunately, he never saw it coming! He didn't know *what* had just hit him…where it had come from…,nor why most customers were laughing! He didn't know what to think!

Laughter, soon, spread, uncontrollably, from the customers, to the staff, and on to the cooks in the back! I was still in shock, and turned a deep red with embarrassment. I wanted to crawl under my table and hide, or just mysteriously disappear! I thought about slithering out a nearby window to make my escape! Instead, I meandered over to offer my apologies to the innocent victim.

There was nothing else I could do; but, confess my error. The kind-spirited man smiled and, courteously, accepted my explanations, and my apology. He jokingly said, "I didn't know lobsters could be so dangerous!"

Dad insisted on buying the man another bowl of oyster stew. I wanted to ask if I could have my last piece of lobster back. But, my dad's "don't you dare" stare sealed my lips. The innocent victim turned out to be a very gracious man, who, gladly, offered the remaining piece of the wayward lobster to me. Addressing my dad, he said, "It's, too, expensive to waste!"

Dad thanked him and ordered him another bowl of oyster stew.

When all the hilarity subsided, a calmness was restored as everyone went back to eating their meals. We consumed a lot of seafood and hush puppies that night! We flushed it all down with several glasses of sweet tea. With all the eating and slushing, it was only a matter of time before some of it would have to go….somewhere!

Whenever dad acknowledged a '*nature*' call that meant he *had* to go. He, usually, waited to the last moment; because, he hated to miss anything being said, or done, at the table. So, when he had to go, he would be about ready to bust! Under those hurried conditions, he stood to be excused.

During his eating frenzy, he had tucked his cloth table napkin into his belt. At least, he *thought* it was his table napkin. In reality, he had, inadvertently, tucked the *table cloth* into his belt!

That night, the restaurant owner had decided to use cloth dinner napkins that perfectly matched his red checkered tablecloths. When dad stuffed his 'dinner napkin' into his belt, he was, actually, stuffing the edge of the tablecloth into that secured position! With it tucked tightly in his belt, he was poised for disaster, and didn't know it!

Much to the shock of everyone at his table, as he turned to walk away, he started taking the whole table cloth with him! Mom yelled, "Julian! Julian!" But, he didn't know what for! He kept turning around trying to figure out what "in heavens name" was happening! His rotating action was wrapping more of the tablecloth around him, pulling more, and more, stuff off the table!

Aunts and Uncles were grabbing their plates of food, while trying to catch their drinks at the same time! Some were not fast enough! Items began to fall to the floor. Mom's yelling, other's laughing, plates clanging and tea glasses spilling only caused dad to get more confused and, deeply, frustrated.

After a moment of pandemonium, and above all the excited clamoring, mom yelled, "Freeze, Julian!" Recognizing the source of that piercing command, he, finally, froze in a most befuddled and embarrassing position. In his frozen state, he paused enough to help avert further disaster; but, the main damage had been done!

Aunt ML was laughing and snorting so hard that tears streamed down her blood-red face. She could, hardly, catch her breath! With dad frozen in place, mom got to laughing. She laughed so hard, she had to sit down to avoid an "embarrassing" accident of her own! Dad, red-faced and hot as a firecracker, was getting angry and ready to pop! He couldn't figure out what in the world had just happened!

Of course, this great calamity could have happened to anyone. Something similar may have, even, happened to you. It may have just *seemed* that this kind of stuff followed us each time we got together, and wherever we went! Maybe, that's why some restaurants shuddered when we came to visit!

The restaurant owner was just about as embarrassed about the event as my dad. His crew, quickly, cleaned up the mess, and replaced the food. The only good thing from all this was that the restaurant patrons enjoyed both acts of the floor show! I think some finished eating, then sat waiting to see what might happen next!

The restaurant owner insisted it was his fault and vowed to never to repeat that mistake, again! Uncle G made the comment, "This is going to demand a big tip!"

If you think about it, the Church is, sometimes, guilty of the same thing! It takes on the appearance of the world around it. On occasion, it has tried to blend itself back into the society, and worldliness, from which it was redeemed!

Some think it is best <u>not</u> to "stick out," too much. If we are not careful, however, the important differences between the ways of God and the ways of the world can get blurred beyond recognition. When this happens, it becomes hard to see any measurable differences between the lives meant to be holy and those living in the world, outside the realm of faith.

When this happens, is the Church being honest? I mean, isn't the Church *supposed* to "stick out" from the world? Isn't it *supposed* to look different?...Isn't it *supposed* to act different....and not be the same!?

How can light and darkness blend together? Or, as Paul puts it: *"Do not be unequally yoked together with unbelievers. For what fellowship has righteousness with lawlessness? What communion has light with darkness? What accord has Christ with the devil? What part has a believer with an unbeliever?... Therefore, come out from among them and be separate, says the Lord'"* (2 Corinthians 6:14-17, NKJV).

It is befuddling for the Church to look just like the lost world around it. This confuses those who are seeking a difference in their lives. The fellowship of redeemed believers, the Church, should offer them a difference that could change their lives. We should be unashamed to stand upon the guiding principles of our faith, in all areas of life.

When we look the same, act the same, think the same and react to life the same as those outside the Church, then we set the stage for confusion, disappointment and discouragement. We must not be afraid to be different from the world in a loving, redeeming way.

What does your Church look like?

FIRE DRILLS

Remember the drills we used to have in elementary school? In the 1960's, St. Marys had bomb drills and nuclear fallout drills on a regular basis. We were only a few miles from a big naval base and shipyard located in Mayport, Florida. Being right on the Florida line meant that we were not far enough from Cuba during some troubled times.

It was believed, if Mayport *was* targeted, *we* had to be ready. The thought of nuclear war was frightening, even to a child. That's why we felt like we were fulfilling our civic duty by drilling and being prepared.

My personal favorite among these drills were the fire drills. It got us out of class work, and offered a trip out-of-doors for a while. Fire drills were, always, conducted in an orderly, and proficient, manner. When the fire bell rang, the teacher would, calmly, instruct the class to stand beside their desks. With everyone standing, we were to exit, slowly, by rows in single file.

In the hallway, four lines of orderly elementary students converged, vacating the building through the nearest exit doors. Once in the school yard, each class was assigned a designated rallying point. We were to wait there, until the "all clear" signal was given.

Some teachers were disturbed by the drills. It was fun to me!

Anything that took up class time, and got us out of school work, was fine with me. I loved all the drills; but, I <u>loved</u> fire drills!

As in anything else, after you've done drills for a while, you tended to get used to the routine. They become monotonous, mechanical and mundane. The thrill of the moment began to fade. This was especially true when teachers were alerted, in advance, that a fire drill was coming. Once alerted, they began to give the class advance warning of an impending drill.

It became like a private contest among the teachers. They 'calmly' rushed us through the procedure to see which class could get to their rallying point first. There must have been a prize for the teacher who was the first to have their class in place!…Well, I'm not sure about that. I just know that *our* only prize was getting out of school work, which was, still, fine with me.

Personally, I think it would have been a lot more rewarding if the fire trucks were allowed to participate. All we got was the fire chief, accompanied by his friend, the chief of police. They didn't, actually, attend every fire drill. When they did make their appearance, they would calmly stroll across the street from City Hall bringing their coffee cups with them. In a way, I kind of felt sorry for them. They gave the appearance of being bored and bothered.

With each new fire drill, I had reoccurring phantasies about new ways to become the hero who saved the class…or school…or some special girl from peril. The saved, indebted female, of course, would always reward me with a kiss.

Some might would debate if I were the hero type. In reality, I probably created more disasters, than I really want to admit! Though I wouldn't want to name them, I'm sure there were *some* who felt that way!

The more I pondered it, the more I wondered: what would *really* happen if we had a *real* fire? What if the teachers didn't know the fire drill was coming? What if it all was a big surprise!? What would *really* happen then!?

All were good questions that had no good answers. For the safety of all students and teachers, *I* felt these were good enough questions that needed to have good and sure answers. I realized that there are those who would not agree with me. And, that was OK! A lot of my reasonings got that kind of a response from others in my earlier years.

The burning question became: How could we see what would really happen? Also, how could this be done without hurting anybody... and without destroying school property?

Just pulling the fire alarm was out of the question! I had, already, learned a valuable lesson in a J.C. Penny's store involving that small curious red lever on the wall!

One day, while shopping with mom and dad, a little red lever on the store's wall caught my attention. I, barely, remember pointing at it... maybe, even, touching it, while asking dad, "What is t...?"

I never got to finish the question! The next thing I knew dad's firm hand of correction knocked my fingers away from this imposing red device on the wall. I can still hear his stern, strong voice commanding, "Don't touch that!"

You better believe, whatever that red thing was, I was **not** going to touch it! It might have caused the building to fall down...a bomb to go off...or, something else more terrifying! At the time, I didn't know, for sure! And, I didn't care! I just knew, I wasn't going to touch it!

He, later, explained that it was a fire alarm. But, he had already, definitely, put the fear of the red lever in me. There was *no way* that I was, ever, going to touch one, much less to pull one. Not even if there *was* a fire! No, sir! *Someone else* would have to do that!

The perplexing situation called for a great deal of fourth grade strategy. How could I get smoke without a *real* fire? Was there a good smoke substitute that could be used? I didn't want any real destruction of property, nor anyone to get hurt. All I wanted was a more genuine test of a fire drill. So, what could I use for my test?

Dry ice came to mind. Lunch room workers often used dry ice for some reason; then, they would discard it behind the lunch room. We would find it laying on the ground. We, also, discovered that if you put water, or a human water *substitute*, on dry ice, it *would* smoke. Getting dry ice when you needed it, however, would be difficult. Not to mention that the transportation of it posed several problems.

I had to ponder on it for a while. "What else would 'smoke' without a real fire?" This concept consumed my thoughts, night and day. It didn't keep me up at night; but, it was on my mind.

One evening, while pondering on this matter, I saw my mom fluffing powder under her arms. For a moment, or two, the powder puffs looked like smoke. Something like that might be the very thing that could work! However, her little box of powder wouldn't be enough. I would need more…a lot more!

My chemicals offered some food for thought as an alternative. There were some of them, when mixed together, would cause smoke of different kinds and colors! Of course, I would have to be careful using my chemicals; because, mom and dad had, already, informed me that most of my self-produced smoking results were poisonous. I, certainly, didn't want to poison anyone!

After spending a good bit of time pondering on it, the possible answer hit me out of the clear blue! Of course! The chalk dust from the electric blackboard eraser cleaning machine would be a perfect smoke substitute!

It was collected in a big red bag, and then discarded after it was full. I could collect it for a while, and get a huge bag of this chalk dust, then use it in my experiment. It seemed like a great idea! There was only one flaw in that solution, only a few *elite* students had access to the cleaner. I, unfortunately, was not counted among them; but, I had a friend who was!

David *was* among those elite students. He and I had partnered on some experiments in the past. We, often, would combine our chemistry sets and concoct many chemical combinations with various results. He was <u>always</u> interested in a good experiment.

When I asked him to collect the chalk dust for my undisclosed project that I wanted to conduct, for humanitarian reasons, he was more than happy to help out. He was a bit curious as to what I planned to do with all that chalk dust; so, he asked me what I intended to do with it. When he, justly, asked that question, I, honestly, told him I wasn't sure, just yet! I just knew I would need a lot of chalk dust to conduct my experiment, successfully. He seemed satisfied with my answer, and pledged to help.

Whenever he was allowed to clean the erasers, he began to empty the bag of dust into a large paper bag, and then he would hide it behind the air conditioning unit. With great precision, and stealth, he filled two big grocery bags with chalk dust.

No one noticed the paper bags hidden behind the air units in the same equipment room where the electric blackboard eraser cleaning machine was housed. I admit, the collection process did take a while. It was near winter's end, when the paper bags were ready and waiting for my experiment. By this time, I had decided on my delivery system for the dust. The only thing needed, now, was the opportunity.

Opportunity was going to be difficult. The equipment room was always locked; and, <u>only</u> the elite students could handle the key. They were sworn to loyalty to the teacher who had entrusted them. They, rarely, broke that trust.

I had been in the equipment room once before; but, it took a chicken pox epidemic to allow me that opportunity. Now, everyone was immune. Of course, there *were* the mumps and measles; but, no one was feeling sick!

Just when it all seemed hopeless, my fourth grade teacher, Mrs. W, 'commanded' me to stop what I was doing and go clean the erasers. I couldn't believe it! At last, the opportunity had, unexpectedly, fallen into my lap! Could this mean Providential approval! I didn't know for sure…and I really didn't care!

The equipment room was just across the hall; so, I had to act quickly. As soon as I had finished cleaning the erasers, I emptied the dust bag into the paper bags already filled with chalk dust. They were *exactly* placed where David said they would be.

The plan that was first devised back in the Fall was, now, about to take place as early Spring approached. It was a simple plan. I was going to vigorously shake the chalk dust in the paper bags in order to loosen it up. Next, I was going to, carefully, empty it into the dormant air conditioning main air duct. The air duct had a small door on the side of the upper portion. I guessed it was there for cleaning purposes. For whatever reason the door was there, it made the perfect entry door for the chalk dust to be placed inside the air duct.

The air conditioning unit had not been used all winter. Our heat for the winter came from the boiler room through baseboard radiators into each classroom. The weather was such that we were still using the heat. I thought that the chalk dust would sit for days, maybe weeks, before the air units would be kicked on. When they did come on, *sometime in later spring,* the chalk dust would be stirred up and delivered to some of the rooms along its air duct trail. Hopefully, it would resemble smoke…just enough to make the experiment work! Then, we would get to see what would *really* happen in a more realistic fire drill.

It seemed to be a good plan, from my perspective. The delayed action would cover my connection to the chalk dust. I would *not* be the last one in the equipment room. Not to mention that many others would have had time to go in and out in that elapsed time span. No one would know *who* might have placed the chalk dust in the air vent. It was a good winter plan.

Did I mention that I was living in the coastal town of St. Marys, Georgia? I had forgotten that the seasons change quickly there. It could be winter cold in the morning, and summer hot by the afternoon. Some years the summer heat would slip up on you making your spring feel like summer!

I had no sooner placed the stirred up bag of chalk dust into the air conditioning vent, when the air unit awoke from its winter hibernation. "Days" and "weeks" later, *suddenly*, became "then" and "now"! It shocked me, so much I almost swallowed my butter rum lifesaver. Whole!

Confused, I ran back to the classroom and returned the erasers, and the key, to Mrs. W. I took my seat sweating out the next few moments. I didn't know what was going to happen, nor how long it might take. I would just have to wait, and sweat it out!

Waiting for something you weren't sure about, and not knowing what might happen, was like waiting for fish to bite a baited hook....only worse! I couldn't concentrate on the teacher's lesson. Sweat covered my brow! I sat there for the longest time staring at the air vent in our room; but, nothing came out! I was about at the point of giving up and accepting the fact that it was a bogus plan, when things began to happen!

From the rooms on the opposite side of the hall you could begin to hear rumblings. You could hear girls chirping like excited marsh hens. All of a sudden, we heard a repeated cry of, "Yahoo! Yahoo!"

It was SB. He came bursting out of his classroom headed for the nearest fire alarm. Without hesitation, and with great pleasure, he pulled the alarm screaming at the top of his lungs, "Fire! Fire! Hot dog a fire!"

His previous record of pulling fire alarms in other places was known only to the teachers, and our principal. SB had never pulled one at our school. None of us knew of his obsession with fire alarms, and SB never mentioned it! But, as I recall, now, he, always, had to touch each fire alarm unit as he walked down the hall. Now, he was rejoicing; because, he felt justified in, finally, pulling the alarm...for real!

I hadn't planned on SB's reaction, nor his enthusiastic participation. He ran up and down the halls, continually, screaming at the top of his lungs, "Fire! Fire! Get out! There's a fire!"

His screaming inspired the janitor to join in the enthusiastic call to safety. He insisted that everyone get out of the building, as quickly as possible…by any means possible! This confused the teachers who wondered why they had not been alerted to a practice drill.

Students, and teachers, began to panic. The janitor's insistence became more frantic! He began to rush things along, demanding that students get out…*any way they could*!

Some students ran down the halls, searching for any exit they could find. Some were climbing through the V-angled windows to exit the building. Some tried the windows, but got stuck in them! Mrs. W made us march out in single file to our rallying spot. She insisted we wait there for further instructions. From there we had a good view of what went on. It was <u>not</u> a pretty sight! Not many teachers were following the fire exit plan.

The arrival of the first fire truck brought some excitement to those of us who admired the massive red trucks. The other fire truck came later. It was delayed while waiting for its crew to show up. The volunteer firemen had to leave their jobs to come help.

The paper mill blew its mill whistle, usually reserved for noon, or a community emergency or crisis. It was signaling a warning that some emergency was going on. It was all very thrilling! But, now, a sense of fear and doom began to creep over me!

The building was, finally, cleared of all students. The volunteer firemen worked, quickly, as they checked every room. Every nook and cranny was examined. No fire was found! Not anywhere! They *did* detect, however, a heavy smell of chalk dust in the air, which they couldn't explain.

At first, all eyes were turned toward SB. His past history made him a prime suspect for a mischievous prank. As the investigation progressed, student and teacher witnesses mentioned that the "smoke" appeared to come from the air conditioning vents <u>*before*</u> SB pulled the fire alarm.

When they inspected the equipment room, they found chalk dust residue still piled up in the vent. No one could determine how the chalk dust got there, nor how long it had been there. They *did* know that SB was <u>not</u> among the elite students who had access to the equipment room.

It got to be late in the day; so, they let everyone go home, while they continued their investigations trying to figure out what had happened. The rest of the afternoon, and into the night they went over the building, again, and again. They wanted to be sure that they hadn't missed anything.

I was restless all night long! I was worried about what the next day might bring. I decided that I should ask the Lord to keep me out of any impending trouble…but, *that* prayer didn't seem to go beyond my bedroom ceiling! No comforting answer came. No peace. Just more worry!

The next day at school everyone who had <u>ever</u> cleaned an eraser, from the third to the seventh grade, was summoned to the auditorium. We were lectured about the abuse of fire alarms. We were threatened with being arrested and "institutionalized"! (We didn't know what that meant; but, it didn't sound good!)

A local minister, Pastor Mc, explained why the whole event was morally wrong, and an offense to God. "God does not like pranks like this," he bellowed.

He put it, plainly, to us! This 'prank' had caused confusion, which led to panic; and, could have caused someone to get hurt. "God is not the author of confusion," he proclaimed, "so, it must have come from someone <u>evil</u>!"

Oh, boy! This had just become more of a spiritual war than I had anticipated! I was gripped with guilt and shame. I didn't want God mad at me; but, how could I make things right without getting myself *murderized*? I mean, God wouldn't listen to my earlier prayer! Would He help me, now!

The answer came in his next words, *"But, 'if we confess our sins, He is faithful and just to forgive us our sins and to cleanse us from all unrighteousness',"* (1 John 1:9, NKJV).

So, in order to get God's help, I was going to have to confess! It sounded a little goofy to me at first; but, God had always worked in strange and mysterious ways. It took a while to sink in; but, it began to sound good to me. So, I confessed to God, in Jesus' name, and asked Him to forgive me, and let me live to the fifth grade!

Was I forgiven? Perhaps, I was; but, there was no peace. To find peace, it appeared as though I was going to have to go a step further. I had to get some sixth and seventh graders off the hook. Our principal was convinced that one of them was the culprit.

After a second day of praying, and looking for some other way out, I, finally, decided to stop by the principal's office. I told him that I *might* know *something* about the incident. I tried to explain that it was an experiment, for the benefit of all mankind, that went terribly wrong.

He nodded his head and told me that I was the fifth student to confess! Boy! I wished I had known that! Evidently, there was a _lot_ of chalk dust that had been piled into the A/C ducts over the whole winter period.

Mr. T, the principal, said, "However, I'm glad you confessed. I appreciate it, and I'm sure God does, too; but, you know squaring with God is between you and Him. Squaring with me means I paddle you."

Deep down, I knew that! I asked if I might make <u>one</u> request. He acknowledged that he, rarely, granted requests. I guess I could understand that; but, I asked, anyway: "Please, use your regular paddle, and *don't use* the electric paddling machine!" (It was rumored to be somewhere in his office.) After a moment of silence, he rubbed his chin and nodded, slightly.

He, finally, said, "I guess I can do that."

He complied to my request; and, I, willingly, took my punishment from him…then, I took it from mom…and, then, from dad. I never repeated that experiment, ever again! After my repentance and confession, peace was restored.

I learned that if you want to get, completely, square with God, you must get square with others, too. That's when we find peace and forgiveness.

I had learned a valuable lesson at a terrible price! The price that Christ paid to secure my forgiveness and peace, however, was much greater! Praise the Lord! For His mercy endures forever!

First Dates

Valentine's Day always makes me remember 'first' dates. To me first dates have, always, been an awesome, yet frightening proposition.

Do you remember your first date with "the" girl of your dreams? Do you recollect your first double-date? Do you remember your first solo date? Sure you do! It was a special event filled with excitement, nervousness and uncertainty.

Most of my first dates were like religious experiences. I called them the "alpha and omega" dates…"the first and the last"! Each one taught me a valuable lesson. I just wish I could have remembered that lesson from one date to the next! My "re-caller" button malfunctioned, a lot, in those days. Hopefully, I've learned how to learn since then.

When my brother was up for his first date, mom wanted to help. She pulled Floyd aside and gave him some 'private' instructions. I am not sure what she told him. Neither one would ever talk about it. When it was my turn for a first date, she did not have that discussion with me. I guess she thought I picked the information up by observation, or osmosis!

Uncle G, mom's youngest brother, had a discussion with me about personal hygiene. He told me that I needed to change my underwear…often…like every day! And, use deodorant…and, some kind of aftershave or cologne.

This was important information. I guess it must have taken the place of mom's discussion. All I got out of that particular discussion was the need to take a bath...and put on clean underwear ....and the other stuff....often!

I guess he thought I had a problem with that kind of thing! Maybe, he was afraid I would stink the girl unconscious, or to death! As unnecessary as *I* thought the discussion was at the time, it was instruction I have always remembered, and still practice to this day!

After mom spoke to Floyd, privately, it was time to go pick up his date for the evening. That's when it became apparent that _we all_ were going to take him to get his date. Floyd was not a happy camper about this!

He was not old enough to drive; so, mom had to drive him. That was bad enough! To make things worse, Dad was fishing and my sister was spending the night with a friend. So, that meant I had to come along, too. Floyd objected, vehemently, with these arrangements; but, there was nothing that could be done about it. Mom was not going to call in "markers" for a babysitter for such a brief time. Floyd would just have to deal with it!

I was assigned the back seat. I was, also, told, or commanded, to keep my mouth shut! Boy! Did they mean business! Every time I cleared my throat I was cautioned, "Not a word!" All this concern was baffling to me. I couldn't understand what the big fuss was all about. I just knew it sounded pretty serious to me!

With no other option available to me, I decided to put myself into a learning mode. I kept quiet, with listening ears. If I couldn't participate, then I had best try to learn something, partly for the sake of fear, if I did speak ; and, partly to observe this strange phenomenon in which I had no previous experience...nor, any confidence!

The way it was panning out, this dating business seemed to be a much graver situation than I had first imagined. It became evident that a person had a lot to gain...or to lose, in this endeavor. There seemed to be a lot being laid on the line here! I decided the best thing for me *was* to sit back, keep quiet and observe every detail.

When we arrived at the young lass's house, my brother asked mom to beep the horn. It sounded like a reasonable request to me. Mom, however, almost went ballistic! She, sternly, responded, "No sir, young man! You go to the door to get her; then, you escort her back to the car."

I wondered "why"? What was the big deal? Was the girl not able to make it to the car? Had she been injured in some way? Perhaps, there was some unseen peril lurking about! I looked around the yard for any obvious signs of danger: thugs, bears, gators, dogs…but, I could see none!

When someone came to pick _us_ up at our house, they would, usually, blow their horn as a signal for us to come out to the car. I always thought it was a universal signal used throughout the known world. I thought everyone knew what it meant. Why wasn't that alright, now?

Reluctantly, and with evident shyness, my brother opened the car door, and got out of the car. He stood beside car for a while. Then, he, slowly, made his way towards the sidewalk leading up to the door. With each step, we could hear him murmuring, "She said, 'just beep the horn' and she'd come *right* out…I don't see why I have to…" Before he could finish his thought, He arrived at the door.

He, sheepishly, looked back at us. Now, I could see the beginnings of a grin that, eventually, stretched from ear to ear. He coughed… shined his shoe on his pants leg; then, he boldly rang the bell…with trembling hands!

He thought for a moment of how he and his friends had often rung someone's doorbell at night; and, then ran off! He felt the strong urge to run, here….now! But, for some reason, he was compelled to stand firm, and hold his ground! It was one of those defining moments when I was proud to call him my brother! I regarded him, that night, as someone I could, really, look up to! His expression of boldness and courage was inspirational.

The door, slowly, opened revealing the father of the girl. He was a tall, grisly man who towered over my brother. Floyd's eyes got "way big" as he tilted his head upward to view the full scope of this giant of a man that stood before him. I wanted to shout, "Run for it!" But, my lips had been sealed shut by mom's clamped fingers. The father politely asked, "Yes?" It was as if he was saying, "What do <u>you</u> want?"

Floyd mumbled something; but, I couldn't make it out. Whatever it was must have included the secret password; because, the girl's father let him in the house! Once inside, he was on his own. There was no way for me to know what was going on! And, there was definitely no way to offer him help to make his escape!

A few moments later, he, and his date, re-emerged from the captive's house. He seemed to be unscathed and smiling. I, often, wondered what terrible things might have happened behind those closed doors. He never told me; and, it would be a while, yet, before I would learn for myself.

Having escorted his date safely to the car, Floyd opened the car door and jumped in the middle allowing the girl to have the "shot gun" seat. I thought, "Hey! He must really like this girl!" He <u>never</u> gave up the "shot gun" seat to *anyone*!

Mom had other thoughts on the matter. He had no sooner gotten in, when mom ordered him right back out! "You **always** let the girl get in first!" She was very stern in her instruction.

This was a shock to us all…including the girl! My brother was totally caught off guard, and totally embarrassed! The girl was embarrassed, too! I was embarrassed for the both of them! I mean…my goodness! Riding "<u>shot gun</u>" (by the door) was the *primo* place to ride. *No one* wanted to sit in the 'middle'. The middle was, always, cramped, hot and uncomfortable. The siblings in my family would, almost, draw blood fighting to see who would get to ride "shot gun". Offering her <u>that</u> seat seemed, to me, to be a good way to impress a girl and show her that she was special! It was offering her the best seat in the car! What was so wrong with that!?

Dating was, definitely, becoming very complicated and confusing. Not only did you have to bath, put on clean underwear, fresh clothes, deodorize with new deodorant, cover yourself in costly colognes, brush your teeth until your gums bleed and comb your hair, *all* to impress the girl; *but*, now, you had to risk it all by condemning her to sit in the middle seat!

To some of the girls we knew, all the smell goods, clean clothes and baths in the world wouldn't undo the degradation and humiliation of condemning them to sit in the middle seat. Something was, definitely, odd about all this!

Floyd, who was nervous and painfully self-conscious, still, obediently, jumped out of the car, allowing his date to get in first. He was, obviously, upset. I could see the *steam* building up all the way to the movie theater. Neither one said a word, until we arrived at our dating destination.

At first, I thought the event was, almost, comical. After thinking more about it, my heart went out to Floyd....and his date. I didn't; but, I almost cried on his behalf!

After we dropped them off at the theater, I climbed over the seat and, quietly, stared at my mother. My silent stare became, obviously, irritating to her. Suddenly, she stopped the car and quipped, "What!?"

I puckered my previously sealed lips and asked, "Why? Why did she have to sit in the middle? He went through all that stuff to impress her, and you made him give her the worse seat in the car. What's with that?" She tried to explain that it was "customary" and "polite" to open the door, and let the girl go first. It was something a *gentleman* does for his special lady.

I was still puzzled. It made no sense to me. After a moment of pondering, I asked, "But, if going in 'first' means you get the cruddier deal on the seat dibs, shouldn't the guy go first and let his girlfriend have the better deal with the better seat?"

She gave no response. Her continued silence meant either she didn't have a good answer; or, the conversation was over.

When dad got home from fishing, he and mom had a private conference in the bedroom. When he came out, he stood between me and the television and asked, "You got any questions about dating?"

My first answer was, "No, sir!"

He said, "OK".

Mom said, "Julian…"

When he pressed the matter further, I posed to him the events of the evening. I gave him my observations, and revealed the still unanswered question that I had put to mom.

His response was, "When you get older, the girls appreciate sitting in the middle more than they do, now." It was, clearly, one of those, "This too shall come to pass" moments. The answer was quick, to the point and futuristic in nature. It was enough to satisfy my young inquiring mind. I think he was relieved. It was never mentioned, again.

As I ponder upon it now, I realize that my mother and my brother were trying to do the same thing; but, in different ways. They were, each, trying to show honor and respect to the girl. Their ideas on how to do that went in opposite directions!

One way may have been more accepted than the other; but, neither way was, necessarily, wrong. In fact, my brother was enacting the *Golden Rule*, though he may not have realized it at the time. "*In all things, whatsoever you want men to do to you, you do it to them, for this is the law (of love) and the prophets (of justice)*" (*Swamp Version*, Matthew 7:12).

He was giving his date the best, and most prized, seat in the vehicle. A seat that, usually, he fought very hard to attain for himself. In his own mind, his heart was honoring and respecting her in a way he hoped she might understand…at that particular age. I guess there are times when we can, only, hope that the motivations of our heart can be, clearly, seen by those who have loving eyes and a caring spirit.

Later, I began to understand what dad and mom were talking about. They were trying to reveal the respect and closeness you feel in relationships, as they had come to understand them on their way to adulthood. They wanted these things to inspire us to be the 'gentleman' they spoke of…and, open the car door for the girl to get in first. Then, the genuine motivations of a true heart are rewarded, usually, by her sitting in the middle to be nearer to you.

On this Valentine's Day, relive your first date with your loved one. If you can't remember it, then go out and have another first date! Do it today, with a true heart that honors and respects the one you love.

Just remember this: If he goes first when you think *you* ought to, he may be trying to give you the *best!*

May God bless you all in His love that never fails.

FIRST DATE

Shaking, trembling, jerking

Sitting in a pool of sweat!

Rubbing, scratching, stammering

Wondering if my hair is set!

Remembering, reciting, forgetting

Things I want to say.

Biting, dreaming, thinking

Why do I feel this way?

Walking, stumbling, slumping

To the dreaded door I go.

Stuttering, muttering, shuttering

Mumbling each phrase just so!

Quivering, weakening, squeaking

Crashing to the floor with a pout!

"What in the world just happened!"

Oh, he just passed out!

R.P. Wildes
(2009)

GRANDPA McGHIN

Grandpa McGhin was old! The first time I saw him he was sitting on his porch looking older than dirt, and stiff as a board. I had just turned ten years old. He had been ninety for a while. He was, definitely, old! He knew it; and, I knew it!

I rode my J. C. Higgins bicycle up to his front steps, and dropped it onto the ground. He never looked up at me. He just stared in a different direction, as though I didn't exist. I was trying to make a statement with my frustration; but, he wasn't listening to it.

He wore a white, opened collar shirt with dark stripes running up and down it. His dark dress pants were held up by suspenders. He sat propped up on his cane staring straight ahead into space.

His white hair was combed neatly. He had shaved; but, there were some gray whiskers still on his chin and neck that he had missed. And, there was a wart on his ear that had matured grey hairs sticking out from it!

The whiteness of his aged hair made the small brown stain in the corner of his mouth stand out like a sore thumb. It looked like the same kind of snuff stain that my Aunt Frankie used to have. At least he wasn't as messy with his snuffing.

I was <u>not</u> real happy to be at his house; and, I wanted it to show! You see, my mom had 'lent' me to the McGhins to walk with the elderly man for his exercise. The other adults were at work, and didn't want him to walk alone.

It was not uncommon for us children to be 'lent' to family and friends for favors. It was not something we got paid for, nor did we ask to be rewarded in any way. It was a favor extended from one family to another.

The decision to lend was never placed into the child's hands. It was made by our parents based upon necessity. Needless to say, I was not happy about my assigned task. I had other, more serious, things to do…at least, they were more serious to me. This intrusion was going to put a severe crimp in my meaningful afternoon of play and adventure time!

I wanted my discontent to be obvious; but, it was not being acknowledged. When I asked if he was Mr. McGhin, he looked straight ahead and didn't respond. So, I asked again. Still, no response. I thought, "Great! He's old and deaf!" Staring straight ahead, he asked, "Who is it?"

My next thought was, "Oh no! He's old, deaf and blind, too!" What had mom gotten me into!? I could, hardly, take care of myself; and, now, I had to care for a ninety year old man who was deaf and blind! This just wasn't fair!

He asked, again, "Who is it?"

I took a deep breath and yelled, "Hi. I'm Ronnie. I've come to walk you for a while."

"What am I…a dog!?", he quipped. "You've come to *walk* me?…And, why are you yelling? Is something wrong with you?…Or, do you think I'm deaf, or something!?"

My thoughts were, now, even more terse, "Oh, great! He's old, deaf, blind and senile!" I wasn't even sure what 'senile' was; but, Grandpa had been accused of it by Granny when he didn't think straight!

My thoughts were altered by the expression on his face. It was clear that I had offended him, which I *really* didn't mean to do. I wasn't mad at him. I was mad at my mom who had obligated me without my consent. I apologized for my rude and selfish behavior. I felt bad that my words had been so harshly spoken. I admitted that my sentence construction didn't come out right. I restated that I had come to walk *with* him, and keep him company.

"Well," he continued, "what if I don't want to walk with <u>you</u>?"

My subdued, delayed, and submissive response was: "I guess, then, we'll just sit on the porch, and stare at the graveyard across the street."

"If we do walk…you know, we could walk anywhere…even by one of your friend's house, if we wanted to," he offered.

It was a nice suggestion. I told him that St. Marys wasn't very big, and anywhere we walked wouldn't be far from *somebody's* house! That's when he realized that my youthful wisdom had confounded his!

I began to notice, as we talked, that his eyes would move a little back and forth. So, I asked, "Are you blind?"

He quickly responded with, "Are you stupid?"

I said, "No, sir!"

To which he quipped, "Well, there you go."

"If you're not blind, then why do you just stare out in space?", I queried.

He informed me that it was obvious that I didn't want to see him; so, he wasn't going to see me, until *I* saw him. It took me a while to figure that one out! Eventually, it began to sink in and make some sense. It was obvious that our walk was beginning on shaky ground.

At first, not much was said by either one of us. He mumbled, every now and then; but, I couldn't understand a word he mumbling…and, I wasn't about to ask him!

We walked towards the Oak Grove Cemetery. In the daylight, it was a beautiful historical cemetery. The oak trees stood tall with wandering limbs, covered with Spanish moss. The grave sites were old. Each one told a little of the history of the one buried there. If you took the time to read them, they revealed a little bit of the history of St. Marys, which was self-proclaimed as the "second oldest city in the United States".

As we stood at the stone wall surrounding the cemetery, we began to talk about different items we saw in the graveyard. We agreed on its beauty. We, also, agreed on how spooky it got after dark. I told him of some of the 'ghosts' that I had encountered, as well as, some of the stories associated with the old cemetery. He seemed to take joyful delight in my informing him about some of the eerie, creepy things I had, personally, encountered within it.

As we continued our walk, he tried to make lighthearted conversation. He would state things like, "I understand this graveyard is a very popular place…People are *dieing* to get in!"

With that, he cracked a smile, and offered a little giggle under his breath. Although the joke was older than he was, I realized this guy *did* have a sense of humor. I felt better about walking with him, and a little relieved. It became evident to me that he was going to be alright!

We walked every day for quite a while. As we walked, he would talk; then, I would talk. We talked about many things…anything! Nothing was off limits. I, even, asked him how it felt to be ninety years old. After he pondered the question for a moment, he said, "I'm not sure!"

I was a bit perplexed at his answer. If he *was* ninety years old, how could he not know what it felt like! Then, he continued, "I've never thought of myself as being ninety. The mental pictures I have of myself are those of a twenty-five year old man. When I glance into a mirror to fix my hair, or straighten my clothes, I don't see an old man there in the mirror. I see *me* at twenty-five. Now, if I pay closer attention to my image, I see that the young man has aged…But, I don't dwell on it. I'd rather think, and feel, like the younger man within me."

I guess I looked puzzled; so, he explained that he knew he *wasn't really* twenty-five. He acknowledged that he was wise enough to know that there were limits to what his body could do at his current age. But, he made sure that the things he *did do* at twenty-five, and still could do at ninety, were still done. That image kept him walking every day, and feeling younger than his years may suggest.

I don't know how, exactly, but it made sense to me. His words made an instant, and lasting, impression on me. From that time on, age has never made much difference to me. Living a quality life is what makes all the difference.

There are times, even today, that I forget how old I am; <u>because</u>, I don't dwell on aging. My circle of friends have no age limits. Without realizing it, a whole new world was opened up for me. A world which, now, allowed me to receive, even, more wisdom and counsel from a *friend* - not from an old man!

I began to look forward to our walks. I *wanted* to learn more. Some of his bits of wisdom may have sounded silly to some; but, I was storing them up for later! I was certain they would make sense later! I felt as though I was, really, learning a lot! I know, now, that there was a purpose in our walks. In many ways, Grandpa McGhin was helping me to become wise. I needed him in my life.

By age ten, both my grandfathers had passed into eternity. At an age when a young boy might would have listened to a grandfather's wisdom, the Lord put me with Grandpa McGhin. I think he sensed that connection as well.

Later, I saw our transfer of wisdom to be a little like Solomon sharing his wisdom to his young son in Proverbs and Ecclesiastes. When citing the reasons for writing the Old Testament book of Proverbs, Solomon wrote, "*To know wisdom and instruction; to perceive the words of understanding; to receive instruction of wisdom, righteousness and justice and equity; to give prudence to the simple, to the young man knowledge and discretion,*" (Proverbs 1:1-4, NKJV).

Time passed quickly. It didn't seem like it was, too, long after our walks began that Grandpa McGhin completed his life journey. I'll be honest, I missed our walks. I missed him...I still miss him. But, you know what? The Lord is gracious and kind; because, I have been blessed with many more sets of adoptive grandparents along the way. Men and women of faith, love and charity have blessed my life throughout the years beyond measure. Each one has contributed something to my wisdom; and, I have loved them all for it.

As I age, I have a desire to have the grace of Grandpa McGhin, and the fervor of Caleb! In the Book of Joshua, having been denied entry into the *"promised land"* by the lack of faith of others, Caleb asked for the land of the "giants" to be his inheritance...at age eighty! He was ready to take on the obstacles that had kept him from receiving his blessing of *promise*. With God's help, he was able to do so.

How old am I now? Does it matter? In my mind's eye, I am still that six year old boy who said "Yes" to Jesus, or the twenty-one year old who trusted God, completely, as I embarked on a life of serving the Lord in ministry. I have never regretted it. I have never looked back. And, serving has kept me younger than my years!

How old are you? Does it matter? What matters is living a quality life in the Lord's blessing.

MY GREATEST DESIRE

My wonderful Lord has given to me
Abundant grace beyond measure.
His mercy and loving-kindness
Is valued more than any treasure.

His strength and might are powerful,
Able to destroy any foe.
Yet, it is His tender love and compassion
He would rather to freely bestow.

When I need His immanent guidance
As I face a darkened way,
His precious Spirit directs me
Into His footprints safely to stay.

Though I may not know
Which way I will from here aspire,
I know I shall trust in Him
To lead, protect and inspire.

What is my greatest desire?
Why, to see Him face to face,
To forever be in his presence
In my eternal resting place.

R.P. Wildes
(1998)

KEVIN

As a child, I must confess, I did <u>not</u> possess a lot of patience. It was something I had to, really, work on. It developed slowly as I experienced life. In my youth, I found it hard to perfect patience. However, I must admit, I didn't work very hard at it. That came later.

My delayed development made me a very impatient person, especially, with some situations…and some individuals. One person that used to try my patience, more than any of the others, was a boy named Kevin.

Kevin was a "special" person. He was older than the rest of the children in years; but, his thinking and reasoning ability was that of a younger child. His speech was slurred and hard to understand. When he spoke to you, it made you stop what you were doing and concentrate on what he was saying in order to make sense of it. It took time to communicate with him…time that I didn't think I had, nor wanted to give!

When children and youth shied away, or ran from him, it, often, angered Kevin. When he got angry he would act up. At times, he would get uncontrollable. We thought he acted like a spoiled brat… demanding a lot of attention! At least, it *seemed* that way to us! We never considered his emotional and physical limitations as our concern.

Even though he got frustrated and angry at our selfish actions and impatience practices, Kevin still wanted to hang around with us. Whenever friends would meet up at the church, he wanted to be included. If we played games, he wanted to play, too. It made going to church a little more difficult, since church is where we saw him, most often.

We would sneak around and hide in order to avoid him. When we could, we would go the whole Sunday and not interact with him. Still, at some point in time, he seemed to find us. In fact, he got quite good at finding us! Then, when he had found us, he'd laugh at us, as if, finding us was the game.

I grudgingly admit: at first, I did not enjoy his company! I know, now, that seems very shallow to admit. I'm not proud of those selfish feelings. They came from a youthful, inexperienced heart. The only thing that I could see was that Kevin slowed me down, too much! My activity was *fast paced;* and, often, required a quick get away!

My good friend, Lamar, felt differently. He was much better at including Kevin, than anyone else. Lamar was a bit laid back and easy-going. He was a year, or two, older than me. In those two advanced years, I guess he had developed more patience than I. As friends, he and I were a good balance.

Kevin's parents wanted him to be involved in the children activities at church. In order to insure this, they involved themselves in teaching classes, and being chaperones. This enabled them to help others deal with Kevin. There were times, however, when <u>they</u> were the *only* ones who *could* deal with him! One of those times was when Kevin got angry, really angry. When he reached that point it was hard to calm him.

Kevin's dad was one of the leaders for the Royal Ambassador chapter of our church. Our R.A. chapter rivaled, and competed with, the Boy Scout troop across the street at the Episcopal Church. While some were trying to keep up with the Jones', our Royal Ambassadors tried to keep up with the Boy Scouts, and *vice versa*!

Our R.A. group had similar meetings and projects to do. Like the Boy Scout troop, we had cook outs, camping trips, badges to earn, knots to tie, and pins to be awarded. Kevin could do very little of these things without a *lot* of assistance.

No one was more consistent in their participation, however, than Kevin. He was, faithfully, present most <u>all</u> the time. If his dad was able to come, Kevin was there ready to participate in any way he could.

It is cruel to confess; but, most of the R.A. guys didn't want Kevin around. Some of my good friends wouldn't go on our outings, if Kevin was going. It didn't matter that much to me, if Kevin went, or not. I just didn't want to have to be tied down by his presence. As long as there was food and a good time to be had, *no one* kept me from going!

Some adults weren't much better at dealing with Kevin. You could tell that many of them just tolerated him, or were afraid of him. They couldn't enjoy being with him. They understood he had special needs; but, they didn't want to be responsible. Plus, I think, they were afraid of his fits of rage. The truth is, there were only a few adults who acted as though they *really* loved and appreciated Kevin. Those people were special leaders.

I did not realize how lonely Kevin must have felt. In my early years, I could be quite thoughtless, at times. Then, at a drop of a hat, I could be the defender of the weak, especially, if they were girls! I was not that concerned about Kevin's feelings. I was only concerned about him being a nuisance, and interfering with *my* fun.

Whenever he wanted to play football, or baseball, with us, no one picked him for their team. He acted, and reacted, so slowly that the speed at which we played the games was beyond him. His sporting abilities were, nearly, nonexistent. However, he loved to be given the chance to try. When I think about it, now, I realize he was just trying to have fun and fit in! At the time, that was hard for most of us to understand.

When you took the time to get to know Kevin, you discovered that, basically, he was a nice guy. He was much smarter than we gave him credit to be. He had a big heart towards the needs of others. He *did*, however, have a little evil streak that surfaced, every now and then; but, who didn't!

In many ways, he really wasn't, too, different from us. It just took us…me… a while to figure it out. I think his "evil streak" was mostly intended to be kidding around. You know, like he was playing a joke on someone. His timing, however, was not good! And, the degree he took it, usually, ended with people getting upset, or angry, with him. This made him feel angry, or sad.

It frustrated him a lot when people didn't understand his intentions. It was hard for Kevin to draw the line between being good, and being bad; between right and wrong. He had to learn most things by experience, not by instruction. That meant he *did* wrong things before he learned that they were wrong to do! This, in turn, *tried* people's patience. Mine, included!

After a while, I learned to accept Kevin with his "special" circumstances. It was through the influence of friends, like Lamar, and the compassion demonstrated by my parents, whom Kevin loved dearly, as well as, those special church leaders, that I learned to love and appreciate Kevin.

Mom and dad welcomed him into our home, and treated him like one of the family. Kevin would ride his bicycle over to our house, and walk right in without knocking or being announced. Many a time, one of us would just look up from what we were doing, and Kevin would be standing there! There were times it startled us. Other times it was a bit upsetting; but, he was just being "at home".

He would, always, ask, "What ya doin'?" Or, he might just come in and sit down in the living room without saying a word. He might just sit there, quiet as a mouse and watch television; or, he might just stare into space. Mom would offer him something to drink, or eat, which he, gladly, accepted. After he had sat for a while, he would get up and leave, never saying a word.

Kevin and I never became "best friends"; but, I *did try* to be more understanding towards his limitations. I stopped trying to avoid him all the time. I began to choose him for my team in church play. When other kids got carried away with their harassing, or 'bullying' him, Lamar and I would step in for Kevin's defense.

Even though I got better with Kevin, Lamar was, still, the best! He was a lot more compassionate than I. Although I was trying, I kept my experiences and exposure to Kevin brief. I tried to be as pleasant as possible in my encounters; but, Lamar was willing to take it further and include Kevin, more.

Defending Kevin, usually, meant diffusing misunderstandings, or cooling tempers down, before Kevin exploded into a rage. His mental abilities may have been challenged, but his physical strength was not! He was as strong as an ox! The fact that he was taller than most of us gave him a clear advantage in overpowering any of us. If he got angry, and lost control, Kevin could do some serious damage before cooling down, again.

This was demonstrated one cold October night on a R.A. camping trip. We were to spend the night at <u>Camp</u> <u>Pinckney</u>, which is a landing along the St. Marys River. During our play time, some of the guys got carried away picking on Kevin. The adult counselors were meeting in their tent to plan out the fishing details for the next day, while we told stories around the camp fire.

Things started out as just fun stuff, then escalated from there. Things got rocky; yet, still stayed within the "OK" level of fun. Eventually, I had to answer the call of 'nature'. Being a primitive camping area, when "nature" called, you had to go find a tree, or some bushes, to "answer" the call. While I was away doing just that, some of the big bullies made their move on Kevin.

That's when things, quickly, got out of hand. Kevin lost his temper. These bullies had resented Kevin being on the camping trip, claiming that he was limiting what the 'others' of us could do. By the time I returned, a full scale assault was in progress.

I, immediately, tried to step in and cool things down before the counselors were forced to come out of their tent to attend to it. But, I was, too, late. Kevin had lost it! He threw two guys into the cold St. Marys River. He took a jacket from one of the guys, which had been used to pop Kevin, and threw it into the campfire. We, all, stood by the fire, stunned; and, watched it burn up, completely!

Nothing was left of the *brand new* jacket, except the metal zipper. Kevin smiled; but, the owner of the jacket became furious. Losing *his* control, he attacked Kevin with fists swinging and feet kicking. This level of attack, completely, surprised Kevin. He was not able to handle that highly intense attack. We, mainly, wrestled and wrastled! *Wrastling*, which is a swamp version of television wrestling, was fine; but, this event had gone beyond that! There was some seriously heavy hitting going on.

I knew something had to be done! I tried to intervene with a pause in the action; but, my efforts were not effective. So, I had to pop a few heads to get things back under control.

Our pastor, Bro. Dave, seemed to always have a "built in" *trouble radar*! He could sense when situations needed his attention. Before we knew it, he was standing among us. All the action stopped! It was a good thing, too! Kevin and I were about to pop a few more heads, and re-toss a few guys back into the river! But, when Bro. Dave said, "Stop!" We stopped!

Kevin and I were brought into the counselor's tent. It was, almost, like standing before a mini tribunal. The tent was a large Army surplus tent. It was large enough for the whole group to squeeze into, which we did.

Kevin, immediately, began talking, trying to explain the situation. He was so excited, and upset, that you couldn't understand what he was trying to say! They were <u>forced</u> to hear from me, the only other witness for the defense!

I explained that things started out playful; then, they took a nasty turn. In the process of unfortunate events, it became apparent that

Kevin needed some assistance; so, I stepped in, trying to settle things down.

Kevin's dad assumed that Kevin had annoyed the others, provoking them to get angry. I had to inform him that his assumption was incorrect. Kevin was just trying to fit in, and defend his right to be on the camping trip. In this incident, he had been more of a target than a provoker.

Kevin's dad thanked me for defending Kevin. I told him, "Hey, no sweat!" The way I had begun to figure it, Kevin was Kevin. God had made Kevin unique, or special. I don't know why; but, there must have been a purpose in it! So, if Kevin wanted to fit in, why not let him try? Besides, no one likes to be left out! Not all the time!

Kevin's dad thanked me, again. Then, Bro. Dave took the floor. He began by saying that fighting was not a good idea, nor a good way to settle things. Then he said, "Ronnie, I've known you for a long time. I can see that you try to care for the underdog. I've heard you pray for the bird with a broken wing, or the baby rabbit without a family. You try hard to 'fix' things, and defend others, which, sometimes, gets you into a lot of trouble! I can, at the least, appreciate that you are learning to care for others. I just wish you would be more careful at it!"

I wasn't sure if I had just been reprimanded or complimented!

Throughout the years, Kevin stayed a part of our group. When we graduated up to the Youth Department, *we all* insisted Kevin go up with us.

Slowly, Kevin was maturing. He accepted Jesus Christ as his Savior, and was baptized. It was his desire to be a good Christian. He was a constant helper at church functions. When our youth group got·on fire for the Lord, and began to do outreach, Kevin got on fire, too!

For his outreach visitation, he would ride his bike around to homes of people he knew. As he did at our house, he would come in and sit down without saying a word. People would wonder why he was there; but, many were afraid to ask.

After an hour, sometimes two, Kevin would say, "I'll leave if you come to church Sunday!" Most, readily, agreed! And, most came to church the next Sunday!

Though I didn't realize it at the time, I learned a lot from Kevin. His love for others was simple and pure. He had a desire to be a part of what you were doing, which was important to him. Being a part of the Family of God was a sincere devotion within him. In many ways, I learned how God deals with me by learning how to deal with Kevin.

I *needed* a lot of love that would cover a multitude of wrongs. I *needed* people to be patient with me, as I *needed* to be patient with Kevin. I *needed* to learn longsuffering in order to put up with failures and imperfections. I *needed* grace greater than what I could generate on my own!

Maybe, the Kevins of this world are meant to remind us of how much God loves us and wants to include us. Maybe, they help to jog our memories of how much patience God has with us, especially, when we don't "catch on"! Maybe, they help us to remember how much longsuffering God has shown us in order to put up with our failures and imperfections. Maybe, they help to show us how much grace God gives us -- grace greater than all our sins!

If that were *all* that the Kevins of this world did, it would be enough to say, "Praise the Lord", for them! But, I'm sure there are many more reasons than that!

May God enrich your living by allowing you to learn some valuable lessons from a "Kevin" in your life.

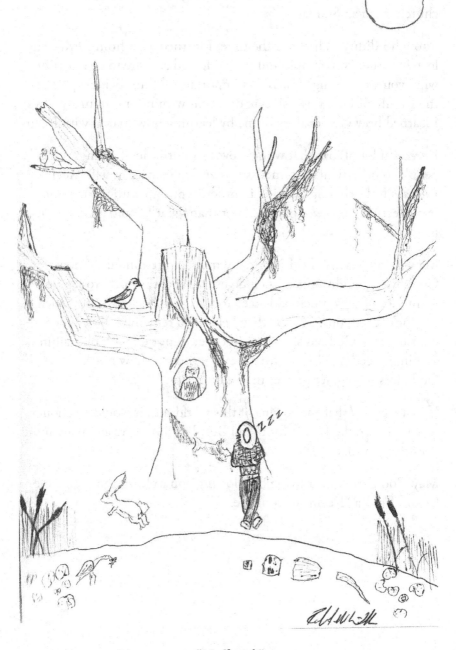

"Nuff said!"

MISS TUTLEYBELLE

If there ever was a saint in Saint Mary's, Miss Mae Tutleybelle had to be <u>one</u>. She was the most loving, and kind, person you could ever meet. When I came to know her she was, already, in her late seventies and was loved by all who knew her.

To a child like me, she was old...really, really old! However, she never acted old. She was always in good physical health. Well...I guess she had to be in good health just to get in and out of her house! You see, her house stood upon stilts. These stilts were twelve feet off the ground. Every day, several times a day, she would traverse those stairs.

Her house was the only one in St. Marys built upon stilts. I, often, wondered why. One day, as my Dad and I rode past her place, I started pondering about that very question...why was her house so uniquely built? After a moment, or two, the ponderance got to be more than I could bear; so, I asked my Dad about it.

I always thought Dad was pretty smart. He always had an answer to all my questions; and, he had an answer to this one. He said that when her house was built, it was, actually, built *in* the marsh. He thought it had been built upon stilts to prevent flooding during storms, and to give her a commanding view overlooking the marsh towards the North River. The other houses that, now, stood around her stilted house were built years later. The marsh had moved further out by then.

You see what I'm talking about! My dad was smart about a lot of things. That's why I asked him a lot of questions. What he said made sense to me; so, I never asked anything else about it, nor gave it another pondering thought. Her unusual house was just one of those things that made living in St. Marys unique.

In those days, most kids that were born and raised in St. Mary's were, eventually, 'kept' at some point in time by Miss Tutleybelle. At some time, or the other, she babysat, watched over, or tended to most of us. I, too, was one of her many 'tendees'.

Mostly, my mom was a homemaker, house wife, or stay-at-home mom. At times, however, she worked outside the home. She helped in stores during seasonal rushes, or when someone was out sick, or on vacation. She was a dependable and honest worker who was a valued fill-in for the local merchants.

Whenever she had to work, and relatives were not available, I would gladly stay with Miss Tutleybelle. I never minded staying with her. For one thing, her house amazed me! That, and the fact that she could bake some of the most awesome cookies, made staying with her very acceptable to me.

She was a woman who loved keeping busy. She was an avid gardener. She loved to work in her yard. Planting various seeds, caring for her azaleas, begonias and hyacinths were acts of dedicated love and devotion.

It was not unusual to see her climbing up into high tops of her pear tree, harvesting fresh pears. It was important to her to pick them before they hit the ground. Her neighbors would be scared out of their wits seeing this old lady squirreling around in her pear tree! One neighbor would, always, call the fire department to come get her out of her tree; but, she never allowed them to help her down…And, she never fell!

It was her custom, at some point in the day, to walk to town to buy groceries. Town was only a few blocks away. She believed in doing her shopping daily, in order to keep her cooking fresh. So, each day, she would walk through town loading up her little "Red Flyer" wagon with her daily goods. She pulled that wagon wherever she went. When she completed her shopping, she would head for home with her wagon full of stuff she needed for the next day, or two. If she had kids staying with her, we would all walk to town with her. It was fun!

She was very careful with children. In order for us to go to town with her, she would tie a ribbon onto our belts, or around our waists. Each boy was tethered to another boy with a blue ribbon. Each girl was linked to another girl with a pink ribbon. This helped to keep us all connected together for our walk into town. It, also, made 'potty' stops easier for her to command. If one boy had to 'go', we <u>all</u> went. It was the same with the girls, too!

Whenever one group had to use a store restroom, she would ask someone she *knew* to hold the other ribbon. They had to commit to watch over their 'ribboned' group with complete attention. If no one was available, she would simply tie the ribbon to a door knob, or some immovable object; then, dare us to move!

Miss Tutleybelle was always very careful to attend our every need. She, especially, took our safety <u>very</u> <u>seriously</u>. Her trouble radar was always turn on…high! Non one messed with "her" kids without her expressed permission…not without *consequences*! Everyone who knew and loved Miss Tutleybelle honored her rules with "her" kids. Without a doubt she was one of the most respected individuals in town. She spent her whole life gardening and caring for others, especially, children. In later years, when she became unable to care for herself, the whole town helped to take care of her.

It was often said that <u>no one</u>, not even Mr. Seals (an elderly man of constant complaints), could get Miss Tutleybelle angry, or upset. No one, that is, except one person!

I never *tried* to upset Miss Tutleybelle. I loved her. Somehow, however, it just happened! Even at my best behavior, no matter how hard I tried otherwise, I still managed to do things that upset her. My inquisitive nature, and mischievousness, was hard for her to understand!

Once, after she had spent all morning planting in her flower beds, I went over to see what she had done. Not being able to see much but rustled dirt, I dug where she had been digging. Up came some of her prized bulbs! Not wanting to be discovered, I, hastily, replanted them…upside down!

I have no idea how; but, she discovered the upside down bulbs! When she did, she was "miffed"! She seemed to know, right away, who was guilty! She didn't need anyone to tell her. She came straight to me, and asked if I had messed with her flowers. Not wanting to get, too, far on her wrong side, I answered her carefully. I was honest in my answer. I, simply, said, "Most likely…" After our following "*discussion*" about it, I never bothered her flower beds, again—ever!

I guess the most upset I can recall ever seeing her, occurred on one of our trips to town. We were all going grocery shopping with her. This particular day, we went to the Suwannee Store, which was owned by my grandpa and his brother. While gathering things in the store, the girls needed a 'potty' stop. There were only two girls with us that day; so, she tied the boys to a grocery cart and asked my grandfather, "Catfish" Lewis, to watch us.

Grandpa "Catfish" was a great guy…but, I had always heard that his attention span was about as long as a "New York minute"! Now, I have never known, exactly, how long a "New York minute" was; but, it must have been *really* short! His intentions were to help out; but, his attention was directed towards making a sale in the meat department. He was always looking to make a sale of some kind, to some one!

On this day, some, unsuspecting, customers came up to the meat counter asking questions about a good looking cut of steak. Since he worked, primarily, in the meat department, he knew a lot about the different cuts of meat. He was more than willing to address the customer's questions. As was his custom, he, often, got carried away explaining why one cut was better than another. During his detailed explanations, we discovered that the cart was not anchored down. It was movable! And, so were we!

I was very familiar with the store and knew the layout, well. I had been over it many times. I decided to lead the boys to the corner where the magazines and comic books were displayed. We couldn't read; but, we loved looking at the cartoons and pictures. We would make up our own stories to fit the pictures in the little cartoon frames! It was fun!

Miss Tutleybelle, however, didn't appreciate our creativity! She got a little frantic, when she realized that Grandpa "Catfish" hadn't been watching us like he had promised to do! He had not seen us sneak off, and had no idea where we were. A store-wide search began, under the direction of Miss Tutleybelle.

The comic book stand was in the front corner of the store, right next to the front plate glass window. We sat on the floor huddled together looking at one of the "Black Hawks" comic books imagining our own story line. The stand must have shielded us from the view of volunteer searchers. Everyone was looking right over us! It wasn't until Miss Tutleybelle ran outside the store, and, slowly, turned back towards the plate glass window, that she saw us huddled together viewing the comic book…still tied to the shopping cart!

She pressed her pretty little aged face against the plate glass window. Frustrated and out of breath, she fogged up the window, more and more, with each breath she took. With each pant, her face got redder and redder, scarier and scarier! When she spoke, her voice came through the plate glass very plainly!

"Ronnie!" After that her words were not as clear, as she turned away from the plate glass window to come back inside the store. You could tell…She was *not* happy! Not at all! We, suddenly, were gripped the possible reality that our cookie privileges *could* be on the line!

We, hurriedly, crammed the comic book back into the stand. We thought we might have time to push the grocery cart back to its original spot. If we could do that, we might could *try* to convince her that we were there all the time! But, we were too slow! Or, she was too fast! She caught up to us before we could get away from the comic book stand.

Her eyes were like liquid fire! Her stare burned a hole right through us! It was quite frightening! Her heavy gasps for air were like a dragon breathing fire and hazing smoke! She had transcended beyond her normal "look" of mere disappointment into a new look we had never seen before! A look reserved for very disobedient children. She was, now, at the point of crossing over into the realm of, "I'm to going to *kill* you!!"

Knowing we were caught, and knowing things didn't look good, I tried to sound compassionate by asking, "Are you alright, Miss Tut? You don't look so good."

Before she could answer, Grandpa "Catfish" came up to Miss Tutleybelle, and said, with a smirk, "Well, there they are…I told ya they were alright."

The look she gave in response could have killed ducks. It scared him! It seemed to slice right through him! Without saying another word, he, quickly, retreated back to the meat counter citing, "Ah! Some customers!"

I'm not sure if he, actually, saw customers at the meat counter, or was wishing them to be there! But, in a flash, he was gone! He left us to fend for ourselves!

Miss Tutleybelle slowly looked back at us! Now, there was a different look about her. Another look we had never seen before! Some of the 'liquid fire' had turned into tears that began trickling down her red cheeks. This new look broke our hearts. It seemed to be saying, "I'm so glad you are all safe…I'll kill you, later…"

We, the perpetrators, still dared not speak a word. We, silently, prepared ourselves to be 'blasted' away! Instead, she said, "Well, are we all here?"

Still silent, we nodded "yes". She took charge of the blue ribbon, which had never been untied, nor broken. In a clear stern voice, she commanded, "Follow me!"

Without a word, and without question, we obeyed her command.

One by one, we filed out of the comic book corner. In unison we followed her lead without missing a step. She stopped, briefly, to pick up the girls pink ribbon that had been entrusted to Mrs. Betsy for safekeeping while she searched for us. Miss Tutleybelle thanked her, kindly, for her assistance.

She, then, marched us to the check-out line. Her groceries were checked out by my Granny Bertha, who always ran the register. After paying for her modest groceries, Miss Tutleybelle asked, "May we have a woman-to-woman chat?"

Granny told her, "Of course.

"Mrs. Bertha…I have some words for Mr. "Catfish" Lewis…Would *you* convey them to him?"

Without Miss Tutleybelle speaking another word, Granny promised, "Yes! He *will* be told every word, exactly as you mean them!"

To this day, I don't know *exactly* what Grandpa was told; but, I'm glad I wasn't around to here it! If I had, my ears might *still* be burning!

When we got back to Miss Tutleybelle's house, the girls were released from their pink ribbon and allowed to play. The boys were not! We had to sit on her tall steps with our blue ribbon still knotted together.

Later, the ultimate punishment came! The girls were given fresh milk and some her home-made chocolate chip, and oatmeal chip cookies. The boys were only allowed a glass of water!

It was torture in the first degree! Her home-made cookies were heaven-sent, melt-in-your-mouth, slap-happy good! This ultimate reward, given to the girls for being in her good favor, was denied us as a result of our wayward actions. It hurt as we watched the girls eat every last one of those precious, mouth-watering cookies.

Miss Tutleybell turned to us and said, "I love you guys; but, you will not be rewarded for bad behavior. Don't disappoint me, again!"

After that, we *really* tried not to disappoint her, again…at least, not to that degree!

Now that I have had time to ponder about it, Miss Tutleybelle's response reflects an important Scripture verse: "… *'My son, do not despise the chastening of the Lord, nor be discouraged when you are rebuked by Him; for whom the Lord loves He chastens…'*" (Hebrews 12:5-6, NKJV).

Miss Tutleybelle's chastisement was enough to get our attention! Does the Lord have to chastise you to get your attention? If so, pay attention. You don't want to miss out on the cookies!

MR. SEALS

Growing up in a small town had its advantages and disadvantages. The small town I grew up in was located on the southern coast of Georgia, nestled between the marshes of Glynn and the Okefenokee Swamp.

Its traditional claim to fame used to be written on its city car tags: "The Second Oldest City in the U.S.A.". No one ever questioned that historical assertion....At least, no one in St. Marys. I'm not sure why the slogan is not still being used today! Maybe, they found another city with the same claim!

There were other historical distinctions about St. Marys, Georgia. Each one made the town a bit more charming. It was a community of distinction....a classic small town.

The St. Marys that I grew up in had its share of "almost" historically exciting events. Many were historical events that were related to other more important events; but, never brought any fame to our fair city.

For instance, Aaron Burr is reported to have come to St. Marys. He is best noted for his duel with Alexander Hamilton, the "Father of the Treasury System". They had severe disputes over political differences. Burr challenged Hamilton to a dual for his slanderous accusations that were politically motivated. The dual took place in New Jersey, which had outlawed duals. When Alexander Hamilton died of his wounds, Aaron Burr, once a noted Presidential candidate and the third Vice President of the United States, became a fugitive of the law. He fled to South Carolina, where his daughter lived, and visited areas in Georgia. Some speculate that he may have spent the night in St. Marys then.

Most likely, his visit came when he was being indicted for treason by President Jefferson and fled to the "Spanish Florida". Most concur that he stopped in St. Marys and spent the night at the old McDonald House. There is a bronze plaque on the house to commemorate the event; but, not the year.

Another historical tidbit is the story of the "Washington Oaks". When the nation's most venerated general, statesman and citizen, President George Washington, died, the residents of St. Marys held a "mock" funeral in his honor. A casket was filled with "unlisted" items to commemorate the event. The funeral procession paraded down Main Street, from the water front all the way to the old city well. There they buried the casket and planted three oak trees on top of it. Later, the main road was divided into two, one way roads, around the trees, with a grassy median in between.

These oaks grew into huge, majestic trees. Their limbs grew out and around, up and down, until they covered both sides of the divided Main Street, providing a welcomed shade to passers-by. When a tree disease took two of the trees in the 1960's, special care was given to the one remaining "Washington Oak".

As historical fate would have it, these oaks happened to be the same kind of rare oak that the battle ship, U.S.S. Constitution, known as "Old Ironsides", was made from. The keepers of "Old Ironsides" came from Boston, and asked permission to harvest the remaining tree to be used as spare parts for the historical battle ship. Permission was granted.

Also, a few blocks off Main Street, the first pecan tree planted in America is commemorated by a historical marker. The marker is registered by the State of Georgia and resides in the back yard of the property owner. There are still pecan trees there today.

See what I mean! Almost famous stuff; but, not quite earth shattering to put us on the tourism map. There are other little known facts about our small historical city that were sources of civic pride; but, too, little known outside our fair city to generate much national interest.

We may not have been blessed with much historical recognition; but, we were blessed in other ways. Our city had some of the most colorful characters you could ever hope to encounter, and was a town filled with caring citizens.

The old downtown area was a cluster of small shops and stores on either side of Main Street that ended at the river. At that end of town, there was a pavilion built out over the St. Marys River. It was a nice shaded area to sit and enjoy the view of the wide salt water tidal river. Some have likened it to a classic fishing village. No matter how others viewed it, it was just home to us.

There were not many places to stay in St. Marys, even if you did want to visit. We had two boarding houses that remained active. Only one offered a meal for its customers, and town folk, too. There *was* an old hotel facing the waterfront that used to accommodate visitors. In fact, the Riverview Hotel was featured, and made a little famous, in the syndicated newspaper cartoon *Wash Tubbs & Easy*. The cartoonist, Roy Crane, spent some of his winters there, as did some other almost famous people.

In the 1920's and 1930"s, a little vehicle that was half bus and half train brought visitors to St. Marys from the main rail road stop in Kingsland. It was called the "Toonerville Trolley". The cartoonist wrote about the many comical encounters that took place while riding the trolley. He included several of the colorful, local characters in his comic strip, as well. When trolley was retired, the old driver bought it and lived in it for several years. It, now, has been restored and encased in its own special place on Main Street.

There were a few family-owned eating places....some might call them restaurants. These served as hubs for civic activity and gossip gatherings. The food was, usually, good; but, locals like my family, rarely, frequented them. Mom cooked our meals. When we "out" to eat, it had to be at a *bona fide* restaurant. That meant we had to be *out* of town to eat!

As a young boy in St. Marys, I grew use to my surroundings. I thought all small towns were like ours. I thought all communities had colorful characters that made life exciting. I, even, came to think that all colorful characters had to be senior citizens! That's the way it seemed to me! The more colorful, lovable characters, in our town, were the older senior adults! The older they got, the more colorful they became. Some were sweet; some were wise, and some were onerous old cusses!

One of the 'old cusses' was a man named, Mr. Seals. I never knew his first name. I'm not sure that many did. Out of courtesy and respect for his age, he was always called, "Mr. Seals". When I was eight years old he was already old…very old! It wasn't that he just seemed old to an eight year old. He was, *really*, old! In fact, no one knew how old he *actually* was. All who knew him as a younger man had already died… of old age! And, they weren't talking!

Mr. Seals had a regular routine. Every day, like clockwork, he would walk the downtown streets with his crooked, knobby cane clicking as he walked on the sidewalk. He wore a long-sleeved shirt, dark pants with dark suspenders and a straw hat. The only thing that was different from one day to the next was the color of the shirt. It might be white, dingy white, almost white or white with thin dark stripes in it! That was the only change!

As he slowly strolled through the town, he would mumble…a lot! He would mumble louder when people passed by him. Many would, politely, ask, "Were you speaking to me?" or, "Sir?" or, some other kind query.

To which he responded, "What's it to ya!" or, "Here comes a fly, better close your trap!"

To most he seemed to be a mean, rude, nasty old man. He was, rarely, nice to anybody! And, never spoke directly to anyone. When he did, it was rude, or crude! Most everyone began to think of him as an offensively revolting old cuss! In reality, well....that's, mostly, what he was!

Whenever he would see children, like me and my friends, walking towards him, he would get this sneering grin on his face. He'd check his straw hat, like he was fixing to tip it; then, say, "You look better going than you do coming!"

We found it hard to respond to that. We wanted to say something nasty, or borderline nasty; but, we *had* to be respectful! That was the 'code' for old folks in St. Marys: you <u>had</u> to respectfully respond to them, whether you wanted to, or not!

Most of the time the parents, or other adults who overheard it, would try to make light of it. I guess they thought it would help children shrug it off. They would remind us that he was an old, lonely man who didn't always know what he was saying.

I kind of felt like he knew exactly what he was saying! That's why I was tempted to say *something* back. But, because of the code of respect for elders that my parents had taught to me, I would bite my tongue and respond, "Yes, sir."

My parents, more than others, were very "<u>insistent</u>" (*if you know what I mean*), that I should <u>always</u> show respect to my elders. For most elders that was not a problem. With Mr. Seals, however, it became increasingly difficult!

My grandpa, "Catfish", was old; but I could, easily, respect him! He was another colorful character that people had differing thoughts about. He had many different careers in his lifetime; but, that fact never bothered me. Though he may have had many different careers, he was not rude or crude...not on a regular basis!

One of his careers was as a family restaurant owner. For a while, he owned a family restaurant near the waterfront of old St. Marys. His restaurant became the exception to the eating out rule. We would eat there, regularly. The main reason we ate there was because he was family...and mom had to work there. Mom wasn't, always, thrilled about working there; but, I liked Grandpa owning the restaurant. For me, it meant that I got special privileges!

Yes, sir! It was nice having family owning a family restaurant! I would come in after school, and get a large glass of <u>ice cold</u> milk fresh out of the new refrigerated milk machine! No questions asked! Anytime I wanted it, I could get it. All I had to do was put my glass under the chosen lever, and pull up! The ice cold milk of my choice would come out. I could have regular white milk or rich chocolate milk; or, I could mix the two together! It was an amazing invention, and I used it, often!

Mr. Seals enjoyed Grandpa's restaurant, too. Every day, right around meal time, he would find his way to the restaurant. He would find a place to sit out front in the shade of the covered sidewalk. As people would come in and out of the restaurant, Mr. Seals would mumble something questionable, or snap at them.

Of course, most local customers knew about Mr. Seals, or had heard of him, and paid him no mind. Yet, every now and then, some short-tempered person having a bad hair day would snap back at him. If it became noticeable, Grandpa would come out to try to put an end to it. If he couldn't, he would send Granny out! Granny had a way of ending arguments!

My pastor, Bro. Dave, stopped by the restaurant, every now and then. Each time he did, he would speak to Mr. Seals. One moment their encounter seemed polite; then, Mr. Seals turned it rude! But, Bro. Dave just smiled at him, and told him that he loved him; then, he moved on.

One day Mr. Seals had an obvious bad cold. Bro. Dave asked him if he was feeling alright. Mr. Seals responded, "Does a fish have a watertight butt!" Bro. Dave smiled and offered to take him to the doctor; but, Mr. Seals refused to go. Mr. Seals told him, "I've already settled the matter. Whenever the Lord's stupid enough to take me, I'll be smart enough to go!"

Bro. Dave, rarely, questioned Mr. Seals' readiness; but, he, often, wondered if the destination would be the same as Mr. Seals had in mind! Still, Bro. Dave offered to help, if the crabby Mr. Seals changed his mind. He, then, shared a brief prayer for his health and patted him on his shoulder. Mr. Seals thanked him; then, added with a crooked half-smile, "Your food's getting cold!"

Mr. Seals ate several meals at the restaurant, though I don't remember him ever paying for one! My grandparents, usually, brought him a plate of food, or a bowl of soup, or a container of turnip greens and cornbread for him to eat under the covered sidewalk. Sometimes, Granny would add a desert. Whatever they brought him, he received it gladly. He would tip his hat as he mumbled something; then, he would eat it up, completely. He wasted little time eating! He gobbled it down, quickly, as if he thought someone might ask him to share it, or give it back!

I never heard him thank Grandpa, though he may have mumbled it! When Granny brought him food, it was a different story. He would, clearly, thank her with a smile; then, give her a wink.

From time to time, Granny would catch him smiling at her and giving her a 'look'. When she caught him giving that "*good*" look, she would say, "You'd better pop those eyes back in your head, before I pop 'em for ya." Mr. Seals would giggle and raise his eyebrows. To my knowledge, he never spoke rudely to her. Not even once!

One day, I decided it was time to get the best of Mr. Seals. I was tired of hearing, "You look better going than you do coming!" I was tired of having no response. I couldn't think of anything better, or snippier, to say; so, I was decided to beat him at his own game!

One day, I decided that this was the day. I found a good scouting place in the small alley near the shaded walkway. The alley was a narrowed path between Grandpa's restaurant and the old Catholic Church, darkened by a constant shadow. There, in that shadow, I waited.

Soon, I could hear the tapping of Mr. Seals' old crooked, knobby cane. Whenever he walked, he would tap that old cane on the sidewalk. Just like clockwork, I saw him walking his *usual* route towards his *usual* free luncheon.

My plan was to hide in the shadows, until he got close. Then, I would blindside him, by, suddenly, running out of the shadows saying, "You look better going than you do coming!"

For this to work, I had to be quick! I couldn't hesitate. I had to say it, before he had a chance to say it to me!

I, stealthily, hid in the alley shadows, waiting for him to get to just the right spot. He was not very fast; so, it took a while. But, that was alright. I was ready, and I was committed! I just had to be patient.

At just the right moment, I made my move. I ran up to him out of the shadows, which surprised him. I, quickly, shouted out, "You look better going than you do coming!"

Without missing a beat, as though he planned it all along, Mr. Seals, immediately, responded with, "Well, you don't look good either way!"

I, again, was caught with no good response. I had no choice. I had to admit it. I was beaten by a better snooker! I was out *nastied*! I had to yield to his greater ability to insult. He was, indeed, the unquestionable and unmatched master of rude derision!

Having yielded to the expert, I helped him to his, usual, seat. We sat down together, never really looking at one another. Then, all of a sudden, our eyes met. It was frightening at first! Then, I saw a little curve in the corner of his lips…almost like the beginning of a smile.

I began to sit with him, often, as I drank my ice cold glass of the milk of my choice. When it was all gone, I would, sometimes, excuse myself. Other times, I would sit a little longer than the milk lasted. On those extended stays, we might talk…or we might not!

Oh, he, still, snapped at me. He, still, snipped that same phrase whenever we met, or when I, hurriedly, passed by him. I did notice, however, that when we sat together in front of the restaurant, he would target others more than me.

On some of our sitting occasions, he would bring something to give to me as we shared the same shade. It may be an Indian head penny, or something he had whittled. Once he gave me a small, 'itty bitty' pocket knife, which I still have. Mostly, he gave me marbles…old marbles of different colors and sizes. He loved to talk marbles. He considered himself quite the expert marble player.

In his youth he used to hustle other kids by playing marbles. He, freely, offered hints to me on the best way of winning the game. At times, he acted as though he wanted to get down on the ground and demonstrate his techniques. He, actually, acted kind of nice! His moments of niceness, however, <u>only</u> came when I sat with him in the shade of the covered sidewalk in front of Grandpa's restaurant. Any other time, he was rude and crude, as always.

Miss Tutleybelle, another colorful character who was a dear, old, ageless saint, used to tell him, "Mr. Seals, if you don't *nicen* up no one's going to come to your funeral."

To which he would reply, "I ain't going to die. I'm just going to nasty away!"

One day, that's exactly what he did!

For me, the day started out the same. The cool morning was quite pleasant. The summer heat did us all a favor by not showing up, until the afternoon. Everyone commented on how wonderful the day was panning out. By lunch time, everyone was in their usual place for a good meal. Everyone, that is, except Mr. Seals. No one could remember hearing his cane tapping. In fact, no one could remember seeing him all morning. Even the barber noted that he did not show for his usual free hair cut.

When the regular evening crowd came to the restaurant, a general discussion took place concerning the whereabouts of Mr. Seals. The mayor, who was dining with his family (and consuming a good bit of country fried chicken) decided he would go check on him. Of course, he meant right after he sopped up the last bit of gravy with one of granny's lip-smacking biscuits. One of the other men in the restaurant said he would go with the mayor to check on Mr. Seals. They left their families at the restaurant, while they went to his small, run-down house.

They had to force their way into the house. Strangely enough, the interior was much cleaner than the outside suggested! They found Mr. Seals in his bed. Evidently, at some point during his sleep, Mr. Seals had nastied his way into eternity. No one had been there by his side. No one had been near to help.

Looking back, I, now, believe, in his own way, Mr. Seals just used sarcasm and rudeness to be colorful. I think he just wanted to get a 'rise' out of folks. Maybe, it was his way of kidding around. Or, maybe, it was just his way of getting noticed!

I would like to think that Mr. Seals was more ready to take his eternal journey than he let others know. But, we will never know for sure this side of eternity.

Pondering this made me realize something important. I don't want people to have to wonder about whether I loved the Lord, or not! I didn't want them to wonder if I cared for others! I *want* them to know where I stand on all important issues of life and eternity.

The Bible says, "*Therefore, by their fruits you will know them*" (Matthew 7:20, NKJV). It is <u>not</u> a good thing for our actions and words to make our "fruits" questionable.

Mr. Seals' fruits were shaded by his, unseemly, rituals of mumbling, rudeness and snookering. His "fruits" were confusing to others. He hid his true character and walk of faith, if he, indeed, had one! We, always, need to act, and speak, in ways that leave no doubt about where we stand with the Lord, or with one another.

Because of all the confusion about Mr. Seals' "fruits", there were several stories made up about where Mr. Seals was spending his eternity. Some suggested that neither heaven, nor hell wanted him; so, God and Satan stuck him someplace in between, by himself!

I have a better view. I, kind of, think when he got to the Pearly Gates, the Lord saw him coming, and said, "You look better *coming* than you do *going*!"

I'm sure receiving an affirmation like that couldn't help, but bring a full smile to Mr. Seals' face. I sure would like to see that one day!

I wonder what the Lord will say, when He sees me coming! What will He say when He sees <u>you</u> coming?

Poem And A Locket

As I look back, now, I realize that I, probably, noticed girls a little, too, early in life. That may have been a result of being the youngest of three siblings. My sister was six years older, and my brother was three years older. Maybe, I picked up on their desires and struggles with boyfriends and girlfriends a little earlier than I should. In any event, by the first grade I began to try to express special feelings towards certain girls.

The first special girl was Sylvia. She was a brown-haired beauty that was a bit thin, but strong as a purebred filly. Just my kind of girl!

One day, I decided to introduce myself to her at recess. She had the habit of running close by me, and tapping me on my back, or shoulder; then, run off. So, when she made her swoop past me, on this particular day, I grabbed hold of her pony tail and yanked her down to the ground!

After she quit crying…and, after the teacher's correction, we were special friends. It was so easy, then! It didn't last long, however. Soon, after school started, she moved to another part of the county. I didn't see her, again, until high school.

After Sylvia's departure, my affections were drawn towards a little blonde named Melody. Although we, rarely, spoke to one another, we knew we each had special feelings towards the other. Helpful friends volunteered to convey messages, and deliver notes for us.

We attended the same church, which made things easier. I got to see her, almost, every Sunday. During church, I had to sit with my parents. She had to sit with her mother. No matter where we were seated, we would always find each other. We always knew when the other was there, or not.

People, young and old, knew we were sweet on each other. In fact, if a teacher ever wanted to get me to be quiet, all she had to do was sit me next to Melody. I would get so doggone nervous, and shy, that I would clam up tight! If I tried to speak, it would come out like baby talk, or idiot gibberish.

It is still a mystery to me, even to this day! Why was being around that 'special' girl so difficult? Why did it make me go all to pieces!? Any other girl didn't affect me that way. It was only that <u>one</u> special girl! The one I wanted to like me back in that special way.

My confidence around those 'special' girls of mine only came in knowing, without a doubt, that they liked me, too. Once that was established, I became more normal and, extremely, loyal. I anointed myself their 'lord protector', and the "defender" of their honor. Yes, chivalry was very much alive in me! And, still is!

Many an unsuspecting guy met different levels of fate in the school yard pine thickets; because, they hurt, hit or upset my "special" girl. After a while, the school yard became, fairly, safe for any girl that I had a claim to…or, affections for.

In the forth grade I was introduced to a new experience. Someone, actually, liked **me** first. Usually, I liked the girl first; then, I had to declare my feelings for her. This method was, extremely, difficult for me! With every attempt to declare my feelings, I ended up stuttering, and slurring my words in a nervous jitter. In the fourth grade, however, pretty little Holly dared to like me first! It was a new exhilarating experience for me.

She expressed her feelings for me during a time of "busy work" in

Mrs. W's fourth grade class. Holly sat in the row of desks next to mine. I had noticed her staring at me, from time to time. I thought it was for *other* reasons (hair out of place, bugger on my nose...stuff like that). I was shocked when she leaned over, and whispered her declarations to me. She wanted *me* to be her boyfriend!

It took me by surprise! I didn't know what to do! Before that moment, I had never been nervous around Holly. Now, all of a sudden, sweat drops began to form on my forehead! My vocal cords began to shrink. My hands began to shake. Puddles of sweat began to pool in my palms. I had to take a deep breath! After a moment's recovery, I leaned over to her, and whispered, "I already have a girlfriend."

Have you ever had one of those moments where you wished you could go back in time and do things differently? This would have been one of those moments, for me!

She didn't take this news very well. Her smile became a frown. Tears swelled up in her eyes. Her pretty little lips pouted out in frustrated anger. Then, she reached over and pinched the fire out of my arm. "OWEE!!", came out before I knew it!

Mrs. W. tolerated **no noises** of any kind during "busy work" time. No disturbance was permitted...not for *any* reason! She was <u>very</u> strict about it. My "owee", quickly, drew a response from her. She, always, nipped things in the bud. She never allowed anything get out of hand. She kept a keen watch over the class, at all times.

She demanded immediate information, which had better be pretty darn good...life and death type of information. She, sternly, queried, "What is it, Ronnie?"

Holly, who had never been in trouble at school, never had a spanking of any kind; and, was, always, was one of the teacher's 'pets' turned white as a ghost! Her look of anger, quickly, changed to one of fear!

I, certainly, was not about to get her into trouble! I mean, she had taken a big risk to tell me of her affections. I deeply appreciated her effort. The pain of rejection was quite painful...I was a bit teary-eyed from her love-pinch. Rubbing my arm, I responded, "A bee stung me."

Now, to me, a bee sting had never been a big deal. I had been stung several times. It hurt for a while…turned red for a few days, and that was about it. But, as soon as I said *a bee* had stung me, two of my classmates ran screaming to the teacher's desk diving underneath it!

I didn't know that bee stings, to them, meant doctors, hospitals and a bunch of shots! They were allergic to bee stings. Who knew!

Mrs. W. proceeded to turn the room upside down looking for that bee! She was determined to find it, and any cousins it may have brought with it! Finding no stinging critters, she looked more closely at my injury. She, carefully, inspected my "sting" mark. Upon this closer examination, she realized that it wasn't a bee sting. There was no sting hole evident, and no stinger left in my arm!

She insisted I tell her more, but I wouldn't. The bee sting was my story, and I was sticking to it! She gave me three licks with her purple paddle for disturbing the class during "busy work".

I, willingly, took the licks for someone who had risked a lot by saying she liked me first. At recess, my chivalry had *not* gone unnoticed. A group of girls, including Holly and some of her friends, came up to me, and thanked me for what I had done. Even Melody gave me a smile!

Before I could say very much, Holly popped a kiss on my cheek! With that kind of reward, I began to have second thoughts about being her boyfriend! I mean, Melody had never given me such a reward! Holly's kind offering was not appreciated by Melody, who stared at her with a burning desire to rip her pretty little lips off!

By the fifth grade, Melody and I had decided to be just 'friends'. This freed us up to look around at other options. By that time, Holly was the girlfriend of buddy of mine. That meant, "Hands off!" (That was another unwritten code that we followed back then. The code lasted for many years, and is still practiced by some of us to this day. I wish more knew the code and would practice it today!)

With Holly spoken for, my affections had to seek someone else out. I turned to a girl who was a friendly sweet girl, with a broad smile. She was a cute, popular girl, named Bunny.

This time, I decided I needed to change my tactics. Liking a girl from a distance wasn't working very well. Liking her *first* meant I had to let her know of my feelings. By this time, note deliveries by trusted friends was becoming a thing of past. Actual contact was going to be necessary!

That meant it was going to be difficult, especially for me! Things were more complicated by the fifth grade. Girls were a bit different! Not to mention that my nervousness and shyness had increased. Not only did I jitter, stutter and slur; now, I had added shuddering and enlarged pooling of sweat in the palms of my hands.

The pooling of sweat in my palms was a big problem. When I tried to take a girl by her hand, it would "squish". It was very ichy and embarrassing!

Yes, sir! Letting Bunny know how I felt was going to be a difficult, nerve-racking task! I had no idea how she would respond to my overtures of affection. It didn't matter that it was only the fifth grade! 'Puppy love' meant nothing to me. This was major stuff!

One day, my Uncle G. heard me discussing my problem with my *imaginary* friend, Tommy. I was sitting on our propane gas tank next to my house, pretending it was my silver war horse. As we rode along the lone frontier, I was sharing my thoughts with my imaginary friend, who was riding his imaginary horse.

Unknown to me, Uncle G. was listening to my shared thoughts from the opened window of our bedroom. When he spoke to me, it scared me half to death! I fell off my trusted steed in shock! I didn't know what God's voice sounded like; but, I was about to wonder if that might be Him, when I saw Uncle G's face behind the screen in the window. He, strongly, suggested that I needed to just *tell* the girl how I felt. Part of me wanted to tell him he was crazy! The other part knew he was right, and, nearly, died!

When he saw the disappointment in my face, he came up with an alternative. He suggested that I write Bunny a poem. He said, "Girls, always, like a good poem. It makes them want to kiss ya!"

Remembering how Holly's kiss had made me feel in the fourth grade made the poem sound like a pretty good idea to me! There was just one problem. What in the world was a poem? He tried to tell me about pretty thoughts and rhyming words; but, I figured a better answer to that question had to be at the library.

St. Marys had a small library located in a couple of rooms of an old historical mansion in town. The mansion was named, *Orange Hall*, which I never understood. It had always been painted white! Someone said it was due to some orange trees planted all around it; but, by this time, they were all gone! Still, it was a beautiful, picturesque, plantation type of mansion with large tall columns on the front entrance.

The above ground basement had been used as the servant's quarters. The front steps led up to the main floor, which was above the servant's quarters and as high as a second floor normally stood. The second floor, which was as high as a third floor, was where the bedrooms were located. Those rooms were closed off.

The main floor had two large, connecting rooms, with tall ceilings. This became the 'temporary' home of the town library. The previous temporary home used to be at the Women's Club building; but, the Women's Club members didn't like it. They wanted their small building back for social gatherings and special events. That was alright with me. I liked the old mansion as the library a whole lot better. It inspired a lot of day dreams and fanciful phantasies!

For a long time, I didn't know a library even existed in St. Marys. I discovered it when my brother and sister started going to it for school projects.

Mrs. Trapnell was the librarian. She was very strict about noises of any kind. She demanded that you be careful with *her* books. Some were very old. We had to promise to take *proper* care of the library books before she would let you take one home. She had the authority to make all the rules, and make them stick! She could call your parents, file a complaint, or ban you from the library, if you violated, too many, of her rules. And, she would, too!

I knew Mrs. Trapnell from church. Her husband was a deacon. He was very kind and likeable. She took a little longer to like! When you came to the library, or when she substituted as a teacher at school, she acted like she didn't know you. She wanted to treat everyone the same way. She was one of the few teachers, or substitute teachers, who truly treated everyone the same. She was just as strict in her class room at school, or at church teaching a Sunday School class, as she was in *her* library.

I knew quietness had its place. In fact, the church and the library were the two places I, really, <u>tried</u> to be quiet. Even then, I got called down a few times for snickering, or whispering, too, loud. But, I never did anything to cross her strict lines…well, not too, severely!

In the library, I could sit, quietly, for hours and look at the pictures in the books. My imagination would run wild as I placed myself in the Revolutionary War, or the Civil War. I have been a Roman soldier…I marched with Hannibal over the Alps…I was a witness to the Crusades…I had seen the seven wonders of the ancient world… Each visit to the library inspired another great adventure; but, poems had not been part of my fanciful experience.

Oh, for your information, I didn't *just* look at the pictures! I did some reading, as well. Like during the summer. Mrs. Trapnell encouraged us to join a reading program by awarding movie tickets for reading a certain number of books. I would, always, validate that I had read enough to please Mrs. Trapnell. She, in turn, would award me with a certificate, which had the movie tickets attached to it. Yet, in all the books I read to get my movie tickets, books of poetry were <u>never</u> among them.

Nonetheless, I was convinced that, with so many books available, some of them had to have poems in them. I figured Mrs. Trapnell would know which ones I needed to read. She liked to help people find things; so, I was sure I could get her to direct me to some books that would help me learn more about poems that would get me another kiss.

One evening, while accompanying my brother and sister to the library, I asked for her help. She looked surprised!…Stunned!…No, I think it was closer to _shock_!

She thought I was a bit young for poetry; but, she did not want to quench an inquisitive spirit. I told her I needed to learn how to write poems, in a hurry! Without much questioning, she set out to help me.

She gave me books of poems by Poe, Keats and Shelley…which to a fifth grader made little sense! Not to mention, Poe was a bit scary! She, then, pointed me towards the poetry section and turned me loose. I read Longfellow, Walden and Burnes. I had been told that they were great poets; but, I still had a hard time understanding them.

I kept on reading all kinds of authors who wrote poetry. Their sentiments were complex. My sentiments were simple. I was convinced that, somewhere, there was a resource of simple poetry that would meet my needs. That's when I discovered the greeting card rack at the Rexall Drug Store!

Greeting card poems were simple. They sent clear messages. Though I had never bought a greeting card before, I began to read every one of them on the rack. The drug store attendant, Mrs. Wheatley, didn't mind, as long as, I had clean hands, and was careful not to damage the cards.

After doing some intense library researching, and reading at the Rexall Drug Store, I felt I was ready to start writing my own poems. I began writing in seclusion. I didn't want anyone to know what I was trying to do. I was a bit embarrassed at putting my thoughts down on paper; so, I kept it very private.

At first, I had a hard time making things rhyme. If it did rhyme, it didn't make sense. In the process, I discovered that there were some words that just didn't have a rhyme to them. None that I could think of! And, none that made any sense!

Mrs. Trapnell offered to assist me. Her assistance came in the form of critiquing and grading my poems. After several attempts, and several failing grades by Mrs. Trapnell's high standards, I, finally, came up with a poem that passed her inspection. She even smiled signifying that it had made the grade! From all indications the poem was good to go!

I was proud of my efforts; but, I wasn't convinced that a poem alone would be enough. I needed an edge…a bribe of some kind to go along with it.

So, I went down to the "5¢ & 10¢" Store. With my saved allowance in hand, I browsed through the yo-yo's, spinning tops and plastic army men. Somehow, I wasn't convinced that these were the things that would impress a fifth grade girl. It became obvious that I needed some advice. I needed a little help.

One of the store clerks volunteered to be that help. Pretty soon, all of the store personnel became involved in the search process. They chose pretty…sissy stuff that didn't appeal to me, or was, too, expensive. I, finally, settled on a pretty bonze locket that Bunny could wear around her neck. It was cute. It was cheap. It *was* the perfect gift! The whole store staff confirmed that my choice was very appropriate.

At long last my poem, and prize, were ready. Now, I needed a delivery system. How was I going to present my treasured items to her?

Some of the options I entertained included just going up to her and handing the package to her; but, I was afraid the sweat in my palms would make the ink run and distort my poem. I *could* let a friend deliver it; but, then they might, accidentally, get the credit for it. After my long hours of hard, deliberating labor, I could not let that happen!

I thought about riding out to her house on my bike and leaving it in her mailbox…or, I could leave it at her front door; but, she lived, too, far in the marsh. Her house was outside my permitted bicycle riding limits. Oh! And, what if she saw me dropping it off! Or even worse, what if I encountered one of her parents! That would be a disaster!

After giving the matter a lot of thought, I decided that the best delivery system was the "run-by" method. It was a simple method that had been used with success by many preceding generations.

The "run-by" method involved waiting, until the perfect opportune moment to make your delivery. A time when she wasn't looking at you, nor for you. When that precise moment came, it required you to spring out from nowhere, and run towards your targeted sweetheart with your message ready in your hand.

As you *ran by* your sweetheart, you would throw the message, wrapped around a rock for a more accurate throw. Then, you would run away as fast as you could. After she recovered from the hit, she would read the message and respond to your advances.

The "run-by" method was my choice. Afterwards, hopefully, she would want to kiss me. The "run-by" worked well, in the past, with paper notes. Certainly, it should work even better with a poem and the added locket boxed and ready for delivery. To be sure my precious cargo was accurate in its targeted mission, I added a small rock to the package. Now, it would be easier to throw!

I was, now, set! The day for the delivery had, finally, come!

I was nervous all morning long. It was hard to concentrate on the school subjects. Each minute seemed to be an hour long! When recess, finally, came, I hid in the pine thicket, next to the play yard. There I, nervously, waited for just the right opportune moment.

As I waited in the pines, a good friend of mine wandered into the same pine thicket. He was very sad, and nearly in tears. I asked him what was wrong. He told me that he liked this girl; but, he was, too, afraid to tell her. He was very upset; because, he couldn't think of what he could do about it.

I felt bad for him. I told him I was in the same boat! It surprised him. I decided to let him in on my secret plan. He was every interested, but didn't have a clue as to what a poem was; and, he didn't have time to learn about poems and stuff, now.

I felt his frustration. I had been there! I knew his anguish first hand. Since I was *so* nervous, and looking for any excuse to delay, I decided my delivery could wait. This guy had been a good buddy of mine throughout the years…You know, the few years getting to the fifth grade! I hated to see him suffer and hurt like this. So, I gave him my locket and poem, and instructed him how to use it.

His frown turned to a smile. He vowed to pay me back. I told him to execute the plan right then, without delay! With great boldness, he ran out of the pine thicket straight towards a group of girls standing in the school yard. Oddly enough, it was the same group of girls that was standing with Bunny. I thought, "Well, he must like one of Bunny's friends."

I thought that could be cool: two friends liking two friends! That could have some promise in it.

As he commenced his run-by, I thought, "Boy! He must like the girl standing right *next* to Bunny!"

His hand was locked and loaded, as he took careful aim. With great accuracy and precision, he delivered a hard, line drive shot…right into Bunny's face!

I couldn't believe it! I went into shock! I had no words to utter! My limbs went numb! He liked Bunny, too!

I watched, intently, from the pine thicket. After she got up from the ground, and quit crying, she read the poem and opened the locket. Her frown and teary eyes were replaced by a big broad smile.

My heart sank. Like a torpedoed ship, my emotions plunged low into a bottomless pit of despair. I sat in the pine thicket the rest of the recess and wept, hoping no one would see me. When I saw my friend later, at lunch, he was deliriously happy. Bunny had given him a positive response.

As they passed in the lunch line, she hauled off and kicked him in the shin while smiling. This was an undeniable response of acceptance, which meant they were, now, boyfriend and girlfriend. My misery was, now, compounded by these obvious facts!

As always, good news travels fast. It wasn't long before other guys found out about my poem and locket system. My little poem got used, and reused, many times over! I, however, never used it!

All the girls seemed to like the poem. Many shared it with their friends, and even their parents! A few parents voiced their concerns about the "run by" method of delivery; but, they liked the poem. My poem and locket system became so popular that some other guys, from grades higher than mine, wanted to use it, too! Who knew it would catch on so quickly!

Before long, no one could remember who had written the poem; but, it was mine. It was a simple poem that conveyed a simple thought:

<u>Just You</u>

My heart shall know no gloom,
Nor feel the slightest fear,
If only you will take my hand,
And stay forever near.

Since the poem was so' surprisingly, successful, I began to write other poems that expressed my feelings. Some were feelings for a girl and some were feelings I had without the girl. I wanted my special girl to know the depth of my feelings. I felt it was important to let her know that I loved her *first*. I hoped it would open the door for her to love me back!

I admit...my ways were not perfect. Still, I wanted her know that by loving her first, I was removing any uncertainties, or obstacles in the path of her love towards me. I *wanted* to leave little doubt about my desire to establish a caring relationship.

In the early years, like the fifth grade, relationships were brief. A boyfriend-girlfriend relationship may last a week, maybe, two. Rarely, did it go much further than that. In the teen years, I wanted relationships to last much longer. As an adult, I wanted them to last forever!

The Bible says that while we were still sinning, God still loved *us* <u>first</u> (1 John 4:19). By loving us first, He left the door wide open for us to love Him back. He desires to establish a lasting, eternal relationship with us.

He has made it easier to love Him, by loving us first! His delivery system was much better than my "run by" method! His delivery system was perfect. The Truth of His love may knock us for a loop! But, His boundless love lifts us up higher than we could ever aspire on our own.

Being loved, on any level is <u>so</u> important. I believe that a loved person can share love with others much easier. That's why the Scriptures say: *"Beloved, if God so loved us, we also ought to love one another"* (1 John 4:11, NKJV).

May I challenge you to love someone first, today. God will bless you for it.

SHARK'S TOOTH ISLAND

Royal Ambassadors were always fun to me. In many ways they were like the 'Baptist' Boy Scouts. We worked hard for badges and pins, just like the Boy Scouts. In those days, the R.A. manual rivaled the Boy Scout manual by those who compared such things. We had recreation, camping trips, and studied about various missionaries.

Part of our reading material was the Royal Ambassador Magazine. It was fun to read. It was filled with missionary stories, *and* a joke page. The jokes were 'baptized', and clean. They were funny, too! If the truth be told, the obvious *is* true…the missionary stories were nice; but, the joke page was the first thing read each month!

I, actually, entered the R.A. program a little early. Bro. Dave allowed me to come to the meetings, promising mom and dad to look out for me. My brother wasn't, too, happy with my early entry; but, I tried not to get in his way, and he tried to make the best of it. All in all, I guess, he handled it, fairly, well.

He just made it a point to be better than me in the games we played, and took every golden opportunity to make me look foolish. I didn't mind. I thought that's what all big brothers did! As far as the other guys, they didn't seem to mind my being there. I got along with most of them, and was able to stand my ground among them!

No meeting was complete without some kind of discussion about our next camping trip. We were always ready for our next camping trip! And, we were ready to discuss its details, anytime! We didn't get to go that often. Our leaders, who would have loved to have taken us, had a hard time coordinating their time off from work. We got to go on just enough camping trips to keep us interested, and hoping.

Part of earning a 'camping' badge was planning the trip in every detail. That's why we <u>all</u> wanted to take credit for planning the event. We wanted it to count towards our camping badge. Since everyone couldn't, officially, take the needed credit, it was, usually, awarded to the oldest one without a camping badge.

Planning was very important. That part of the badge requirement was handled with great proficiency and care. The planner had to decide where to suggest going for the camping trip, and what we would do when we got there. The planner, usually, consulted with the other guys; then, he made his bid for a location with the Counselors.

The first, and *primo,* choice of all camping destinations, for all <u>R.A.</u> boys, was, without a doubt, *Shark's Tooth Island.* It was, also, the absolute <u>*last*</u> choice of all our Counselors!

Shark's Tooth Island was a *real* island. It started out as a large natural sandbar that became, clearly, visible at every low tide. It was transformed into an official island by the <u>Army</u> <u>Corps</u> <u>of</u> <u>Engineers.</u> The Engineers dredged the river bottom to deepen the channel for Army transport ships. These ships were, often, loaded with ammunitions and supplies. Heavily laden with their cargo, they would sit deep in the water. The mud from the river bottom dredging was dumped onto the large sandbar forming a permanent dried mud island. Over the years, it became covered over by sagebrush and other types of bushes.

The name, *Shark's Tooth Island,* came from all the shark's teeth that could be easily found there. The shark's teeth had been in the mud dredged up from the river bottom and piled on the manmade island. The mud was rich with ages of shark's teeth! Hundreds of shark's teeth had been discovered just by walking around on the island. Fishermen would, often, take a break from their fishing, and harvest several shark's teeth in just a few minutes. They would sell them to local venders, or collect them for themselves.

I' m not sure who, actually, owned the island. I'm not even sure if anyone would want to own the island! I only know that it had been open to the public for decades. Anyone could go there, without having to get permission…not even from the Army base!

The Army never minded anyone being on the island. Anyone could visit the island without much cause of concern to them. It was not close enough to the Army base to worry them. Not much of the base was visible from the island. Besides, this particular Army base was not, at that time, a high priority base. It was, basically, an ammunition storage depot facility, with very few men stationed there.

For us, however, it was the hottest ticket around! Especially, for anyone who had a thirst for shark's teeth and adventure. We shot for it every time there was a chance to do so! Usually, we got shot down!

Being an island troubled our counselors, greatly. Boats would be required for transport, *and* for any emergencies. Emergencies meant a forty-five minute boat ride to the nearest public dock. That meant that someone with a good knowledge of *first aid* would need to go with us. Also, timing the tides and watching the weather would be crucial. No one lived on the island. Hard weather flooded it, easily. The packed mud surface was still, too, soft for any permanent structures to be built upon it.

No doubt, there were several obstacles that concerned our counselors. Of all the obstacles of varying degrees of concern, I think the one obstacle that scared the counselors most was the forty-five minute boat ride on the water, especially, with our particular R.A. group!

Truth is, that was a *bona fide* element of concern. If you knew our group, you would not have blamed them for their caution. It took special men, with a great deal of zeal, and patience, to work with our group of misfits and 'would-be' adventurers. Even today, I thank the Lord they were there for us!

One day, while we were partitioning for our favorite camping destination…well begging, bargaining and promising all kinds of stuff would more accurately describe our approach…one of our Counselors surprisingly said, "OK! Let's go!" He must have been the new guy!

We were stunned! The older, more experienced Counselors were stunned, too! They kept looking at each other, as if they were trying to figure out who had, actually, verbalized the agreement! I'm not sure that any of them have ever admitted to, actually, being *the one* who had, finally, agreed to go. Once the promise was verbalized, we had to go! It was one of those unwritten codes! The counselors had obligated themselves. They could not back down, now! It would have to take an 'act of God' to keep us from pressing on towards our desired destination. The counselors did, however, have several extensive stipulations, and, always, maintained the authority to make further demands.

That didn't matter to us. In order for us to, finally, be able to go, we were willing to agree to <u>anything</u>! Taking advantage of our eagerness, one of the Counselors came up with a list of "Must Do's" that had to be completed before we could, actually, go. The list was three pages long!

We didn't care! At long last, the dream of every local adventurer was going to come true. We left no stone unturned! We did <u>*everything*</u> on the list! Finally, the date of our adventure was set. Calendars were confirmed. Permission slips were printed and handed out, which Brother Dave insisted upon having. Everything….every little detail had been planned out, to the 't'! There was little room for error on this trip!

After the fine points were ironed out, and, necessary, deals were struck, the final confirmation among the counselors was announced. We could, at long last, begin to phantasize about our anticipated *Shark's Tooth Island* experience! What a joy divine! To have our own shark's teeth…our own, personally, discovered treasure from *Shark's Tooth Island*! Visions of rapture filled our hearts! We could, hardly, wait to make our plans…our long awaited dreams…a reality!

For some in our group, camping out, itself, was a rarity. My family did not camp out much, as a family; but, my brother and I camped out quite often, even if it was in our backyard! When we went camping, we, often, had to go with friends, or organized groups.

I have, always, thought that family camping was fun. I don't know why we didn't do more of it. It could have been due to the fact that we never owned a tent, nor a sleeping bag! When our family *did* go camping, we made do without them! We used tarps and lean-tos for tents. A reclaimed piece of used visquane gave us some shelter from the dew and the rain. Homemade blankets, folded over a few times, made a nice mattress. Much better than any sleeping bag!

On clear nights sleeping under the stars was neat. Of course, you had to be sure not to sleep under a tree. Bird droppings were no fun! Sleeping out in the open was best. That's not to say it didn't have its drawbacks, too. With no cover meant the dew settled on top of us. This settling of due was not all that bad; but, it did cause an exciting moment with my Dad!

On a family outing at <u>Camp</u> <u>Pinkney,</u> we were all sleeping out under the stars. We were snuggled around the camp fire to keep warm. The early morning in the outdoors could get a bit chilly. That's why we got as close to the fire as mom and dad would allow. Hearing the fire crackle and feeling the warmth of the embers made it cozy and nice. Everyone was just fine, until dad awoke from his deep slumber having an urge of nature. He lay there for a while, contemplating how long he could "hold" things, until he just *had* to find a bush! When he opened his eyes, he realized he couldn't see!

His vision was all a haze…fogged up and blurred! He thought he had been the victim of a stroke during his sleep. He reached for mom, shouting, "Doris! Doris!!"

Mom jumped into the air, then sat up, quickly, asking, "What is it? What is it? What's wrong?"

"I can't see! I can't see! I've gone blind in both eyes!" You could sense the panic in his response!

She, hastily, rolled over to assist him. She, immediately, saw the problem and smarted back at him, "Julian, take off your glasses!" The morning's dew had covered them, completely!

After that experience, he made canvas awnings to shelter our heads from the settling dew. My brother and I were the only ones with a head awning at campouts! The 'Dad-made' awning would be a good thing to have on *Shark's Tooth Island*, since there were no trees to use for stringing up a visquane cover, nor to make a lean-to. Our awnings would have to do.

The *Shark Tooth Island* Planning Committee went all out for this trip! They planned some fun activities; time to work on our camping badges; <u>and</u>, time to do a lot of shark's teeth hunting! You could always count on our planning to include good cookout food and fun!

Our menu for this festive event included roasted hotdogs and potato chips. We, also, made sure we had plenty of ingredients for making 'smores', a popular campfire delicacy. Plenty of eggs and bacon were some other 'musts' on our food list. There is nothing better than fresh eggs and bacon cooked over an open fire!

Oh, yea! As always, we intended on telling ghost stories around the camp fire…after we got exhausted hunting for shark's teeth, of course! It was going to be a great camping trip!

The Counselors decided to use Mr. "R's" large wooden, V-hull cabin cruiser to transport the boys. It was large enough to hold us, the counselors and much of our supplies. A large cruiser would make it easier to get everyone to the island without a bunch of small boats to worry about. Mr. "R", a mill foreman and part-time <u>R.A.</u> Counselor, gladly, volunteered the services of his big cruiser for the trip.

The fact was, it made a lot of sense. It was a huge boat! The size of the vessel would be good for safety reasons, which the Counselors were very concerned about. It was big enough to haul all of the boys, and all our stuff. Not to mention, Mr "R" kept his cruiser in great condition. There was no doubt that it was sturdy enough to be trusted for our excursion.

Bro. Dave was to follow us in his flat-bottom "John boy" boat. He was going to use my Dad's 18 horse-powered, Evenrude, outboard motor. The outboard motor was an antique that Dad inherited when one of my uncles died. Like Mr. "R", Dad kept his motor in excellent condition. It proved able to keep up with the cruiser, quite nicely. The "John boy" boat was our back up in case of engine problems on the cruiser. Every detail for safety tried to be covered.

My cousin Gilbert elected to ride with Bro. Dave in the "John boy" boat. The two of them, and a few personal items, almost, filled up the "John boy". They had, barely, enough room for a couple of coolers to ride with them.

Details and strategies were refined daily. We had to leave the *Crooked River* landing by a certain time, precisely, in order to reach the island at high tide. This was essential! It was a well-known fact that the island had extended mud flats all around it. These mud flats were exposed at low tide preventing landing close to shore. The mud flats, however, were covered at high tide. Shore landing would be much easier, then.

If we missed our timing, low tide would become a problem in navigation. If at all possible, we wanted to avoid the exposure of the slick, slimy, dredged-up-river-bottom marsh mud. No one wanted to contend with that!

That black gummy mud would stick to everything it touched! It was, almost, like glue! Many a fisherman had encountered this kind of mud while fishing in the marshes. It was nasty stuff! High tide would take it out of play. At high tide the water went all the way up to the shoreline. The boats could be pulled up close to shore. This would allow us to leave on the next high tide without any mud complications. That's why the timing of the tides was critical. All the Counselors had coordinated their work schedules to match our timely, and crucial, departure schedule.

Finally, the day arrived! We were all eager beavers! In fact, most of the boys were at the boat landing an hour early. We had time to play some ball, while we waited for the Counselors to arrive.

Mr. "R" was the first counselor to arrive with his big cruiser mounted on a huge trailer trailing behind him. We, eagerly, assisted in the floating of his cruiser and the, careful, loading of our "stuff" on board. We, even, thought to bring our own fire wood. <u>Everything</u> was ready to go…So was Mrs. "W's" *baby*!

Mrs. "W" went into labor earlier that same day. Since St. Marys had no hospital, she had to be taken to Jacksonville, Florida, where her doctor practiced medicine. *Of course*, Brother Dave was with them at the hospital!

It took all day! The baby was a bit stubborn; but, it was, finally, born in the late afternoon. Brother Dave left as soon as he could, and was trying his best to make the forty mile trip back to St. Marys, and the landing. He drove as fast as his old <u>Rambler</u> would take him. He knew how crucial our schedule was!

Some of the boys suggested that we go ahead, and let Brother Dave and Cousin Gilbert catch up later. The Counselors, however, would not leave without their backup. So, we waited!

As soon as Brother Dave arrived, he loaded his stuff in the "John boy" boat; and, we left the landing. We were behind our schedule. This meant, with each passing second, more mud was being exposed prior to our arrival! But, you know what? Even that didn't matter, now! We were on our way to *Shark's Tooth Island*!

For me, the boat ride was half the fun. I chose a seat at the bow of the heavy cruiser. I enjoyed the salt spray mist lightly showering my face. It was refreshing to me. From my position, I could see everything! The sights along the way were great! The beauty of the marsh at high tide has always been an awe-inspiring sight to me. Like a beautifully painted scene upon a canvas, the sight still takes my breath away!

Our journey brought spectators along with us! The soaring seagulls seemed glad to see us. They hovered overhead catching chips, bread, candy, even bubble gum that was tossed up to them! Whatever was thrown up into the air never made it back to the ground! They would swallow it up, quickly; then, beg for more.

As we rounded *Buford's Bluff,* the island came into view for the first time. The sighting was followed by joyful shouting, and clapping of hands. Mr. "R" gave a loud blast from his boat horn, which startled us, but added to our joyful celebration.

The closer we got to the island, the more evidence that our delay had cost us, dearly, was made manifest. The mud flat was much more exposed than we had calculated. Things appeared doubtful! It was enough cause for concern to warrant a side-by-side boat meeting in the channel. Brother Dave had called the meeting after he surveyed the condition of the island.

The two boats idled, attached together, as the Counselors discussed the fate of our trip. We feared the worse! We knew we might have to turn around and go home!

All of the R.A. boys huddled in the bow section, as the Counselors huddled in the stern. We could see that they were, seriously, talking things over. The sounds of the surf made it impossible to hear what they were saying. We watched, intently, praying for a miracle!

When their huddle broke, a bold, new landing plan was revealed! If it could be put into play, properly, our landing could proceed. We were ecstatic!

The bold plan involved running the boats at high speed straight into the mud flat, cutting the engines at just the right moment; then, skimming over the slick surface as far as we could go towards the dry land. I don't know who came up with the plan; but, I was game! It was determined that we could float the boats the next day at high tide, allowing us to leave the island as, previously, planned.

Brother Dave volunteered to be the first to attempt this bold landing maneuver. He opened the little outboard motor throttle all the way. Dad's antique Evenrude made a distinctive high-pitched whining sound as it propelled the flat-bottom "John boy" in a designed pattern towards the shore. Speeding as fast as it could go, the high pitch got higher and higher as Brother Dave made a wide circle at the highest throttle! Coming out of the circle, he aimed the little flat-bottom boat straight towards the mud flat.

We had never witnessed such resolute determination in Brother Dave's eyes before! It was a bit bothersome! Cousin Gilbert's eyes told a different story, however! His eyes were wide open and full of fear!

As soon as they hit shallow water, Brother Dave pulled up the motor. His "John boy" hit the slick, slimy mud at full speed. The gallery of <u>R.A.</u>'s burst into cheers. Sliding, seemingly, effortlessly, the flat-bottomed boat skimmed over the mud like it was a field of ice. The boat traversed the mud flat with unimagined ease. The "John boy" made it all the way onto the shore, and into the bushes beyond!

Mr. "R", now inspired, and not to be outdone by a preacher, was ready to go! He said, "We can do that!"

In the fullest of confidence, he opened the 8-cylinder *in-board* motor as high as it would go. The deep, V-hull cabin cruiser captain took an even larger acceleration circle to get the fullest effect for his speed whip! Coming out of the circle, Mr. "R" headed straight for the shore sounding his horn like a huge freight train barreling down the tracks. Just as the cruiser entered the shallows, he cut the engine and let out a, "Yee Hi!" The V-hull cruiser hit the slick, slimy mud with great force; but, the result was quite different!

The V-hull acted like a farmer's plow, sending mud flying in all directions! The cruiser rolled and pitched, back and forth. The more we advanced, the bumpier the ride. Everyone was holding on for their dear life! When we, finally, came to rest, we found ourselves showered with mud, and about seventy feet short of the shore line. The dreaded slimy mud surrounded the cruiser on all sides. Still, the Counselors seemed quite pleased with the result!

Getting out of the boat, into the mud was the next great hurdle. No one wanted to be first. Mr. "H", a longtime, and trusted counselor, volunteered to be the lead mud tester. He tried to slip, ever-so-easily, over the side of the cruiser and into the mud. He hoped this would minimize sinkage into the grimy pit.

It may have helped some; but, he sank pretty deep, anyway…nearly up to his knees. After getting his footing in the slick, gooey mud, he decided it was safe for the others to venture out, one boy at a time. Following his act of bravery, we each went over the side. One by one, we slipped into the gushy mud. With each boy's slippage into the mud, it got gushier and gushier. Each boy sank a little deeper, and deeper!

The slimy mud acted like a vacuum, sucking off our shoes…then our socks! But, we didn't care! Each "squish" and "fop" got us closer to shark's teeth….and out of the gooey mud!

Once safe on the shore, the mud stayed glued onto our legs. We couldn't wash it off! There was no water on the island, and the river was receding beyond the mud flat. We, only, brought drinking water. There was not enough water for everyone to take a 'shower'! We were going to have to wear the mud all night!

After we thought about it for a moment…we didn't care! Sticky mud, lost shoes, disappearing socks…none of these mattered! We had made it to *Shark's Tooth Island*! We were excited! We were thrilled to be there! And, we were ready for the harvest of shark's teeth! We just were _not_ ready for what followed!

The moment we stepped one foot beyond the shore line, we were, instantly, swamped with mosquitoes and gnats! I'm not talking about small skinny mosquitoes! These blood-suckers were humongous! They were big enough to wrastle! They could, almost, take you down! That's how big those critters were!

We were covered with mosquitoes and gnats from head to toe! There were *zillions* of them! Our eyes and ears were packed full with these flying menaces! They went up our noses, and into our mouths! Bug bites and red dots covered our little bodies! With all of our careful planning and packing, no one thought to bring *insect repellant*!

Mr. "H" built a big fire with island brush and the wood we brought with us. He hoped it would keep the mosquitoes away. It didn't! Instead, it only revealed more targets for the mosquitoes to attack! For the fire to work as a repellent, we would have to stand in the middle of it!

The fire <u>did</u>, however, dry out the mud! Like a kiln, it made it like a plastered coating. The dried, plastered mud coating did help in preventing the mosquitoes from biting. They couldn't get through the plaster! The dried mud, also, restricted our movement. We stiffened as the mud dried.

As painful and, terribly, annoying as the mosquitoes were, it <u>still</u> didn't matter! We were on *Shark's Tooth Island*, and we were determined to find shark's teeth! We were <u>not</u> making this trip and suffer in vain! We were coming home with some shark's teeth, or else!

Venturing away from the fire, we encountered another obstacle: *blade grass*! Blade grass covered the island. It was a wild plant with thin, flat, razor-sharp leaves that, easily, cut the flesh on contact. When we tried to run from the mosquitoes, we were slashed by the blade grass. We were having a *great* time!

The Counselors decided to have another meeting! They were all in agreement that we needed to leave the island, as soon as possible! That meant pushing our boats over the mud flat, down to the water. I, accidentally, overheard their plan. What I heard didn't thrill me! I was not very excited over their decision. In fact, I hated the thought of getting back into that black, slimy mud.

I decided that there was no way *I* was going back into that sticky, stinky, slimy slush. So, I came up with an alternate plan…for myself! My plan was simple and very selfish. It called for me to climb into the cabin cruiser and hide under the seats. I could cover myself with the boat cushions and keep out of sight. I would hide there while the others pushed the boats to the water's edge. When the task was done, I would, mysteriously, reappear.

Admittedly, it was not a great plan. It *was* a quickly devised plan with no time to refine it! For it to work, I had to put the plan into action, immediately; and, without anyone detecting my actions.

While no one was looking, I slushed the seventy feet back to the cruiser. With great difficulty, I climbed over the side and into the boat. Once on board, I found the perfect hiding place. Placing the boat cushions over me, I laid there, quietly.

In a few minutes, I heard the others squishing towards the cruiser. From my secured hiding place, I could hear the sploshing, slipping and sassing. From the sounds of things, I was convinced I had made a wise choice!

As darkness came upon us, Mr. "H" slipped back to shore, unnoticed. He knew we were getting hungry; so, he started roasting the hotdogs. You could smell them for miles…even with mud and mosquitoes stuffed up your nose! When they were ready to eat, he signaled the others. The pushing stopped. I could hear them moving away, headed for shore to indulge in freshly roasted hotdogs. I could almost taste them, myself! Those who knew me, well, knew that I, rarely, missed a meal…especially, hotdogs! Smelling them had made me, even, more hungry for them! But, how could I get to the hotdog feast and not reveal my deception!?

The only answer that I could come up with was that I had to wait, until everyone had left the boats. Only then, could I come out from my hiding place. So, I waited. I wanted to be sure everyone was gone! When it was all clear, I, stealthily, jumped over the side of the cruiser into the mushy bog of stirred up mud.

The force of the jump into the soupy mess made me sink past my knees upon impact. Once in the mud, it acted as a vacuum sucking me into it further. As I wiggled, wrangled, twisted and turned, I sank deeper and deeper into the miry mud. Determined not to be discovered, I kept struggling on my own. I didn't want anyone to know about my deception. When the sinking continued and reached up to my chin I began to worry. A few moments later, I didn't care about being discovered, anymore! I needed help! I sank to the point that nothing, but a small portion of my head, was above the mud flat.

Had I waited, too late! At this point, no one could hear my calls for help. The sound of my pleas was absorbed by the menacing mud and splashing surf! Suddenly, I was gripped by a sense of impending doom! It just came out of nowhere!

I prayed and prayed. When you are nine years old, and your whole life flashes before you, there's not that much to see! I wanted there to be more! I prayed for the Lord to let me have more of a flashback by **living longer**!

I confessed and repented of every sin I could think of…even some I hadn't committed, yet! I re-promised the Lord things I had already given Him! I, even, promised Him things I didn't have, yet! My situation was dire, and it was getting worse with each twitch!

Back at the camp fire, Brother Dave noticed that I had not shown up for the hot dog feast. He knew this was <u>not</u> normal; so, he began to look for me. Sensing something wasn't right, he, instinctively, came back to the shore line. Cousin Hubert joined him there. They looked up and down the shoreline, thinking I might be picking up shark's teeth. Then, Brother Dave looked closer towards the cruiser.

At first, he couldn't see much of anything. Finally, he noticed what appeared to be a coconut on the mud flat. He could not hear me yelling; but, when he saw the "coconut" move, he feared the worse! The "coconut" was me!

The two rescuers, quickly, sprang into action! They stomped, slushed and swam in the mud to reach me! Their yelling and commotion was noticed by the other Counselors. They dropped what they were doing and came to help.

Once at my side, Brother Dave and Cousin Hubert began pulling on anything they could grab a hold of: my hair, my nose, my ears, even my mouth! Everything was covered with mud and, too, slippery to grasp! Yet, they kept their efforts in motion! They were bound and determined to keep my head above the mud's surface. With one of their hands, they held my head up, while using their other hand to drag mud away from my face. It turned into a "Mexican standoff"! Every handful of mud moved away was replaced with the same amount of mud oozing back.

The suction of the mud wouldn't let me go! It was as if the mud was trying to claim me for its own! Thank Goodness, they, frantically, held on, and did not give up!

Soon the other Counselors arrived at the scene and joined in the rescue effort. With their help, they, finally, began to make some positive progress. Slowly, but surely, they struggled, ever so diligently, to extract me from the grip of the mushy, miry, marsh mud.

The ichy marsh mud, finally, gave up! At last I was free! Free from the mud's death grip! Everyone cheered! A sigh of relief was expressed by all!

Now, a new sensation was taking over. I was cold and shivering. They became afraid that I might go into shock. It was determined that I needed warmth; so, they brought me to the soothing heat of the camp fire. Believe me! It felt good!

It didn't matter that the mud, which now covered me from head to toe, was being baked into a crusty shell. I was safe! I was happy! And, now, I wanted my long awaited hotdog!

The dried mud made movement a little difficult; but, I could, still, reach my mouth! My fresh roasted hot dog and potato chips tasted of marsh mud and grit; but, I didn't care. My NuGrape soft drink flushed it down with the sweet soothing flavor of carbonated grape!

As I sat, covered in dried mud, I noticed something: I had discovered the perfect mosquito repellant! They, barely, bothered me at all! Of course, I looked, and felt, like a walking statue; but, I could eat my meal, and drink my drink, without mosquito interference! Life was good!

After eating a couple of hotdogs, I was ready to start fulfilling one of my promises to the Lord made in the mud pit. I yelled out, "Let's go guys and get these boats down to the water!"

After a mini-pep rally, we were all raring to get back to the boats. We had gotten some shark's teeth, eaten some hotdogs and were raring to go home! With a new sense of enthusiasm we started out towards the boats. When we got to the cruiser, Brother Dave and Mr. "H" grabbed me, and placed me inside the big boat. I tried to get back out to help; but, they forbade me to get out of the cruiser!

I began to cry. They didn't understand! I had _promised_ the Lord to partake _in_ what I had 'weaseled' _out_ of before! Their resolve, however, was firm.

I was overcome by guilt and shame. I <u>wanted</u>, desperately, to pay my vows; but, they wouldn't let me! I _needed_ to do this; but, they didn't understand. I had sown seeds of deception and trickery. Now, I was reaping a broken heart, riddled with remorse. I realized that night, like never before, the Bible was true in saying, "_Do not be deceived, God is not mocked; for whatever a man sows, that he will also reap_" (Galatians 6:7, NKJV).

I didn't know, until years later, how much Brother Dave blamed himself for my near demise. He thought he had walked off, carelessly, leaving me behind. It was a hard thing to do; but, years later I, finally, 'fessed up' to the truth about that night at _Shark's Tooth Island_.

He said, "Well, Ronnie, the Lord just wasn't through with you yet!"

The Lord is, still, not through with me…nor you!

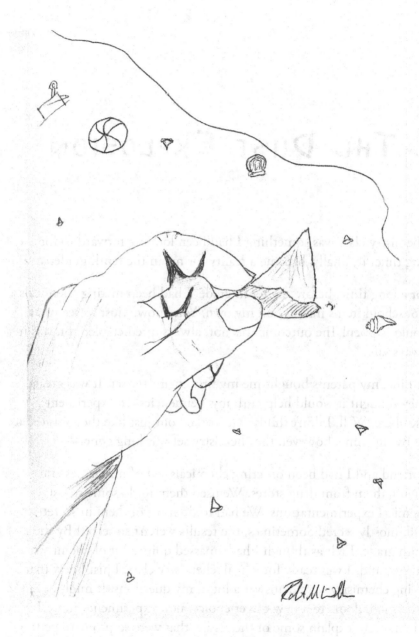

"Shark's teeth were everywhere!"

THE DUST EXPLOSION

Chemistry class was something I had been looking forward to for a long time. It, finally, became a reality for me in the tenth grade.

For a long time, before the tenth grade, I had been mixing chemicals (household items mainly) on my own. You know...just to see what would happen! The outcome was not, always, predictable; nor, was it always safe.

At nine, my parents bought me my first chemistry set. It was great! They thought it would help curb my "tendencies" to experiment elsewhere. Well, I don't think that worked out just like they wanted it to! By this time, however, the chemistry set was long gone.

A friend and I had been ordering chemicals out of magazines and buying them from drug stores. We used them to do some self-styled chemical experimentations. We had to do most of them in secret... well, mostly secret! Sometimes, the results weren't so secret! By the tenth grade, I felt as though I had amassed quite a bit of chemistry background. I was ready for a 'real' chemistry class. I just knew that taking chemistry would answer a lot of my questions. It might, even, open more doors to a new career choice, new experimentation...It might, even, explain some of the results that were so prone to getting us run out of houses, and forcing us into hiding!

Our class met in the lab, which was perfect for me! We sat on stools at lab tables. We received our lectures, and did our lab work from the same lab tables. I loved it! What a perfect working environment!

Everyone was assigned a lab partner. I couldn't wait to see who might be mine. I was hoping for a pretty girl that I might 'woo' with my chemical expertise. I was a bit surprised, and a little disappointed, however, when many of the females shied away from being my lab partner. In fact, no one seemed eager for that challenge! Wayne was the only one brave enough to answer the call! He proved to be well able for the task!

Our tables were surrounded by all kinds of interesting things: cabinets filled with beakers and flasks of all sizes...condensers that my uncles, in the swamp, would have loved to have used distilling some *swamp water* (home brew)! There were many other appealing things, as well.

In the back of the class was a chemical room filled with all sorts of awesome chemicals. My table sat right in front of it! I would have loved to take a peek into its inventory; but, no one was allowed in there, except the teacher. Placed around the room were several pretty red fire extinguishers that varied in size from small to large. In the corner, near my table, sat the 'queen mother' of all fire extinguishers. It was a humongous monstrosity, begging for someone to take her for a ride! But, it had a big sign across it saying "HANDS OFF! - THAT MEANS YOU!"

All of our experiments were under strict controlled conditions. Some proved to be very interesting. Some were boring as all get out! Our teacher was a stickler for safety, and was very strict about her commands being followed to the "T"!

Our lab table was equipped with a faucet, a cute little baby-sized sink and a Bunsen burner. The Bunsen burner could only be used when our militant teacher, Mrs. "B", was present. She had the key that turned on the natural gas. As you can guess, she was not going to entrust it to *any* student.

We tested it, often, just to see if the gas might have been, *accidentally,* left on; but, it never was! Mrs. "B" was, rarely, forgetful...about anything! She had been around students long enough to know our inquisitive nature. She had seen her share of mischievous, well-intending students making inappropriate actions. Plus, she had me for geometry, earlier!

It was hard to get things past her. She was often accused of having an extra set of eyes in the back of her head! It remained a rumor, of course. We were, too, afraid to look! *They just might have been looking back at us!*

As the school year proceeded, I could tell she had mixed feelings about my participation in class. On the one hand, I annoyed her with my many questions. On the other hand, she was favorably impressed at my knowledge of chemical reactions. In fact, the extent, and detail, of my knowledge, in this area, may have bothered her to some degree.

This, most likely, resulted in her being 'inspired' to pay special attention to my table during <u>all</u> experiments. As a precaution, she hung out at, or near, my table, nearly, all the time. In reality, I think she, actually, liked hanging out near us. She listened to <u>every</u> <u>word</u> we spoke, and, instantly, corrected our misperceptions. Having her so close by was kind of neat….and kind of creepy!

From my table, in the back of the classroom, I commanded a good view of everything. I could see where all the instruments were housed, the placement of Mrs. "B's" fish tank, and where everyone was seated. An added bonus, and a great thing for me, it was located near the extra "EXIT" door!

I paid closed attention, especially, to those the things of great interest to me. One such thing was the periodic table. I know the periodic table doesn't turn some people on. I can understand that. I, however, looked at it and studied it, often. It was just by coincidence, that it happened to be on the wall right behind where Holly was sitting.

I had known Holly from my elementary years, and had watched her blossom into a very attractive, desirable young teenage girl. Many of my friends and colleagues 'lusted' after her! It was fun to phantasize about getting Holly to go out with you; but, a phantasy is all that it could be! She was claimed by a rough, and tuff, sports jock named, Doug.

Doug didn't trust anybody with Holly. He had let it be known that no one was allowed to, even, talk with her, without his expressed permission. I was an exception, only; because, she lived across the street from me. It would be difficult to live that close, and not speak to one another. Plus, Holly and I had shared an encounter of friendship in the fourth grade that we never forgot.

It was obvious that she was an attractive girl. Of that, there was no dispute! You'd have to be blind in both eyes not to see it; and, completely, deaf not to hear it in her sweet voice. It was a fact that you couldn't help noticing. Yet, she was a taboo you didn't want to risk your life for!

I found that I, often, had to look at the periodic chart for long periods of time. The nature of the class demanded it! Sometimes, Holly would catch me looking; and, smile back at me. She was a very friendly person, who welcomed a friendly distraction from her class work, not to mention her trapped relationship. I didn't mind offering her that distraction. In fact, I felt it was my duty, as a good neighbor, to offer her such a distraction…from a safe distance, of course.

I hate to admit it; but, as pleasant as she was to look at, I, almost, got the same pleasure looking at the huge fire extinguisher standing in the corner of the lab! I know! It's sickening, isn't it! But, I had to consider that she was a taboo that could have led to physical dismemberment! The fire extinguisher just meant detention!

Besides, the fire extinguisher was awesome! I mean let's face it! I had a great view of one of the largest fire extinguisher I had ever seen in my life! It was four foot tall and twelve inches in diameter. It was so heavy that it had to be mounted on two, three-inch wheels just to move it around. As class progressed, the huge extinguisher became more and more interesting to me. As I mentioned, there were other fire extinguishers in the room; but, this one was, without a doubt, the most intriguing! It had a large, cone-shaped nozzle. It was said to be able to project a flow of foam-coating over ten feet. I caught myself thinking, "Boy! Would I love to see that!"

Every day I hankered over that giant fire extinguisher. I wanted to get my hands on that gigantic tank of foam, *so* bad! It proved to be as much of a distraction to me, as Holly! Well, OK! Almost, but not quite!

Whenever it needed to be moved, I volunteered my services; but, Mrs. "B" would never allow me to touch it. Being the responsible teacher that she was, she would always move it herself. There were only two times that it was ever used. One of these times was related to one of *my* experiments.

As I remember it, my lab partner and I were charged with the responsibility of explaining, *and demonstrating*, how a dust explosion takes place. We were, of course, thrilled with the assignment. Mrs. "B", however, was a bit cautious of our enthusiasm. She <u>*carefully*</u> instructed us on <u>every</u> detail. We were to obtain a metal coffee can, opened at one end, and empty it contents. We were to keep the plastic snap-on lid that came with it, which would be needed for our experiment. We were, then, instructed to drill a small hole in the metal bottom of the can, centered, and just large enough to stick a match into it.

Our dust for the experiment was to come from a household vacuum cleaner dust bag. A measured amount of the dust was to be placed inside the can. The plastic lid was to be fastened, tightly, onto the can after we had filled it two-thirds full with vacuum cleaner dust.

After shaking the can of dust, to stir it all up, a lighted match was to be placed through the drilled hole, into the metal can. The heavy concentration of dust was supposed to ignite inside the coffee can, causing a "puff" ignition…barely, strong enough to pop the lid.

In our test trials, everything worked just like Mrs. "B" said it would. The "puff" effect was cute, though a bit disappointing. Mrs. "B" insisted that the "puff" would be all that would be needed. We, however, were <u>not</u> convinced. We thought it should be more like a

"PUFF", or a little "pow"! To gain this added effect, we tried stuffing more dust into the can. The result was still a little "puff"; or, at times, no "puff" at all. We tried dust from different sources; but, it, still, didn't give us the effect we were looking for. No matter what we tried to do, it, pretty much, came out the same. It looked like the "puff" would have to be it.

Even though I knew our results would be alright for our grade, I wasn't *really* satisfied. It wasn't quite up to my personal standard! I kept pondering on it. I tried to come up with some idea of how to get more "puff" in our bang…or, bang in our "puff"!

The night before our presentation, I pondered about it, until the wee hours of the morning. I tossed and turned, not able to sleep. I couldn't even dream about it; because, I was staying awake! At some point during the night, however, a solution popped into my mischievous head.

When I arrived at school the next day, I alerted my lab partner that I had made a slight modification to our dust mixture. I told him, I didn't have time to test it; but, I was sure it would increase our "puff" to a small "pow".

He was in complete agreement. He wanted to get more out of it, just as much as I did. I didn't have time to discuss it, or explain it before class. I just gave him my personal guarantee that it would be a little "puffier". He said he was OK with whatever I had done. The late night modification remained a mystery to him; but, it didn't matter. I was sure he would have, still, agreed even if he had known.

The modification revelation that came to me during the night should have been obvious from the start! It was, simply, to add a little bit of gun powder! So, in those early morning hours, I borrowed a 12-gauge, "00" buck shot shell from my Dad's closet. Carefully, I retrieved the gun powder from it. I knew this _had_ to help us get the response we were looking for!

When Mrs. "B", finally, called upon us to give our demonstration, we were more than ready. After our thorough explanation of how a dust explosion occurred in nature, we proceeded to demonstrate our man-made dust explosion. Still, thinking "puff", we, actually, apologized for our 'small' scale demonstration. We moved a few people back a few steps to allow some room for the lid to pop off. In cautious care, I, firmly, gripped the coffee can, and shook up the dust mixture. I made sure it was stirred, thoroughly, into a volatile state. Wayne lit his match and, cautiously, inserted it through the small drilled hole.

The result was immediate! <u>Much</u> <u>more</u> than we expected! When it exploded, it sounded like cannon fire! Flames shot out the drilled hole burning the hair off Wayne's hand, and part of his arm.

The plastic lid was blown across the room, followed by a spiraling trail of thick smoke. The coffee can tried to kick out of my hands; but, it got so hot my fingers were fused to it! I danced around the lab table trying to shake it loose; but, my burning fingers were melded to the can!

Everyone in the lab, instantly, and instinctively, hit the floor! Screams were heard up and down the hallway. Without missing a lick, Mrs. "B" ran for the huge fire extinguisher.

She could not find anything on fire; so, she foamed the coffee can. A good layer of foam was applied onto the can. Then, she turned on the water faucet at my table, allowing me to cool the coffee can even more. Very carefully, she helped me get my fingers loose from the coffee can.

It took a while for the shock to wear off! Things, finally, began to settle down. Everyone got back up from the floor. The unsuspecting students brushed off their clothes and began to look around the room to assess any damage. After having been stunned into silence, some began to laugh! Others applauded!

Our ears were a bit deafened by the blast; but, Wayne and I knew they were cheering for us. There was no doubt that we were a huge success among the students...at least the ones in class! As we turned towards Mrs. "B", however, our smiles were, quickly, erased. If looks could kill, we would have dead on the spot...three times over! We knew we were toast!

She demanded to know "what in the world" had we done to our dust mixture! I, justly, explained that in order to get a better "puff," I had added some *extra special* "dust". When I told her where the 'extra special' dust had come from, she exploded <u>*all*</u> <u>*over*</u> <u>*us*</u>!

You could tell that there was much more she wanted to say...and do, to us; but, just then, the Woodbine Volunteer Fire Department arrived on the scene! Needless to say, we were glad to see them!

This Volunteer Fire Department, like most in our area of the state, was made up of a batch of men from various backgrounds. There were a few business men, a few retirees; plus, a few county workers and some civic-minded school teachers. They were all anxious to help, and seemed disappointed to find that there was no fire to put out. We tried to make them feel better by thanking them for coming. Not wanting to waste the trip, they decided to use the event as a training exercise.

Though they did not find any fire, they *did* find six expired fire extinguishers in the lab, and wrote the school citations for each one of them. The principal, <u>*Mr.*</u> "B", was not a happy camper!

The County School Superintendent, and his whole office staff, ran the three blocks to the school to inspect the "damage" first hand. They seemed, partly relieved, and, partly disappointed to find none. The county ambulance that was in route from Kingsland, eleven miles away, was radioed to turn back. They had to return to the funeral home, where they were housed, empty handed! All in all, we thought the experiment was a great success! At least, it was in our eyes!

For a while, we were heroes among the student body, and scoundrels to the faculty. Mrs. "B" was crabby and upset for the next few days. She moved her desk to the back of the class. Right behind our table! I could feel her cold, glaring stares, piercing my back, like sharp knives piercing the flesh! I kept wondering what might she be thinking, or planning to do us...Yet, I was afraid to look her in the eye for fear she might tell me!

At the end of the week, she asked Wayne and I to stay after class. We felt this was it! The axe was fixing to fall! We just knew we had failed the class! Since the principal happened to be her husband, we felt that we might be expelled, too!

Wayne and I had discussed those plausible possibilities the whole week. As we waited for the verdict, we began to plan what we might do with our spare time. We, also, knew that our parents would want to contribute, ever further, to our woes with stern correction... because they "loved" us, of course!

Mrs. "B" overheard our discussions. She told us to stop making plans; because, we were not going anywhere!

With a half-ugly smirk, and half of a cracking smile, she preached to us about the dangers of our demonstration. She explained how innocent people could have been hurt. Wayne looked at his hairless arm, as I looked at my bandaged fingers and thought, "Could have been!?" We assumed we were <u>not</u> counted among the "innocent".

Mrs. "B" went on to say, that in all her twenty years of teaching, she had never seen such a display of carelessness. Nor, had she seen, or ever wanted to see, a better dust explosion! She gave us an "A" for our effort; then, she subtracted two letters from our grade for our 'carelessness'.

We, happily, accepted her verdict! Any grade would have been fine, as long as it kept us in school! We offered our apologies and vowed never to demonstrate a dust explosion like *that one*, again!

Looking back, I realize that I was so obsessed with accomplishing "my" will...to attain "my" self-glory...that any regards towards safety, for myself or others, were thrown out the window. I did not take into account <u>all</u> of the consequences of my selfish actions. I became "unwise", bordering on sheer "foolishness" for not seeking proper counsel on my self-conceived path to glory.

The Scripture says, "*Therefore, do not be unwise, but understand what the will of the Lord is*" (Ephesians 5:17, NKJV). To "*understand*", means "to bring together into oneness". I was *not* <u>one</u> with anyone on my decision. It was all about me!

I did not seek wisdom, nor counsel; because, I didn't want anyone to change my mind. Nor, did I pray over my decision; because, I knew the Lord would not have approved it. The result was a near disaster!

I hope, in your case, it doesn't take a disaster, nor a near one, to make you realize how important Godly counsel is. When you are determining a course of action, or making a big decision, seek Godly counsel. Being one with the Lord, and His will, brings guiltless peace to our hearts…a peace that surpasses all understanding. It's, definitely, something worth pondering.

THE ELECTRIC BLACKBOARD ERASER CLEANER

Her manner was gentle, yet her voice was commanding. She stood six foot tall…a giant to a third grader! Her name was Mrs. "V", and she was my assigned third grade teacher.

From the very first day of class her eyes were fixed, suspiciously, upon me! Every move I made was measured and calculated. She seemed to map my every position in the room. It was kind of spooky! I could 'feel' her looking at me. When our eyes met, I would smile and, sometimes, wave. She would, kindly, acknowledge it; then, I would return to my assigned work. For some reason, she seemed to be very cautious with me; but, she never mistreated me. She just watched me….as though she was waiting for something to happen!

She began the year telling us that she would be seeking out volunteers for helpers. For whatever reason, I was never selected as one! I was never asked to take the lunch money to the office. I was never commissioned to deliver notes to other teachers. Nor, was I chosen to alert the library that our class was ready to invade the book shelves.

Some of my friends were chosen; but, I was never allowed to

volunteer. It didn't bother me, too, much. It just kept me from doing the <u>one</u> thing I *really* wanted to do…the *primo* choice of all volunteer tasks…*cleaning the blackboard erasers*!

It may not sound like much, now; but, then, it was the pick of the litter. It was *the* most fun thing to do. Sure, it was a little lung-choking, and a very dusty thing to do; but, it was fun!

You see, in order to clean the blackboard erasers, we had to beat them on the exterior brick walls of the school. This left residue on the walls to doodle in…You know…To make your own mark, or personal designs. You could express yourself in the chalk residue. It was <u>fun</u>!

It became even more exciting when the Principal, Mr. T., decided he had seen enough of unsightly, chalk-battered walls on his precious school house. Enough was enough! He decided it was time to bring this small elementary school into the twentieth century. It was time to purchase a brand new, state-of-the-art, electric blackboard eraser cleaner!

No more embarrassing words, humiliating pictures or awkward designs in battered out chalk dust. No more chalk covered students leaving traces of chalk dust on the interior walls and chairs. From now on, chalk dust would go to where it belonged: into a dust bag that could be emptied into the trash!

Rumors spread, like wild fire, about this new machine. Each rumor made it more, *more* desirable to see….to touch….to use! Ah! But, only the *elite*, the <u>most</u> trusted volunteers, would be able to use it. Teachers were instructed to, *carefully*, chose responsible volunteers, which needed to be trained in its use

Those who were chosen, gloated over it. They rubbed their 'eliteness' into the faces of those of us who were deemed "unworthy" for the task. To make it even worse, the machine was placed in the 'Equipment Closet' next door to my classroom! It was so close; yet, so far away!

The closet was locked to protect it from thieves, and those who would '*misuse*' the new electric blackboard eraser cleaner. Each teacher had a key to the 'Equipment room', which was only to be entrusted to a reliable volunteer. The whole volunteer system was a 'closed' system. I was on the outside! It would take a miracle to get me beyond the obvious barriers that kept me from my imagined bliss of using the electric blackboard eraser cleaner! Yes, a miracle!

I used to pray, in my third grade splendor; "Lord, Please send a miracle!" I believed in God and His miracles! (I still do!) But, none came! But, that didn't stop me from praying! My young impetuous prayers for that miracle continued, daily, for a long time. Eventually, they, almost, ceased due to not seeing any "positive" result. In fact, my *daily* prayers for a miracle turned into a prayer, *every once in a while*. I figured the Lord had better things to do than be concerned about who could use the new electric blackboard eraser cleaner, or not. I was about to give up hope when something happened….a miracle in disguise!

My long awaited and prayed for miracle seemed to have come in the form of an outbreak of *chicken pox*! The *pox* invasion of our school was devastating. Nearly, half the students from the first grade through the fourth were infected. Classes continued; but, some had to be combined, since they were down to just a few students.

Thanks to my older siblings, the *pox* had already invaded our home leaving me immune at this go 'round. No matter how small the classes dwindled, we kept on having school. Having classes meant that teachers kept writing on the blackboards; and, the need to clean blackboard erasers was never abated.

With normal volunteers absent, the cleaning frequency slowed, dramatically. Erasers in our class became filled with used chalk dust. They got even worse when students dragged them through the chalk treys to build mounds of dust that could be used in a chalk dust fight.

Each time Mrs. "V" used an eraser, a cloud of dust surrounded her. She became so frustrated with chalk dust on her clothes, and in her hair, that she, absentmindedly, beseeched the class for a volunteer to clean the filthy erasers. In her moment of despair, she had forgotten that all of her "pet" volunteers had the *pox*. She became gripped with remorse when she saw that my hand was the <u>only</u> one raised to volunteer.

She pleaded for others; but, none came forward. Her eyes became filled with terrified surprise. She was, almost, in a state of panic! She turned towards me, and tried to project a smile, which came out quirky and crooked. Reluctantly, she assigned the task to me!

I was ecstatic! She was cautious! I was ready! She was hesitant!

She placed the filthy erasers in a paper bag, and placed the key, that was on a chain, around my neck. She lectured me for several minutes about not losing the key; about wasting time, and about being careful with the machine. Repeatedly, she pounded me with, "All you have to do is…" I knew the drill by heart from quizzing the other chosen volunteers. It was a simple task; and, today, I was <u>the one</u> to do it.

I, almost, had to pry the bag of erasers from her hand. Her expression still haunts me, even today! I tried to ease her concern by patting her on her arm saying, "Don't worry. I'll take care of it." Maybe, that's what she feared the most! With no further word, I vanished out the door. I wanted to get out before she could change her mind. A few steps beyond the closed classroom door, and I was there!

At last I was standing before the doorway of my dreams. Using the key, I thought I'd never touch, I opened the door. I switched on the light. There it was…the most beautiful sight I had ever seen! That is up to the third grade!

It was even more majestic than I had imagined! It, clearly, overshadowed any interest in anything else in the room, including the once coveted electric waxer /buffer machine. As I stood there in awe, I was, almost, certain I could hear the electric blackboard eraser cleaner call my name! It was begging me to turn it on. So, I did. It ran smooth as silk and quiet as a mouse. It was every bit as exciting as I had imagined

I wasted no time at my assigned task. In a few minutes <u>every</u> blackboard eraser was, thoroughly, cleaned…and cleaned again! They, each, had been vacuumed down to their back bindings. There wasn't a speck of chalk dust remaining on any of the erasers. They were so clean you could have eaten off of them! I was, thoroughly, amazed!

There were no dust clouds flying up into the air. Every particle of dust was siphoned into the red cloth, collection bag. I stood in wonder at the sight; but, only for a moment. Having completed my task, I, quickly, turned off the wondrous miracle machine…turned off the light…checked for my key…locked the door and returned, with great haste, to the classroom.

Mrs. "V" was astonished! The whole class was amazed! A few of the students looked out the windows, as if they were expecting something to happen! I placed the bag of super-cleaned blackboard erasers on her desk and returned the key, safe and secure, into her hands.

Mrs. "V" appeared to be afraid to look into the bag, at first. When she did, she smiled, and said, "Good job!" That was enough for me.

When the *chicken pox* epidemic ended, students began to return to class. The teacher's "pets" were healthy, again. I knew my volunteer days had, now, passed. That my golden opportunity had passed; but, that was "OK" with me. I was content. In a moment of a chalk dust crisis, I had been available and ready to serve! I was happy, and at peace.

Pondering about that moment, now, I am reminded that good things come to those who wait upon the Lord (Lamentations 3:25). My "*good thing*" didn't come right away; but, in God's due time. When it did come, I was flying high and smiling big; because, the Lord had allowed me to take part in a great experience and adventure.

He *still* does that, today! The greatest adventure is life, itself. May your adventure be as exciting, and fulfilling, to you as dusting with the electric blackboard eraser cleaning machine was to me!

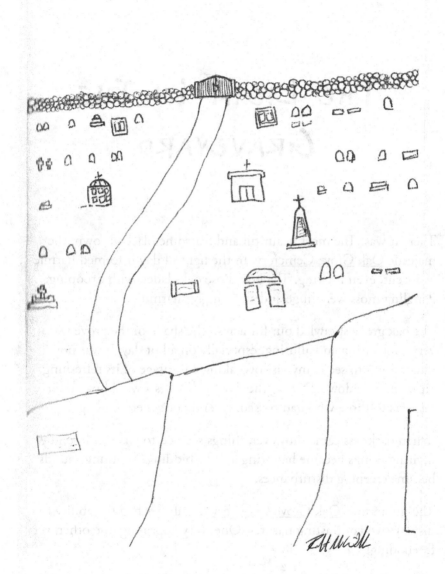

"Oak Grove Cemetery: inviting during the day....spooky at night!"

THE LIGHT IN THE GRAVEYARD

There it was. The most beautiful and fearsome place in town: the majestic <u>Oak</u> <u>Grove</u> <u>Cemetery</u>. In the light of day it seemed harmless, innocent, even inviting. The grandiose oaks laden with drooping, dangling moss were huge and stunningly charming.

The oak grove sprawled out for acres. The shade of the grove was very captivating and alluring, especially on a hot day. It was not uncommon to see many visitors taking advantage of its refreshing, air-cooled shadows. During the day many guests would pay their respects to those who had passed, recently or generations ago.

When darkness came, however, things seemed to change. Friendly, inviting things became haunting and forbidding. Soothing sounds became creeping disturbances.

The mysterious <u>Oak</u> <u>Grove</u> <u>Cemetery</u> has always had the ability to display two contrasting natures: One, very appealing; the other, very foreboding!

Of course, now, I know that nothing *really* changed after dark; but, in the proper setting, the mind can play tricks on you. This historical cemetery offered that perfect setting for the mind to run wild after dark. Added to its nightly ghostly appearance were the haunting stories generations old.

At a young age my mind ran wild anyway. It didn't need much incentive in that direction. Every time I walked to the movie theater, I had to walk by that bewitching cemetery. Really, though, walking <u>to</u> the theater wasn't *so* bad. Usually, there was still some daylight that caught the cemetery's alluring charm. Walking home <u>after</u> the movie, in the dark, especially after a horror movie, was the problem.

Walking past the graveyard at night, required a group. A group of like-minded guys that you could trust was always a big plus. The best guys were those that you could count on in a pinch. You know…guys that wouldn't let you down.

The fact is, walking past the cemetery at night was the main reason we *would* group together after a movie. It wasn't to do mischief, although some mischief may have been included. No, it was for safety from the ghost and goblins that, sometimes, came out of the graves on foggy nights after a horror movie! The number needed in your group depended on the intensity of the horror movie. Sometimes, two or three would be enough. Other times, it required a lot more. We felt there was strength in numbers. Plus, the slower ones could be sacrificed…if needs be!

One night, after a double feature of <u>Frankenstein</u> and <u>Dracula</u>, a *<u>large</u>* group was required. Six of us banned together for the dreaded walk home. We ended up having a, fairly, gifted group. We wanted it to be a comprehensive assemblage that would provide for our various needs for survival. We had a strong guy, two scrappers, a runner, a radar man and a sacrifice…if needs be.

Most of our group had to walk by the graveyard. It was our only way home. For Sammy, and his brother Russell, it was a little out of their way. However, after seeing the same movie we had just endured, they didn't want to walk home by themselves.

Joe and Lamar insisted that Stanley be in our group. Stanley boasted of having 'radar toes' that could sense ghosts and specters, before they actually came out of the ground! The claim was never proved, nor disproved. If it were true, then the only thing we needed to know was, whenever he started sensing stuff! That was the signal for us to start running!

We trusted Stanley's radar toes to work. To us, it was obvious that they had worked before. I mean, it was obvious that a ghost, or specter, had never caught us, nor eaten us alive! To us, Stanley's radar toes seemed to be, fairly, accurate; and, that was good enough for us!

The group didn't have to sit together during the movie. That was not necessary. We, usually, sat in different places in the theater. Each of us had our own special seat, especially, for horror movies. Some liked to sit up close and pretend to watch the scary parts! (But, they really had their eyes shut tight!)

Some liked the middle section, or one side wall, or the other. For me, I preferred the darkened back corner. Everything was in front of me from there. Plus, no one could tell if I had my eyes closed, or not.

After the movie, our group, officially, formed at the front lighted entrance of the theater. We would be hyped up, full of cola, popcorn and candy! We tried to psych ourselves up for the challenging walk home.

After our group was accounted for, we felt strong and confident. We joked about the "sissy" double feature horror flicks we had just seen. We belittled them as being 'kiddy' stuff, knowing all along that we had just been scared out of our wits!

Beyond the lighted area of the theater, the road became dark and haunting, very quickly! Only one street light was on the road. It was located at the corner way down the road. It stood right where we turned towards the graveyard. The darkness between the theater and the light seemed to be pitch, black. Each of us wondered, silently, whether there could be any forbidden creatures hidden in that darken trail!

We were hesitant to leave the safety of the theater lights; but, we all knew we *had* to start towards home. After viewing a double feature, we knew it was getting late. It was a common fact that the later we delayed the more ghosts, goblins and specters there would be waiting for us to encounter. So, taking a collective deep breath, we ventured our first steps towards home.

It wasn't long before we entered the first darkened area. Our courage quickly transcended into nervous laughter. Still, we were, somewhat, confident in our numbers, and in our gifted abilities. Huddling close together, we entered the darkened trail. The way was, indeed, dark; but we emerged out of the darkened area safe, without any incident. There were no ghost, nor any specter attacks! Not even a goblin showed its face. There wasn't even an eerie noise to taunt us!

The street light glowed brightly in the dark. It seemed to be our friend as it called out to us. It served as a regrouping point, helping us to reaffirm our confidence for the next leg of our journey home. We stood under its comforting glow dreading our next steps.

As we examined our infamous turn towards the graveyard, we noticed that the fog, that dreaded complicating menace, had already begun to settle in. We knew that the denser the fog, the more frightening the graveyard became! And believe me, *this* fog was thick! It was *really* thick! That meant it *could* have all kinds of hidden "things" within it.

Was it just a coincidence that in both of the horror flicks, the fog had hidden Frankenstein and Dracula from some of their unsuspecting victims!? We weren't sure. What we had just witnessed on the big screen could have been a warning to what all this fog *could* hide. This made us ponder upon the kinds of "things" that might, *actually,* be hidden in *this* particular fog! Each one of us knew we had to be ready for anything!

With the fog coming in like it was, some of us wanted to camp out, for a while, at the street light. We felt safe and secure there. But, with each passing moment the fog thickened. That meant more spooky critters might be on the rise. Plus, the hour was growing later. We *had* to move on, ready or not!

In times like these a weaker person might suggest a "run by" the graveyard. A "run by" meant what it said; but, it included throwing things at the shadows, and screaming out defensive swamp calls. It was a bit noisy, especially for those living around the graveyard; and, it was not something a brave man would do, or even suggest.

That night, however, we were hoping that there *was* a weaker person among us. And, even though, he might be labeled a "whimp", or a "sissy pants" for a while, the rest of us would have graciously granted his wish.

To our dismay, however, no "run by" was requested. That meant a "walk by" was mandatory. A "walk by" was much more traumatic; but, it *was* the braver thing to do. And, as you know, the brave thing was always automatic with guys like us. Being brave was the first thing on our list of things to be...unless, some whimp made it easier for us! Since no whimp spoke up, we were duty-bound by the code to do the brave thing!

Slowly, yet cautiously, we began our walk away from the safety of the street light. We took baby-steps into the dense fog...in the direction of the, now, terrifying graveyard!

The darkness in, and around, the graveyard seemed the darkest that any of us could ever remember seeing. And, as we feared, the graveyard darkness was filled with the thickest fog we had ever seen! That made it much, much more spooky than we had ever encountered! This began to have all the elements of a *bad* "walk by".

As dreadful as the thought of danger was to us, the "walk by" started out quite well. We, nervously, joked as we approached the ghastly graveyard entrance gate. Yet, we pressed on! When we were about a third of the way along the wall of the graveyard, we all began to notice the same thing. There were no strange noises, nor motions, coming from the graveyard! None at all! "Things" that could have complicated *things*, were nonexistent. Everything seemed to be working out for a much better "walk by" than we expected.

With each step, our confidence was increased a little more. We breathed a little easier…laughed a little louder…boasted a little more. We, even, got a little cocky!

We were, nearly, done! We were at the midway point, which meant that we could run to safety, if needs be, without far to go! We, all, were about to breath a sigh of relief, when a voice, out of nowhere, made a dreaded suggestion, "Let's walk *through* the graveyard!"

We couldn't believe it! It had happened, *again*! It seemed to happen every time we tried to walk by that spooky graveyard. *Someone,* from *somewhere,* had made that fearful suggestion of walking *through* the graveyard!

Everyone knew that walking *through* the graveyard was regarded as the total test of maximum courage. We, also, knew that we had all done it before. Yes, we had lived to tell about it. Those other nights were not like this night. This night was different! The ingredients for safety and fun were all wrong! It was <u>too</u> dark and <u>too</u> foggy for us to have any kind of an edge, <u>even</u> <u>with</u> 'radar toes'.

We weren't sure who had, actually, made the suggestion! The squeak of the voice was not, easily, recognizable. For all we knew, it could have, even, come from the fog! Once the challenge was spoken, however, *the code* demanded we act upon it. To say "no", or not embrace the challenge, meant we were <u>*all*</u> "whimps" and "scaredy-kats", which were labels of ridicule that no one could live down, easily!

I had hoped the challenge would <u>not</u> be issued that night. Not on this particular occasion, not this particular night. But, there it was! To this day, I wish I knew who spoke those dreaded words!

The only brave, and manly, response that could be given stuck in our throats for a moment. Then, one by one it squeaked out, "Sure!... Why not!"

It was at this particular time that Stanley was to play his important role. With his 'radar toes', he was drafted to be the lead man. Voicing one protest after another, he was pressed into, reluctantly, accept his assignment. While voicing opposition, Stanley angrily plopped down on the street, and started taking off his shoes and socks. Bare toes were better radar rods! And, believe me, we wanted those bared-toed radar rods out in front of us that night! We needed our best radar sensor sensing for ghosts, specters and goblins. Any doubts of his ability were set aside. That night we were all depending upon his uniquely gifted toes to be accurate and true.

When our radar toed front man was, finally, ready, we, slowly and painstakingly, crept over the old tabby cemetery wall into the dark, foggy graveyard. We kept alert for even the slightest sound, or most minor movement. Our ears were finely tuned, and our ears were wired for the most, minute sound. We wanted to be ready for _anything_. Deep in our minds, we knew the only thing we were, really, ready to do was to run...and sacrifice the slowest among us...if needs be!

In those days, it was well-noted on our city car tags that St. Marys was the second oldest city in the United States. To us that meant we were, now, entering the second oldest graveyard in the country! That was _not_ a warm fuzzy feeling!

Once inside the graveyard, you could, easily, see that there was no shortage of graves. Some graves and tombstones dated to the early 1700's. Some graves were so old that their markers were long gone! Some graves had decayed and caved in over the years making pit holes in our path. Others were bricked up high above the ground... High enough to be housing dead corpses waist high! And, some of the antique bricks were missing on quite a few!! This knowledge only made our journey through the graveyard more, dreary! Besides, _everyone_ knew that unmarked graves were the _most likely_ graves to have angry ghosts or specters rising up from them! (This was a well-known fact among elementary school students.)

The dense fog made it very difficult to see. This meant that goblins could sneak up and play tricks on you! Goblins, of course, were the less aggressive of the three. But, you still didn't want _anything_ sneaking up on you in this place, not at this time!

The instant Stanley's toes hit the ground on the other side of the wall, he began his radar sensing. Our group now resembled a condensed wad…an agglomeration of human flesh, fused together by fear, with Stanley's toes poking out front…as far as he could stretch them! We were, solidly, back-to-back and belly-to-belly as we baby-stepped our way into the depths of the dark, misty, fog-filled graveyard.

We didn't have to travel far, before the dangling moss began to take on the forms of ghosts and specters hanging from the trees…hovering all around us! They seemed to be watching our every move! Waiting for just the right moment to strike, and take us away!

We were afraid to look anywhere, but straight ahead; yet, our eyes still wandered in every direction. We were, totally, committed to following Stanley's 'radar toes'. When we heard strange noises, we tried not to look directly where noises arose. As you all know, it is another well-known fact that a specter wouldn't gobble you up, *if* you avoided direct eye contact. Also, a ghost was less likely to rip you apart, if you didn't look at it squarely into the eyes! You all knew this, right!

It, all, must have been true! None of us had *ever* made eye contact (not once, not even in the theater); and, we hadn't been gobbled up or ripped apart, yet!

Onward we pressed. Stanley, vigilantly, guided us around graves, monuments and above-ground burial chambers. Every "hot spot" his little 'radar toes' detected, we avoided! No questions asked! We were forced to trust our guide; and, it seemed to be working!

We were, nearly, two-thirds of the way through the old graveyard, when Joe, frantically, yelled, "Stop!"

We all, instantly, froze in our tracks. Nervously pointing in the distant fog, Joe, fearfully, queried, "W-w-what is that!?"

None of us wanted to look! The whole idea was to avoid eye contact! But, Joe kept questioning, insisting; then, demanded that we look in the direction he was pointing. What he was demanding would take a great deal of courage. We had to force ourselves to do it! When we, finally, did, we could see what Joe was so concerned about. In the distant fog there appeared to be a light, or lantern hanging in an unusual place! There had <u>never</u> been a light there before! Each of us knew most of this graveyard inch by inch, and <u>that</u> light was out of place!

We offered weak explanations. It could be a policeman…a night watchman…someone taking their garbage out, or…walking their dog…*anything* but a <u>ghost</u>!

None of the excuses were working for us! Now, we *knew* we were out of place. We weren't even supposed to be *in* the graveyard after dark in the first place. But, that light wasn't supposed to be there, either! It would be bad to be caught where we weren't supposed to be by another person; but, it would be even worse for us to be eaten up by a specter while in violation of authorities. Much worse! I mean what would they put on our tombstone… *"They got what they deserved!"*

We needed time to figure things out; so, we remained frozen. Well, actually, we *couldn't* move! Our knees were locked. We couldn't do anything, *but* stand there and stare at the light! We were fear-frozen in dead silence!

Suddenly, Joe screamed, "<u>It</u> <u>moved</u>!!"

Instantly, Stanley was gone! He just disappeared into the thick fog! We could hear him running, screaming, and tripping over graves. Bouncing off one monument, then another, his screams became faint! We hoped that meant he had cleared the tabby cemetery wall. The wall was the safety line! No ghost, goblin or specter would follow you beyond the wall! At least, that's what we had been told!

In an instant, we were without our specter radar protection! We all panicked! In the midst of Joe's screaming and dancing around, a limb from one of the big oaks popped. When it popped, we froze! When it hit the ground, we all scattered in different directions trying to find some portion of the wall, yelling and screaming all the way!

Joe took off through the briar patch at the other end of the graveyard. Sammy and Russell went screaming back the way we had entered the graveyard. It sounded as though they were tripping over and hitting each gave marker we had missed earlier!

Lamar and I ran towards Mr. McGhin's house. Mr. McGhin was a deacon in our church. Being a deacon, we just knew he had to have some kind of spiritual power over these fearsome spirits. His house sat just on the other side of the nearest wall and was targeted as our refuge of safety.

We stumbled and tripped as we made our way to the nearest wall! Each time we fell to the ground, we'd jump back up and keep on running, until we scaled the outer wall to safety. We didn't stop, until we were standing in Mr. McGhin's front yard. Through all this frantic activity, the light just stood there. It _never_ moved, again! Not an inch, one way, nor the other!

At first, we thought that, maybe, our hysterical response had so, thoroughly, confused the goblin that it didn't know which one of us to eat, or come after! Of course, this was just our own speculations. We couldn't tell for sure. And, we _were not_ going back to check!

Not wanting to become the 'sacrifice' left behind, we ran for home! We didn't slow down, until we reached the street light at Bailey Street. This light was a good safety zone just three houses down from my house. Being safe, again, gave us a warm fuzzy feeling! We took a deep breath, laughed a little; then, we parted to finish our journey home.

When Monday came, our group reassembled at school. We wanted to compare notes and injuries. Sammy, Russell, Lamar and I had bruises and scrapes. Joe had briar scratches all over his face and arms. Stanley was not at school! No one had seen, nor heard from him, since that night. Our imaginations ran wild with possibilities. Had he been gobbled up? Maybe, a specter had ripped him apart! Had he fallen into a grave and couldn't get out? Had we abandoned him in the graveyard needing help? Had _he_ been our _sacrifice_!?

When we went by his house, or tried to call to check on him, his mom would only say, "He's _not_ available." That, usually, meant she was mad at us, and didn't want him to talk to us for a while. At least, she didn't seem to be panicky! That meant he was, probably, safe at home.

What had *really* happened that night? That question was eating us up. We just had to know the answer!

After two days, Lamar and I decided to look into the matter after school. Two days was the established waiting period after a spook attack. That meant a daylight visit would be safe. So, on the way home from school we veered by the graveyard.

Don't worry! It would be safe in the daylight. I mean, everyone knows that ghosts, goblins and specters don't come out in the day time, especially, two days after an attack! With the brightness of the sun on our side, and the authority of the unwritten code, we, gingerly, and courageously, crossed over the cemetery wall, once again.

We tried to retrace our path from that fateful night. It proved very difficult to do! Everything looked different in the daylight, smaller and less intimidating! The fog had disoriented us. We weren't sure which way we had wondered using only radar toes.

We, finally, found the spot where the light had appeared to us. We looked in every possible direction trying to see where the light could have originated. We couldn't find anything strange, or out of the ordinary. Nothing stood out as being odd. We couldn't find any obvious clue that could be used to explain what we saw.

When all else failed, we timidly, walked towards the last known position of the menacing light. It was at the far back corner of the cemetery…an isolated area of the graveyard with many unused spaces. The opened area stretched out, right up to the chain-linked fence that, now, comprised the back boundary of the graveyard.

Beyond the fence was a residential street with new houses. Right _at_ the fence, nearest the graveyard, someone had erected a brand new street light. We had never seen this light before. No one had told _us_ about it! It was the _only_ light we found! That _had_ to be our specter!

The fog, our imagination, and fear had made us believe that it had moved. Joe's, untimely, suggestion had ignited our nightmares, which we let get the best of us.

When we felt we had figured it all out, it became, kind of, funny to us. A sense of relief, and joy, filled our hearts as we left the cemetery laughing.

On the way out, we retrieved Stanley's tennis shoes. He had, evidently, flung them at some "menacing spirit", while making his escape. Stanley's mom appreciated our retrieval of her son's 'radar toe' covers, since they were brand new <u>Keds</u> shoes. Stanley, however, was not so happy. He never wore those tennis shoes, again. He was afraid that attacking "spirits" might have been 'boobie-trapped' his shoes. He didn't want to wear anything that could have been touched by a specter, or tainted by a goblin virus as they lay on the ground inside the graveyard wall.

Since that night, I have had a lot of time to ponder about the events of that night. We wondered in the darkness and fog in a spirit of fear and panic. We were not aware of a light that could have been used as a source of hope and guidance. I keep thinking about what the Apostle John wrote in his Gospel: "*In Him was life, and the Life was the Light of men. And the Light shines in darkness and the darkness did not overcome it*" (John 1:4-5, NKJV).

That street light had pierced the darkness of that night. It cut through the heavy fog and caught our attention. It scared us at first; because, we didn't know what it was. We didn't know why it was there! Our desire to learn about the light helped us to discover the truth: the light was there for our benefit.

Knowing that the light was there, and that it would <u>always</u> be there, made our future trips through the darkened graveyard a little easier. We learned it was best to, always, walk towards the light. The closer we got to the light, the more we could see things clearly. The shadows seemed to run from the light in the graveyard!

The Light of our Lord is like that, too. The closer we get to Him, the more of life we can see clearly. Things, once hidden in darkness, are revealed for what they truly are. "*That was the true Light which gives light to every person coming into the world.*" (John 1:9, NKJV).

Are you fearful of the darkness around you? If so, walk towards the Light of the World. His light chases away the darkness and helps us see life more clearly. Let Him lighten your path, today.

THE QUEEN MARY

Our family was never counted among the rich, nor the famous, in St. Marys. There were times when a few of us might have come close to being 'infamous'; but, that's as close as we got to being people of notoriety.

Dad earned enough for us to live on working at the paper mill. After the bills were paid, there wasn't much left for "extras". Of course, back then, I'm not even sure we knew what "extras" were!

If we needed new clothes, we got 'hand-me-downs' from relatives. On rare occasions, about twice a year, we got new clothes. The rest of our feeble wardrobe was made by my mom...or, at least, she tried to make them! She had women's and girl's clothes down pretty good. Men's and boy's clothing was more of a challenge for her. She was a good seamstress and could make, pretty much, whatever she put her mind to making. She was constantly studying stuff, contemplating on whether she could make it, or not.

Mom was an excellent house wife and homemaker. She kept things cleaned and fresh as she commanded our readiness and movements. It was a well-organized household, except for a little disorganization every now and then. Basically, the house ran according to her design and with dad's permission. To help our cash-flow challenges, from time to time, she would take a part-time job. It helped the local store owners in town, and gave us a little extra. She, mainly, worked around the holidays; but, not on a holiday. Some of the store owners were family members, near family members or close friends who were treated like family members.

Other than holiday seasons, she was called upon in times of illness, or when someone took a vacation. She was an honest hard worker. She had a way with the customers that was fresh and appreciated. She would tell people to wait for the sale coming up, or call someone to let them know there was only one left of a limited edition item. Everyone knew they could count on her help. Besides, to "fill in" when needed gave her a chance to add some variety to everyday experience. She was happy to do it, for a limited amount of time. The little bit of extra money helped with other *necessities*.

Our family had many financial limitations, that's for sure; but, we made do with what we had…and the little bits we could add. The rest…we improvised, or did without! Some people sported new clothes with every new season of the year. We never were able to do that. Our clothes, however, were adequate.

Much of our 'newer' clothes were those well-broken-in hand-me-downs that many of us have experienced at some time, or the other. Mom always picked out the best, or mended what she could. We never wore "rag-tagged" clothes. Of course, some were not appropriately matched for every season and, often, the styles had changed before we got the clothes. But, hey, we didn't care!

On special occasions, like Easter my sister would get a new home-made dress. My brother and I would get *another* brand new pair of white oxfords. (Those white oxfords didn't seem to last very long!) Usually, on the first day of school, or at Christmas, we would get *new* clothes. On our birthdays, maybe, a new pair of tennis shoes would be our present.

As I mentioned, mom tried to make clothes for my brother and me; but, that was not her expertise. She could make new dresses for my sister, and herself, a lot better. Hand-me-downs were our new clothes most of the time. Except for a few summers when mom made us "baggie" shorts!

Do you remember "baggie" shorts? When they, finally, came into style, my brother and I had, already, been wearing them for some time. It was one of the few moments in our lives when we predated something that became popular. Mom was so proud! It made her so happy that she could make us something that was popular to wear… and, without much effort!

Without a doubt, "baggies" were the exception, and the extent, of mom's male clothing production! She could make us "baggies"…and, that was about it! We began to wonder if she thought <u>she</u> had brought the 'fad' into vogue! If so, we never got any royalties! If not, who were we to tell her otherwise!

Baggies were so easy to make, that she had all the teens make their own for a Vacation Bible School project! In case you don't remember, "baggies" were beach shorts with a draw string. They were, usually, made in loud colors, or bright, large floral designs. Mom thought the 'louder' the better!

She started it out that way; because, she could get loud colored, discarded materials pretty cheap at the fabric shop. Sometimes, the prints and patterns were so outlandish that they were given to her, at no charge, just to get them out of the store! As long as she got her free, outlandish, new material, she used it to make us those squared, pull-string "baggies". They were drawn tight by a cotton pull cord that dad brought home from the discard heap at the mill. He didn't like his anchor cord being used for these outlandish shorts; but, mom was on a role! I think, all together, baggies were in style, nationally, for about a month, maybe a whole summer. We wore them for years!

Those homemade, squared-off shorts were some of the ugliest things to wear; yet, they met our <u>need</u> for swimwear, summer work attire and knock-around shorts. We used them for everything: surfing, fishing, cutting yards, playing tennis at the newly asphalted courts, and for pool play at the *Crooked River State Park*.

Mom and dad would have preferred to be able to buy us better clothing; but, they had to save money in order to pay our bills. That's one thing dad was known for…He paid his bills!

His payments were <u>always</u> paid on time! If something was going to prevent a bill from arriving on its due date, mom, or dad, would call the vendor to make *special* arrangements. Local vendors were always willing to help out if they trusted you and knew your payment was on the way. We didn't have many puffy things; but, we had <u>good</u> credit! Dad once told us, "I ain't got no money to leave you when I'm gone; but, I can teach you how to have good credit!" That he did!

Clothes we had…store-bought toys was another thing altogether! Our lack of store-bought toys, without a doubt, reflected our lack of extra income. That meant, for the most part, store-bought toys were non-existent! We made, or imagined, most of our toys. On occasion, we might find, and fix up, an old discarded toy. After fixing it up, we made good use of it as long as we could. As a rule, most of our toys, most of the time, were left to our creativity and imagination.

I must admit that using roots, sticks, discarded building materials, old motor parts, and similar items as toys, may seem a little odd to some, now-a-days! It might, even, seem cruel! But, it never bothered us!

Using our imaginations, we could make our items become anything we wanted them to become. Any time we needed a gun, lance or a bazooka in our play, we imagined the item into existence by using one of our props, or finding a 'new' discarded one.

My, personal, arsenal of play weapons looked more like a batch of through-away lumber needing to be burned, or a glorified junk pile! To me, it was my stash of swords, guns of all ages of history, not to mention, spears, bows and arrows! I could always tell, exactly, what each and every item was supposed to be.

When I played "Revolutionary War", or "<u>Swamp Fox</u>", I had some dried roots that were bent, perfectly, to resemble crooked, flint-lock pistols. When you added a bent nail to the top for a flintlock hammer, it became a complete, functional weapon of that period.

When I played 'Cowboys and Indians", I had a discarded, split piece of wood that had a knot hole in just the right spot for a trigger guard. The advantageous split ran lengthwise, which made a great shape for a slender barrel. When it reached the knot, it fanned out, perfectly, to form the shape of a rifle butt. I had to imagine the lever for cocking the 'rifle'; but, that wasn't hard to do!

In my stash, I had sticks for swords, lances, spears, bows and arrows. Some premium items were the machine guns made from discarded caulking guns. I, also, had magnolia tree cones for hand grenades! Those magnolia cones, with their double-jointed, unbroken stem, made great hand grenades. They were much better than pine cones, and less painful to deal with!

I know it could have been confusing, for some; but, I never crossed up my guns! Neither their era of use, nor the type of weapon it represented was ever confused with another. Plus, I never used a grenade more than once! What was the use? It had *already* been exploded! Once the stem was broken at the jointed section, it became a 'spent' grenade. Of course, all of this was all done in the name of fun and play!

I, really, didn't mind using sticks, and other things, for toys. I thought kids, everywhere, were doing the same thing. In fact, at times, I made them seem so *real* that other kids traded their 'real' toys for my sticks. Of course, the trade was just to use for that day of play. At the end of the war, attack or play day, all things went back to their original owners.

Real toys were nice, but some "real" toys broke, very, easily! For toughness and ware, "real" toys could not compare to sticks and metal. In hand to hand combat, for instance, plastic just couldn't stand up to a good imagined wood or metal toy!

With my imagination, and an excellent stash, I never knew what I was missing, in not having *real* toys! That all changed, however, in one day!

One of our well-intending relatives decided that my brother was old enough to have the *real* thing. So, she gave him a real plastic model of the Queen Mary passenger ship.

The humongous model came in a big, two-handed, toting box!

The huge box was filled with a 'zillion' parts and pieces of all sizes! There were decals of various shapes and sizes included, and a tube of modeling glue! Ah, glue! A wonderful invention that I was not, yet, allowed to possess.

I don't know why *he* got one, and *I* didn't! I know he was three years older than me; but, come on! I have to admit...I was a bit "put out" about it! In fact, I was jealous! Yes! Yes, I was jealous.

Out of the clear blue, "they" decided *he* was old enough to have a model to put together! What "they" were saying was that I was, too, young and ignorant! It didn't matter to me that he was three years older! Why should it matter to them? It, just, didn't seem very fair to me!

Yep. There it was! A big "real" toy for my brother to "play" with! Yep! There it was; and, there was nothing I could do about it. I had to sit by, and watch him work at putting it together...piece by piece. To make things worse, I was <u>never</u> allowed to touch it. Not even to breath on it!

Every time I tried, mom, or dad, would be summoned by my brother. For *some* reason, he didn't seem to trust me with his prized beauty. Answering his call, they would scold me, and warn me about the 'consequences', if I *did* touch it! What was the deal with that! All of a sudden, I had become infected with some kind of 'anti-plastic model disease'!

Every evening, before bedtime, he worked on it a little more. Every evening I wanted to touch it! Each successive evening for a long time, he would work on it, and I would want to touch! It was, almost, like it was becoming an obsession! I felt as though I was being tortured!

We, only, had a two bedroom house! Where could I go to get away from his relentless, steady, meticulous, construction rituals! I was trapped in a labyrinth of desire! I had to be obedient, or my life could have been at stake!

It seemed as though, the whole family had turned against *me*, and favored *him*! And, **yes**, to make matters worse, *they* could <u>all</u> touch it; but, <u>*nooo*</u> - not <u>me</u>!!

When he, finally, put the finishing touches on the ship, it was a very impressive achievement! There were decals and fresh paint on the exterior that made it look very sharp! I have to admit, it looked like it was a very fine sea worthy vessel.

I never realized my own brother was so talented! He had, always, seemed kind of 'fluky' to me! I just couldn't believe he had done all that detail work in such professional perfection. It was quite amazing!

The completed watercraft was about two feet in length. Every special feature of the ship was fitted out, just right! Every detail had been attended to. Every piece had been properly glued. Even the tiny life boats were all in their proper place and in uniform order!

In his short life, up to that time, my brother had put together some smaller models, with much fewer pieces; but, this…no doubt, this was one of his greatest achievements ever! I considered it to be his first great masterpiece of his own handiwork. I couldn't help it…I was proud of him, and for him, though I tried not to show it!

As pretty and fine a craft as she was on her own merit, the <u>Queen Mary</u> had another additional perk to it. It had a small compartment for a battery-powered motor. When you tilted the flag staff, the engine would run, turning the propeller! The paint had made it waterproof, allowing the ship to navigate in straight lines on the water. This, truly, made her a sea worthy craft and qualified her as a "real" toy.

Yes, my friends! You could, actually, float the motorized boat in water! This added feature graduated the <u>Queen Mary</u> from just a "what not" sitting on a shelf, to the "IB-A Toy" for playing category! Certainly, now that she was completed, she could be touched by other human hands. Right! After all, "toys" were made to be <u>touched</u>! Right?… *Wrong!* This toy, *still*, could not be touched…by <u>me</u>!

Something was, definitely, wrong here! Evidently, I was the <u>only</u> one who had knowledge of the '*toy code book*'! I'm sure the toy code must have come from a book, somewhere! The code says, "Toys are made to be touched"! That <u>had</u> to be a rule, or a code of ethic, in some book, in some library, *somewhere*! But, no <u>one</u> in *my* family seemed to have had any knowledge of it. They just didn't see it my way! No matter how much I tried to reason with them…no matter how much convincing I attempted, I was, still, denied <u>any</u> touching privileges! This was an outrage! It was, extremely, unfair!

For weeks after its completion, I was forced to look at the monstrous creation, *but was not allowed to touch it*! Mom started making my brother and I take separate baths; so, my brother could have time to play with his creative masterpiece in the tub. *Playing in the tub!* Before the <u>Queen Mary</u>, *playing in the tub* was unheard of! Now, he could play with my parent's blessing!

These new rules were hard for me to embrace. My parents, and older sister, could touch the ship; but, not me! My brother could play with the <u>Queen Mary</u> in the tub; but, I couldn't play at all! My sister, even, got to *hold* the <u>Queen Mary</u>, but *not* me!

Whenever we went fishing, or out to the *Crooked River State Park*, they allowed him to float his battery-powered ship along the river bank! But, could I touch it, or assist him in playing with it? *Nooo,* not me!

I realized my plight was hopeless. I tried to get my mind off of it. I tried not to let it to bother me, *so* badly. But, every night, there it was on the shelf in our bedroom! Every morning, there it was, again! It was driving me crazy!

Weeks, eventually, turned into months. After a while, the luster of the "new" faded into the dinginess of an old used, scarred up plastic boat. It's majestical grandeur and feel, gradually, lost its luster. It became demoted from the glory of the shelf, to the darkness of the clothes closet! Well, it, really, wasn't just a clothes closet for three siblings. The floor of the small closet was the shoe storage area for piles of used shoes and the inside "toy" closet space for old, unused, discarded, touchable toys.

In the past, the house rules were: once a toy, or a gadget, reached this destination, it became fair game for anyone else! I'm really sure about this! There was an unwritten rule (in that illusive code book) that applied here. That rule, clearly, states: "anyone can touch what lies in the pile on the closet floor." It is, also, inferred that <u>anyone</u> could use it, or play with it. <u>Anyone</u>! That meant, now, at long last, the <u>Queen Mary</u> was available to <u>*anyone*</u>, including <u>*me*</u>!

By this time, the ship was in need of several repairs. The decals had come off. The paint was flaked and faded. Some of it had peeled off, completely. The cute little anchor was missing. One smoke stack was severely damaged, and several of the tiny life boats had floated away. Clearly, my brother had had his fun with the ship. Now, dingy, leaky and with severe motor problems, it had been set aside. It had been replaced by other things.

I wondered how…after putting so much time and effort into constructing the ship…how could he, so easily, lose interest in it! How could he sit it aside, like that! This was something hard for me to understand. But, that's what he did. He set it aside, and forgot about it.

As I ponder on it, now, I am, so, glad that our Creator, who made and fashioned us, ever so carefully, has never set us aside and forgotten about us! When our newness and luster was lost, He devised a way to redeem us, and make us new, again. He picked us back up from the junk pile, and renewed us! He refashioned us into new creations.

I wish I could say that the <u>Queen Mary</u>'s fate was as gloriously redemptive as that of a sinner saved by grace; but, I cannot. When the <u>Queen Mary</u>, finally, fell into my hands, I *did* plan to restore her. My restorations, however, were imperfect. They were, only, temporary and didn't last long.

I did restore the outside using some of the leftover glue and pieces of a smashed model airplane that I had found in someone's trash can. I had hoped this would stop some of the leaks. I repaired a loose wire on the little motor using some of dad's electrical tape, which made it run a little longer.

Being limited in my resources, and my creative abilities, I could not repair the smoke stack. I tried to use an discarded toilet tissue roll; but, it wouldn't fit and wouldn't stayed glued. Nor could I replace the life boats, and other small items that had broken, or floated away. There was just so much *I* could do!

Thank Goodness, the Lord's resources are limitless! He does not lack ability, nor the materials! My feeble efforts to redeem the Queen Mary were admirable, but temporary and short-lived. God's redemption is eternal, and complete.

I did, however, give it my best shot! After many attempts, and unfavorable results, I, too, had to give up on restoring the tattered, rundown ship. I am so glad, however, that God never gives up on us! I admit that I am not as patient and gifted as He is!

The Queen Mary *had been* a good ship. It *had been* a great "real" toy. The thought of putting it back into the closet pile, only to be crushed under the weight of old shoes…well, it just didn't seem right! Putting it back onto the shelf, in its worn-out condition, would be an embarrassment to its glorious past. It had been a 'hands-on' "real" toy that had lived up to its purpose: to be played with. Now, it was, too, fragile for anyone to hold. In every respect, it had fulfilled its intended objective.

Its beauty and luster had, now, vanished. It could no longer function as a "real" toy. It had lasted a long time; but, now, for all practical purposes, it had outlived its era.

In my youthful, chivalrous mind, if a toy had no more play in it, it was best to discard, or destroy it. The ultimate glorious demise of a great toy was to send it off with a great ceremonial demolition. With this in mind, I took the Queen Mary down to the river for its final voyage.

I wish I could say that my idea of final retirement was a genuinely, thoroughly romantic gesture…a notion coated in nautical honor.

That was, only, partly, true. The other, more selfish, part of me just wanted to see what an M-80 (larger than a cherry bomb) would do to a plastic ship afloat in the water!

However, with a great sense of honor and respect, I said my farewells, and offered a brief ceremonial speech. I, respectfully, lighted the fuse, and set the valiant ship afloat with its little motor running full speed ahead.

She had only sailed a few feet when the M-80 exploded. It sounded like a muffled shotgun blast! The force of the explosion sent pieces of the top deck flying into the air. The remaining parts of the ship, quickly, descended to the bottom of the dark tidal river. That was the glorious end of the Queen Mary!

When I informed my brother of the respectful way his 'old lady' had been dispatched, he, suddenly, became interested in having her back! When I applied the 'code' to my actions, he, conveniently, forgot there was a 'code'. When he informed mom and dad about my retiring the vessel, they made their own feelings be made known. The end result was that I had to replace the Queen Mary with another. By this time, there were none available; so, I replaced it with a huge model of the U.S.S. Constitution using my own allowance money. And guess what? I couldn't touch it!

Setting aside the unfairness I felt in the Queen Mary's past, I came to realize that life can seem unfair to any of us, at any particular time. Looking back, I, now, realize that man-made restoration, without true redemption, is only a temporary fix. It, often, ends up with a relapse that plunges us deeper into the darkness of despair.

The Lord's ability to redeem is limitless. His resources have no end. True redemption lasts forever! Self-redemption, however, comes up short! In *His* redemption, we become brand new creations, "*old things are passed away; behold, all things are become new*" (2 Corinthians 5:17b, NKJV).

Uncle Sylvester
Goes To Town

Many years ago, it was not uncommon for someone to drop out of school by the fifth, or sixth grade. When this did happen, it was, often, due to family hardships. During the era of the *Great Depression*, several of my elder relatives had to drop out of school, and find some kind of work, in order to help their family survive.

They were <u>never</u> considered "dumb"; because, they didn't finish school. Nor did they lack intelligence. They learned, on their own! What they needed to know, they picked up along the way. They were just not able to finish school. Some did finish later; or, at least, made sure their kids went to school.

Uncle Sylvester was one of those who had come through that period of time, resulting in very little formal education. He was, however, a very smart man. He was a man who, if given enough time, could figure most things out for himself. That's not to say he didn't have his limitations. He did. In fact, one of his limitations was that he never learned to read very well. He may have been challenged in his reading ability; but, he learned <u>very</u> well by listening! His family and friends respected his self-learned wisdom, and honored his decisions.

He was raised deep in the swamp and, rarely, ventured far from it.

When his father died during those troubled times, he dropped out of school to help work the land, and care for his three sisters and two brothers. His mother made a little money cooking for other folks; but, her full-time job was caring for her family.

Uncle Sylvester never became bitter. He was an easy-going fellow. He never complained about his circumstances. He did his best to care for his family, and made sure his brothers and sisters had clothes to wear, food to eat, and went to school.

When his mother died, the homestead was divided among the siblings. With their blessing, he bought back each one's part that didn't want to work the land. Being a family man of great integrity, he assured all his family that they would always have a home with him, if they needed it.

As a young man he married his childhood sweetheart, Lorraine. She had been raised, even, deeper in the swamp. He loved her, dearly. He, always, respected her, and never mistreated her. It would have been hard to find a more devoted couple than they proved to be.

They went through everything together: good times and bad. Their emotions, and their love, had been tested time, and time, again. Still, their love grew. Through it all, they remained an easygoing, loving couple.

If you felt you needed to do so, you could curse each one, individually, to their face with no rebuttal. But, if you cursed the other, in their presence, you were headed for a 'reckoning', as many found out! It, usually, didn't take more than one "reckoning" to learn what not to say! After a few lessons, "N'ere a bad word" was spoken against either one!

One summer, a traveling preacher ventured into the swamp. He had come to save some of those "unfortunate swamp heathens". Uncle Sylvester invited him into his home. He offered his barn as a meeting place, and sent the word out to family and friends to come to the "preachin' meetin".

From places in the swamp that very few knew about, they gathered into a group of about thirty people. Uncle Sylvester and Aunt Lorraine were the first ones "saved". Others followed. After several nights of holy, evangelistic meetings, it was realized that everyone attending the meetings had been saved! Uncle Sylvester made note of it to the preacher. He advised the evangelist that it was time to move on to some other 'unsaved' spots, which the evangelist elected to do.

The "saved" group wanted to continue meeting as a church. None of them had ever constituted a church before; but, that didn't stop them from getting it done. They realized, right away, that they needed a spiritual leader. Not knowing exactly how to do it, nor if they were doing it correctly, they elected Uncle Sylvester as the lead preaching elder of the Mt. Victory Baptist Church.

They decided he would do the preaching and teaching in between revival meetings. He accepted the "call". Uncle Sylvester knew it would be difficult to accomplish this "called" task with limited reading skills. His daughter, Claudelle, had been to school and could read; so, he had her to read the Holy Bible to him. On Sunday, she would read the Scriptures he had selected for the day; then, Uncle Sylvester would preach his heart on those Scriptures to the eagerly awaiting congregation.

When word got out to Folkston that an un-ordained man was preaching in a self-started church called the Mt. Victory Baptist Church, it aroused quite a stir! Whoever heard of an un-ordained man preaching, not to mention other preacher stuff that had to be done! It was close to being blasphemous! At the next Associational meeting, Rev. Mitchell, the esteemed, and ordained, pastor of the Folkston Baptist Church, decided he would go see what was going on out there in the swamp. He promised to make a report upon his return.

So, Rev. Mitchell, was duly commissioned by the Association to venture into the swamp, with seven of his select deacons by his side, to observe what was going on. They were prepared to witness the worse things they could imagine. Some of them expected to see all kinds of forbidden voodoo, or some other evil "goings on"! Other of his deacons just hoped they would encounter folks who just needed a bit of "straightening out"!

When they reached Mt. Victory Baptist Church, they found a brush arbor church built on the highest spot of dry ground in the surrounding swamp. (That's why it was called "*Mt.*" Victory!) The whole area, under and around the brush arbor, was 'swept' clean of any grass, weeds or foliage. The floor was coated with the purest white sand, which was rare in those parts.

The arbor was freshly, and finely, thatched. The benches were made of hickory which had been sanded smooth as silk and free of any splinters. The pulpit was a large cypress log that had been hand cut and fashioned into a pulpit. It had been sanded smooth and covered with a protective coating. Even in those days, a cypress of that diameter was rare, and beautiful! The kneeling bench was cypress, as well, and honed with the same skillful perfection.

The visiting group had, purposely, come on a Sunday morning. By design, they arrived, unannounced, and in time to witness the worship. They thought they may catch the self-styled church in action; but, they arrived, too, early for that.

The morning fog was lifting. The swamp noises of bugs and critters became silent. Birds stopped their chirping. Pretty soon, people began to emerge from the woods encircling the brush arbor. Each man and boy was dressed in their cleanest and finest pressed overalls. Women and girls had on home-made aprons, bonnets and ribbons. Many changed their shoes and boots upon their arrival. Those that didn't, cleaned what they had on.

Those that had them, came with their Bibles in hand. Some came humming a hymn. Everyone came with covered dish meals and freshly prepared breads and desserts.

Some were wondering who these new comers were. Rev. Mitchell introduced himself, and his deacons. They were all, immediately and overwhelmingly, welcomed. They were given the best benches in the church, and offered a pillow to sit upon, if they needed it. During the service, the delegation was recognized and asked to bring greetings from the Christian brothers and sisters of their church. Rev. Mitchell, on behalf of the whole group, honorably and politely, offered "heartfelt" greetings. After the preliminaries, they <u>all</u> joined in the worship service. They sang spiritual hymns accompanied by guitar, jugs, harmonica and juice harp. Different ones gave brief testimonies of God's blessings and help. From the eldest, to the youngest that was able to speak, they praised the Lord.

Uncle Sylvester told Rev. Mitchell, "I would let you preach today, Brother; but, then what would I do with the Word God gave me?" Rev. Mitchell, graciously, thanked him for his acknowledgement, as well as, his kind explanation. He assured Uncle Sylvester that he had come to witness and participate, not to lead.

After praying sincere heartfelt prayers, and singing hymns that stirred the heart of faith, the Scriptures were read in reverenced silence. After another prayer, Uncle Sylvester preached what the Lord had "laid upon his heart". When the preaching was over, they took up a love offering for the needy of the church at Folkston.

Nearly sixty were in attendance that day, with two of those getting 'gloriously saved'. By mutual consent, they were baptized, immediately, in a nearby natural pool of dark, clean swamp water. Rev. Mitchell was asked to officiate over the baptism. Wearing borrowed overalls, he did the honors.

Lunch followed with laughter and good fellowship. Polite discussions, and questions, were intermingled with funny stories and experiences. When it was all over, Rev. Mitchell and his deacons had all their questions answered, and were asked a few by some of the elders. The delegation returned from the swamp pleasantly surprised, and totally amazed.

About a week after the commissioned group emerged from the swamp, the Association had a "called" meeting in order to hear the delegation's report. Rev. Mitchell was asked to give his report in detail to the whole Association. He stood before his peers in humbled silence and lowly posture. With his head bowed low, and his seven deacons standing by his side, he softly mumbled a prayer that could, barely, be heard by those sitting in the front row.

He, slowly, raised his eyes to the ceiling, took a deep breath, and proclaimed, "Brothers and sisters! As far as the Mt. Victory Baptist Church is concerned, we have nothing to worry about. They are as solid as the divine _Rock,_ upon which their church has been built. We need to do as Jesus told those who witnessed Lazarus coming forth from the grave. Jesus said, '_Loose him and let him go!_' So should we loosen Mt. Victory from any restrictions, and suspicions, and let them go as the Lord leads." No further word was ever spoken on the matter.

As time passed, Rev. Mitchell and Uncle Sylvester became good friends. Every now and then, Rev. Mitchell tried to get Uncle Sylvester out of the swamp. He offered an open invitation for Uncle Sylvester to come into the small city of Folkston and "stay with him a spell".

He was, rarely, successful. Uncle Sylvester had seen Folkston…been there and done that! Too busy a place! Too many people in one spot! Too much mischief by those with nothing to do!

After several years of prodding, Uncle Sylvester surprised everyone, one day, by asking his preacher friend to take him, instead, to Jacksonville, Florida. Rev. Mitchell was shocked! Jacksonville was a much larger city, with many more people. Shocked as he was, he was more than happy to oblige. It was decided that the two families would go together.

The reason for the surprise request, soon, became known. Uncle Sylvester had heard that they had just built a brand new J. C. Penny store, which boasted of having one of the first brand new escalators in town. Uncle Sylvester had heard of an escalator, and wanted to see one for himself. The concept of moving stairs intrigued him. What an amazing idea! So, they all went to see this great invention, now installed in Jacksonville.

Traveling by automobile was another big treat. Aunt Lorraine, and her seven children, had never ridden in an automobile before. Uncle Sylvester had ridden in a truck one time. He was certain that an automobile would be similar; but, this was Aunt Lorraine's first time ever in an automobile, or a truck.

They were used to mule-drawn wagons, bicycles, mule plows and push plows. Their children were bubbling over with excitement at the prospect of an automobile ride! It was a thrilling added bonus to their hour-long trip in Rev. Mitchell's automobile. Actually, it took a little longer than an hour. The 'thrill' of the ride *moved* them greatly! They had to stop at a few 'pucker brushes' along the way!

When they arrived at J.C. Penny's, Uncle Sylvester cornered the first salesperson he could find. He asked for directions to the escalator. After receiving directions, he herded the whole group towards the moving marvel.

You could hear them all gasp when their eyes fell upon it. They stared at it in complete amazement. They watched, in awe, as people got on and off, riding up and down. Rev. Mitchell told Uncle Sylvester to go ahead and try it. The good reverend, even, rode it once, to show everyone how it was done.

Uncle Sylvester called Levis, his eldest son, over to him. He told Levis how much he loved him, and how pleased he was with him as his son; then, he told Levis to ride the machine first. Having never denied, nor disobeyed his father before, Levis, reluctantly, agreed.

Rev. Mitchell explained to Levis how to get on without stumbling. They all waited for Levis to take his ride. Levis, however, was mesmerized as he stared at the moving stairs. He stood there watching the steps appear out of nowhere! The constant motion made him reluctant to take his first step. He tried to step forward, a time or two; but, drew his foot back each time. After a few more attempts, Uncle Sylvester put his hand upon Levis' shoulder, and said, "Son, it's OK. I'll do it."

Levis stepped back, a bit disappointed that he couldn't fulfill his father's wish; but, gladly relieved that he didn't have to go first. A comforting smile from his father made Levis know everything was alright.

Uncle Sylvester looked at Aunt Lorraine, as if it could be his last glance upon her loving face. Her eyes were bulging wide with mystified anticipation. He smiled at his children; then, took his first step.

At first, the movement made him almost loose his footing. He, quickly, recovered his balance, however; then, he rode all the way to the top. His breathes were heavy at the beginning of his ride; then, you could hear him sounding off in a low-toned shrill. At the end, he was hooting and hollering, as if it were a victory cry!

The whole family watched with wonder. When he completed his ride to the top, he yelled down, "You have got to ride this thing! Come on up. I'll catch ya at this end."

Aunt Lorraine, coming out of her shy shell, demanded to next. With a little initial scream, and several giggles, she ascended to the top and into the arms of awaiting, loving husband. Each of the children followed, one at a time, with Levis going last. To them it was like riding a roller coaster. Shrills and thrills were exclaimed all the way up! They couldn't get enough! They continued to ride, over and over.

After a while, Aunt Lorraine, who had never been in a J.C. Penny store, said she needed to do some shopping, while they were in town. Uncle Sylvester told her to go ahead. Mrs. Mitchell showed her around the store, while Uncle Sylvester and Levis stayed there to ride a bit longer. They continued to ride up and down several times. After a while, Uncle Sylvester noticed some tools on the bottom floor. He told Levis to go with him to look at some of the new tools. Levis, however, wanted to ride some more. He had to yank Levis off the escalator!

They were astonished at the spread of all kinds of tools, for all kinds of work. The whole area was filled with nothing but tools and farming implements. Tools were on shelves, hanging on the walls and laid out on tables all over the room! Most of his tools were multi-functional; but, here, it seemed, there was a different tool for every job!

As he examined each tool, he noticed a set of doors that opened and closed, quite often. He began to notice people going through the doors, then different people coming out. It was confusing to him. He stood there for a while and just stared at the doors that led into a small room, opening and closing…watching people going through the doors…and noticing different ones coming out!

He had never seen anything like this before. He called Levis over, and told him, "Watch those doors. They open and close all by themselves! People go in that small room; but, different ones come out!"

Levis stood with his dad watching the doors, but nothing happened. Levis, who had never questioned his father, began to wonder if all the excitement of the day had been, too, much for his dad to handle! Uncle Sylvester wisely discerned the thoughts of his son, and said, "I know what you thinkin'. Shut up and watch those doors!"

After they stood there for a while longer, they saw this very huge, heavy-set woman with a well-weathered face walk up to the doors, and push the button. Pretty soon, the doors opened up. She stepped in. The doors closed.

In just a few moments, the doors opened up, again. Out stepped this very attractive young woman. Uncle Sylvester told Levis, "Go get your momma. She's got to ride this thing!"

Transformations are not easy; but, they are required when we become a Christian. Uncle Sylvester had been transformed by his faith from a lost 'swamp heathen' to a "gloriously saved" child of God…from a lost sinner to a saint saved by grace.

No mechanical device could ever effect such a change in one's life. Only the power of God can bring transformation to His children (Romans 12:1-2).

After Aunt Lorraine rode the elevator several times, this truth, finally, hit home with Uncle Sylvester. In fact, it was such a profound truth that he preached on it when he returned home.

PLOWING A
STRAIGHT LINE

I don't know about your family; but, in our family, it was *not* unusual for the children to be 'leant out' to other family members for chores. Mainly, this was offered to help with planting or harvesting. It, also, included various other routine tasks to be done while in their care.

Whenever we were out of school for the holidays, or spring breaks, some of that time might be spent *on loan* to a family member. It meant hard work and long hours, which was not always met with great joy.

No matter if we liked it, or not, we did it to help the family through a difficult time. When my brother and I had to do it, we tried to make the best of it. We tried to add a little fun to it. It didn't do any good to sit around and sulk over it; so, we embraced the opportunity as best we could.

The help we offered was much needed, and always appreciated. Our labors were never compensated in dollars and cents…Well, at least, *I* never saw any money! There were rewards; but, they just came in other forms. For instance, our family would benefit from the bounty of the fields, receiving vegetables and fruits for our shared labors. Some other family member, who had lakes on their property, would allow us to fish their lakes. Those who slaughtered beef or pork gave a portion to the helping families. When a chicken house was thinned out, we got chickens for the freezer, if we helped out.

When certain commodities were desired among family members; but, no work was involved, we traded items. A relative with beef would trade for pork or chicken…an uncle who worked pecan groves would trade pecans for meats and vegetables. It was kind of like a mini bartering system.

My family offered seafood. Dad owned a shrimp net, which benefited many. We, also, fished a lot in salt water, as well as, fresh water. Since the Atlantic Ocean was our front door, and the Okefenokee Swamp was our back door, we had the family seafood bartering market pretty much sowed up!

My family's primary trading power was in shrimp and oysters. As you might expect, shrimp was our strongest trading leverage. Inland relatives would trade, almost, anything to get some fresh, or frozen, shrimp. We didn't have a lot of property or money; but, we had freezers full of shrimp!

I guess you *would* call this a functional family bartering system. Our parents thought it was one family member helping another, not to mention getting some good deals in return! The benefits of such a system were, mainly, realized at eating time. By trading, or by sweat equity, it worked out very well for our family for many years.

One summer, I was loaned to Uncle Clarence and Aunt Alma. I didn't like it, at first. I mean, they didn't even own a television! All they had was a radio, which stayed on 'old-time' country music all day and all night! I heard enough Ernest Tubbs, Johnny Cash and Patsy Cline to do me for a life time!

They did not have any games to play like Monopoly, Clue, or Scrabble. Plus, they thought playing any kind of card game was a dangerous 'sin'! I began to wonder if I was *really* kin to them, or not! But, it was our custom to follow the home rules of whomever we stayed with.

The 'upside' to it all was the cooking. You see, Aunt Alma was a good cook. If you did a hard day's work, she believed you earned a complete hard day's meal! She prepared chicken and dumplings, fried chicken, fried steak, fried fish, beef stew, turnip greens, butter beans, potatoes of all kinds, rice and a variety of biscuit sopping extras, like brown, white, and tomato gravies.

Each meal was an adventure accompanied by biscuits light enough to float off your plate…cornbread and cornpones that were crisp, and not too sweet…not to mention, the hush puppies, fried corn bread or fresh hoe cakes.

If you could hold it all in, you were privileged to have some homemade cane syrup, or fresh honey to top off your breads! Man! I could eat myself silly, and die happy slapping my face with my tongue at her table!

This spread of food was a common, everyday thing. Meals were, always, mixed and matched by the design and wishes of Aunt Alma. It was not uncommon to have some of all of these items at any meal.

Leftovers were never thrown away. They were carried over to the next meal, or the next day. If leftovers were still available, she made soup from the remains! The soup was, always, filled with delightful delicacies, and tasted very good. And, as soup, it went through another leftover cycle of its own. It was good stuff! Well worth a day's labor!

There was no doubt that Aunt Alma was a great cook. She cooked from the bounty that she had. Our family was very fortunate to be near the Swamp and near the marsh. Our location definitely had its advantages. Inland family had food shortages, from time to time; but, food for our family was never a problem. You had the option of being well-fed with critters of all kinds, if you liked critters from the swamp or the sea.

Since St. Mary's was not a big city, we shared the best of both worlds: seashore and inland. Our area afforded us farm-raised critters, as well as, wild critters. A vast variety of meats were available to us ranging from beef to deer, raised pork to wild hog, chicken to quail, wild turkey and duck, from shrimp and oysters to crawdads and armadillo, which was affectionately called "possum on the half-shell"!

Aunt Alma, however, liked to stay with the more traditional 'country' food. She, always, cooked plenty of it; and, you could have all you wanted, as long as, you worked hard and didn't waste food! Who wouldn't work hard for that kind of delicious reward!

Aunt Alma, for as far back as I can remember, was a sweet, older, loving 'grandma' type of lady…when you were on her 'good' side! Her 'bad' side was not a pretty picture! Let's just say, she was a strict disciplinarian! From my perspective, it was best to stay on her 'good' side; and, that's what I did…most of the time!

Uncle Clarence was different. He didn't say much. He, mainly, let Aunt Alma do most of the talking. That's <u>not</u> to say that she did a lot of talking. They, both, were pretty quiet people. When talking was needed, however, Aunt Alma did most it.

For the most part, they *were* <u>grunters</u>. In lieu of saying words, they would grunt! Their responses and comments to one another were summed up in certain types of grunting sounds and expressions. Things like: "Hmph"; "uh-huh"; "M-m-m-m"; "Ooo-boy"; and, huffs of air, all had different types of meanings. After being with them for a while, you could begin to interpret their grunts, fairly accurately. It was amazing how few words were required to get their point across!

Farming was a family tradition for Uncle Clarence; but, *modern farming* had skipped right over him. He planted and harvested by using the phases of the moon, and the <u>Farmers Almanac</u>. He did not own a tractor. He used a mule named *Sadie. Sadie* pulled a plow that was heavy, and awkward to handle. The land in our southeast area of Georgia was, mostly, sandy loam soil. It was soft and loose soil. In fact, the soil was so soft that many home gardeners and light farmers used a hand plow that required no animal pulling power. In this kind of soil it was not as difficult as it might seem. *Sadie*, however, pulled a heavier plow that dug deeper and displaced more soil.

If the land had been mostly clay soil, it would be much more difficult to work. In fact, my dad used a 'push plow' in his home garden. For years he pushed it through the soil without the benefit of mule-power. When his health demanded a change, we all chipped in and helped him buy an old, really old, _Cub_ tractor. He really didn't need all that power; but, he wanted to please his doctor. The type of soil you had to work made the difference in what you needed to work it.

Uncle Clarence was a master of the mule plow. I loved to watch him work with _Sadie_. It was, truly, amazing to watch the two of them work together in unison. He made it look, so, simple and easy. He would speak to the mule, and she would respond! She, always, started and stopped upon his command. His rows were straight and long. His layout accuracy of the field was unbelievable! You could tell he had done this before; and, he was _really_ good at it!

One day, as he was plowing the field nearest his house, he had a "nature" call. He held it for as long as he could. He had a lot of plowing to do, and he didn't want to fall behind. Eventually, he got to that point of "_gotta go_"! He _had_ to go take care of business!

He, still, hated to stop. He didn't want to risk getting behind; but, the "nature" call was, now, yelling at him! He looked at me, shook his head, and grunted, "Gebebababa....!"

When I heard his grunt, and saw him looking at me, I thought I might have done something wrong. My job for that day was picking out the large, and medium, sized rocks; and busting up clods of dirt. I thought I had been doing a pretty good job at it. Now, I wasn't sure.

After a second, or two, his frown turned into a smirk, as he asked, "Do you want to try it?"

Without batting an eyelash, I responded, "Sure!"

"Now, Ronnie," he counseled, "do ya think you can handle it?"

I proudly stated, "Yes, sir, I sure can."

That's when he grunted, "Hmmff!" (which meant, "Yea, sure!").

I had ridden his other mules, *Henry* and *Gladys,* for fun; but, I had never worked with *Sadie* before. I didn't think familiarity mattered, much. In fact, I thought it would be a cinch! I mean, *Henry* and *Gladys* were fun mules. Why couldn't *Sadie* be fun, too!

With his "nature" condition worsening, he found himself "between a rock and a hard place". He had little time to think about what I could, or could not do. Reaching his 'high water mark', he, hastily, turned the mule around, and set the plow in the ground. He, quickly, positioned the rig in the direction he wanted me to go.

After another grunt, he pointed his finger across the field, and said, "Ya see that fence post yonder? Y'ar pointed right towards it. Ya see it!?"

I *was looking* across the field; but, I could, barely, make it out. I could tell he was beginning to hurt, real bad by this time; so, I said, "Yes, sir."

"Just keep yer eye on <u>that</u> fer fence post. Just <u>that</u> *one*! Keep yer plow in the ground, and <u>don't</u> <u>look</u> <u>back</u>! *Sadie* will do the rest."

Then, he whispered into my ear, "When yer ready to get goin', say, 'Let's go'. That's all ya got to say, and she'll start movin' forward."

His whisper got faster as he continued, "If ya want her to turn right, say, 'Gee'. If you want her to go left, say, 'Haw'. To stop, just say, 'Whoa, *Sadie.*'" As he hurried towards the house, he yelled, "Ya got it, boy?"

I yelled back, "Yes, sir."

There I was. Standing behind a nine hundred pound mule strapped to a plow that, now, was attached to me! What in the world was I thinking! I froze for a moment. My mind went blank. I couldn't remember what I was supposed to do!

It, slowly, began to come back to me. I wasn't sure which words went where! I thought about just standing there, until Uncle Clarence returned; but, I *had* told him I could do this. I, at least, needed to try. So, I, shyly, said to *Sadie*, the mule, "Let's go".

Without hesitation, *Sadie* started moving forward. Remembering his command, I tried to keep my eye on that far fence post (that I could, hardly, see). Uncle Clarence had left me, and *Sadie*, on the right track, pointed in the right direction with simple instructions, and one resonating caution, "<u>Don't</u> <u>look</u> <u>back</u>!"

With a "Let's go", the task began. At first, I started out a little rough. The first few feet, I forgot to keep the plow in the ground. It turned out to be harder than I had thought. Keeping the dancing plow *in* the ground took a little more coordination than I had realized! After that rough start, however, the plow seemed to catch a groove, which made it easier.

It was, much, harder work than it had seemed. Uncle Clarence had made it look so easy! I had watched him do it, so effortlessly. I guess, it's like one of those things I heard about that gets better with experience.

After a few more feet, I began to feel a little more confident. After a few more, I felt like I was plowing, almost, as good as Uncle Clarence.

I knew the rows were long; but, they seemed to be getting longer! Without complaint, *Sadie* kept pulling, although my back began to feel the pressure. Through it all, I kept aiming towards *that one* fence post. With each passing moment, the plowing seemed to be getting easier.

After a while, I began to wonder if I was plowing straight, like Uncle Clarence. So, I took a quick peek over my shoulder. To my amazement, it was pretty straight! A bit further, I looked back, again. This time I could see that I had drifted to one side. I tried to correct my course by "Geeing" and "Hawing", right and left! This only resulted in *Sadie* and I, both, getting confused.

Each time I, finally, got *Sadie* back on track, I would look back to make sure the line was straight. Each time I looked back, I drifted, again. The struggle to stay straight was much more difficult than I had expected!

When I, finally, reached the targeted fence post I said, "Whoa, *Sadie!*" She promptly stopped. A bit tired, yet very proud of myself, I turned to look back at my completed row. It was plainly evident that my end result was not of the same quality as Uncle Clarence's efforts. My row was <u>crooked</u>!

I wanted to correct it; but, I didn't have time; and, I wasn't sure how to make the corrections. Just beyond the crooks, I could see Uncle Clarence walking across the field, grunting and shaking his head.

When he reached me, we stood there together looking back over the plowed row. After a moment of silence, he grunted, "Oooboy! Ya looked back, didn't ya?"

I confessed, "Oooboy! Yep, I did!"

Without saying another word, he plowed over my mistakes making the row straight, just as it *should* have been. It was, too, crooked for him to accept. He took great pride in his straight and narrow rows. It made the whole field look orderly and well-kept. My crooked row didn't fit into his straight row plan; so, he *had* to correct it. We lost precious time, because of it.

Years later, while I was reading and pondering the Scriptures, my thoughts went back to that summer experience. I was reading in Luke 9:62, where Jesus is quoted as saying, "*No one, having put his hand to the plow, and looking back, is fit for the Kingdom of God*" (NKJV). That makes perfect sense to me, now!

Every time I had looked back, when I should have been plowing forward, I had gotten off the right path. I began to drift off course. I had taken my eyes off my focal point; and, had, gotten off the straight and narrow way. Every time I looked away, it took me further off the desired target. I ended up missing the mark!

I, now, understand Jesus to be saying that we *need to focus on Him*. <u>He</u> is our focal point for staying on the straight and narrow path of victory and fellowship. When we look back, we take our eyes off of <u>Him</u>. This sends us drifting off course, into darkness and despair. If we cannot learn to trust and focus on <u>Him</u>, we are not *really* fit for the Kingdom of God.

How about you? Are you plowing a straight line? Are you fit for the Kingdom? Or, have you lost your *Focus*?

TIPPY THE LIZARD

On any given Sunday morning, you could always depend on our family being in church. In fact, I was going to church *before* I was *even* born! Yes, my mom was a dedicated Christian and church attender. I was, practically, raised up in the church. I've been around church people all my life! That might bother some folks; but, it never bothered me. I loved church folk! The only thing that might have bothered me, on occasion, was the fact that we hardly <u>ever</u> missed a Sunday service!

As much as I loved church folk, I, still, have to admit that there were times, when I just didn't feel like going to church. That didn't matter to mom! Whether you *felt* like it, or not, was not good enough to keep you at home! The only thing that might have kept you at home was a fever, or a well-documented sickness! That, and that alone, gave you a Sunday pass.

My brother and I thought that mom's church rule was 'oftly' unfair, at times, especially when we wanted to sleep in. Of course, we never mentioned it to her. There were a few things that you just didn't want to mention to mom; and, not wanting to go to church was one of those things. Plus, our objections were, usually, short-lived; because, after we got to church, we were glad we went.

I probably liked church more than my brother and sister. Most of my Sunday School teachers were very good people, and very patient with us kids. Many are, still, my very close friends. They were, then, as they are, now, interested in what "Ronnie" has been doing, or getting into! I commend them upon their efforts as teachers. I, truly, believe they did their very best to keep things as interesting as possible. When their efforts fell short, however, I was always there to offer my help, whether they wanted it, or not!

Through their undying dedication, and willingness to volunteer, I learned new things about Jesus, and other Bible characters…and about life! I know they must have struggled with teaching us. I mean, it was hard to keep our attention very long. Yet, each week they were there to put forth their best efforts to teach us what they could.

In my case, I would listen for a while, then drift away for a while. I wanted to hear what they had to say; but, I was, also, interested in the squirrel, or bird, outside. Still, I learned a lot from these Sunday School warriors; and, I love each and every one of them.

One way they tried to keep our attention was by keeping the class involved. They did this by asking questions, or assigning 'parts'. 'Parts' were Scripture verses to be memorized, or *parts* of the lesson to be read out loud. Not everybody wanted a 'part'; but, I did. For some reason they were a little hesitant in giving 'parts' to people like me. They didn't seem to trust us to tell a complete Bible story…at least not in our own words.

You see, when *I* told it *my* way, my version ended up with a lot of extra-biblical material in it. To me, it was enhancing the story to make it a bit more interesting and exciting. At that age, 'accuracy' was not as important as hearing the "ooo's" and "ahhh's" of my fellow classmates.

When I was assigned a part, they <u>insisted</u> on me sticking to the printed material. I had to read it, word for word, straight from the book! When I tried to sneak in any extra stuff, I would hear, "Now, Ronnie. Just read your part."

If the truth be known, I think most of the kids in my class liked my action-packed swamp version better! Our teachers, however, never knew of the kids preferences. We loved them, too much, to let them know that a lesson was boring. I mean, we realized they had spent extra time during the week in preparation for the lesson. The evidence of that preparation was very obvious.

At home, getting ready to go to Sunday School and Church was, somewhat of, a 'cat and mouse' game! We had bath and shower competitions each Sunday morning. The earlier bathings got the hot water! The latter ones got cold water. If you got caught in between, starting out with the hot and running into the cold, the difference was quite unbearable!

After we got scrubbed squeaky clean, we were served a good hot breakfast. Every bit of it was eaten, most of the time in haste! (That was to make sure your stomach wouldn't growl during the preaching service. That really got mom's goat!) Then, after breakfast, everyone got dressed in their best Sunday clothes!

Sometimes, I would get dressed first. This was not considered a "good" thing. That meant I had time to spare…time to observe… time to question things…time to explore…and, time to get dirty!

The <u>only</u> television entertainment allowed on Sunday morning was the _Bob Poole's Gospel Hour_, or some other gospel singing program. Our Sunday morning choices were, extremely, limited. Your choices were gospel singing, or nothing at all! That was it!

My parents never could understand that there was just _so much_ gospel music that a child my age could absorb before going into _gospel shock_! They felt any other entertainment was, too, much of a distraction that may cause us to be late for church.

With no other options available, after I got '_gospelized_', I had to amuse myself in other ways. That's when my parents seemed most nervous, or fidgety!

On one of those occasions, I asked mom for permission to sit on the front porch, while I waited for everyone else to get ready. In order for her to be willing to grant my request, I had to promise to sit in the <u>one</u> spot _she_ designated. Any movement from that <u>one</u> spot would bring severe '*consequences*'! It sounded a bit extreme and confining to me; but, I agreed. I didn't like it; but, it got me outside.

In those pre-air conditioning days, it was not uncommon for people to use the "outdoor air conditioner", which was a good shade tree! It was, often, cooler under a good shade tree, than inside the house.

Our front porch sat near one of those good shade trees. Knowing this, Mom cleaned off a nice, cool spot, *of her choice*, and sat me in it. She put on her 'stern face', when she commanded me to stay "right there". That meant, I had better do what she said!

Dad did his part by backing her up. He dared me to move from that chosen spot. I was a bit mischievous; but, I wasn't stupid! I, rarely, ever took dad up on one of his dares. <u>Once</u>, and only once, I double-dogged dared him back...I, barely, lived to tell about it!

The spot mom chose was a good spot. It was a cool and refreshing spot in the comforting shade that graced our front porch. From there, I had a good view of our neighborhood on Bailey Street. I could see and notice everything. I noticed the neighbor's dog chasing his own tail. I noticed the cat, of another neighbor, sneaking up on the dog in preparation to jump him, when he wasn't looking. I noticed some pretty birds flying over, and wished I could fly with them. I noticed some doodle bugs and ground puppies digging in the sand, next to the porch, making new homes for themselves. But, what *really* caught my attention was a little baby lizard.

It was an amazing baby lizard. It amazingly changed colors, when it moved from the green grass to a brown stick. It was, amazingly, friendly. It came, amazingly, close to me; then, it would dart away with amazing quickness. It, amazingly, did that over and over, getting a little closer to me each time. It got, amazingly, close to me. So close, in fact, that I was, amazingly, able to catch him without even moving from my designated spot!

As I held this amazing creature, it, amazingly, started to change colors, again! I was, indeed, truly, amazed by this baby lizard! I wanted to show it to somebody...anybody; but, none of my family would appreciate it as much as I. As I held the amazing lizard in my hand, I remembered that our Sunday School lesson for that week was about the amazing things that God has done.

I hadn't, actually, read the lesson. I had overheard mom telling dad what their lesson was about. That's so he could act like he had read it when he got to church. With his work schedule, gardening, fishing and household chores he rarely had time to read the whole lesson. So, mom would help him out.

Usually, all of our Sunday School lessons were on the same theme. I guess that was so we could discuss it, if we needed to. I was pondering the lesson theme, when I realized that this lizard *was* an amazing creature that God had created. It could do amazing things! It was, so amazingly, beautiful! And, amazingly, it didn't bite and wasn't poisonous!

It sounded like a 'show-and-tell' opportunity to me! That meant that this amazing lizard had to go with us to Sunday School. It just *had* to meet my class! Certainly, my friends would see and appreciate this wonderfully amazing creature that God had made, and I had captured!

I named him, *Tippy*. In order to get *Tippy* to my Sunday School class, I had to hide him in my pocket. I knew I wasn't supposed to hide things from mom and dad; but, it was for his own safety that I did. You see, mom put all lizards, worms and crawly things into the same category as all snakes. She believed that the only good snake was a dead, chopped up snake! *Tippy* fell into that dangerous category; so, for his own safety, and mine, I had to hide him in my pocket.

When we, finally, got to church, I got so caught up in seeing my friends, not to mention my "girl friend" that I never spoke to, that I forgot about *Tippy* hiding in my pocket for a while. It wasn't until Mrs. "B" began her lesson about "the amazing things of God", that I remembered my amazing new friend I had brought for 'show-and-tell'. I hoped he was still alive; because, I hadn't felt him move in quite a while!

Mrs. "B" shared about the "amazing things of God" that she had seen. Her things *were* all nice and amazing, in their own right; but, I felt mine was better. After a while, she asked if any of us had encountered any "amazing things of God".

I, quickly, raised my hand. As was her custom, she looked for *other* hands first. When no other little hands went up, she smiled and said, "Alright, Ronnie. What 'amazing thing of God' have you seen?"

I, proudly, stood up and walked towards the front of the class. As I walked, I dug deep into my pocket trying to find my friend, *Tippy*. I started out mentioning the pretty rocks, colorful butterflies, lightening bugs, cute furry rabbits, squirrels, "and *Tippy*".

Mrs. "B" looked puzzled and asked, "What is a *Tippy*?"

I told her that was what I was trying to show her, as I reached further into my pocket. I tried to grab *Tippy*; but, he was twisting and turning inside my pocket. He was a bit slippery; so, his evasive movements weren't helping matters! I couldn't get a good hold on him. I, certainly, didn't want to squeeze him, too, tight! That might hurt him; and I didn't want that.

Mrs. "B" kept saying we had to hurry; because, we had more to share about the truly "amazing things of God". In order to hurry me along, she bent over and tried to help me. That's when I brought out a squirming, slippery *Tippy*.

When *Tippy* touched her nose, Mrs. "B" went ballistic! She let out a loud, blood curdling scream! When she screamed, the whole class screamed. In all the commotion, *Tippy* squirmed loose, and hit the floor.

What happened next resembled an excited version of musical chairs. As Tippy ran around the room, screaming girls kept popping up out of their chairs, and running to other chairs! They sat on tables and stood on chairs. Some carried their chairs in their hands as they ran about the class room, so they could jump on them, if needs be!

It wasn't long before the Sunday School Director, Mr. "St", came into the classroom to see what was going on. When he opened the door, *Tippy* ran out into the hallway. Before long, pandemonium broke out as every classroom in that building began running to and fro, looking for *Tippy*.

By this time, our pastor, Bro. Dave, joined the search. He was a bit confused as to what we were looking for….was it a snake, a rat, or a lizard? When he asked me, I told him it was an "amazing lizard that God had made". Cautiously, he responded with, "Oh-h-h!"

At first, most people thought I had perpetrated a prank designed to disrupt Sunday School. Those who knew me, well, knew that I *did not* want to get on God's 'bad' side. No way would I have, *purposely*, disrupted <u>His</u> Sunday School! This was, certainly, not a prank!

I was relieved when Bro. Dave and Mrs. "B" affirmed that they did not believe it was a deliberate prank. They even found a way to laugh about it…later.

Sadly, we never found *Tippy*. I guess his amazing talents allowed him to hide, so well, we couldn't find him. We found other things…nasty things, including spiders, roaches, centipedes and some pocket change with gooey stuff on it; but, no *Tippy*!

By the morning worship time, people were in an uproar about what had happened. Whispers and murmurings were all over the sanctuary. By the time of Bro. Dave's sermon, it was obvious people were still unsettled. He felt compelled to clear up the matter. He wanted to reveal the facts about that morning's events. He felt it was best to tell the truth in order to settle some of the intensifying rumors that had been spreading like wildfire.

No names were mentioned in his explanations; but, all eyes seemed to be zeroed in on *me*! Bro. Dave told how every class in that educational building stopped what they were doing, in order to help search for *Tippy*, the amazing lizard.

He said he was amazed at the turn out of volunteers. "In fact," he said, "if the same effort everyone put into finding this amazing lizard was put into finding lost souls, our church would be full every Sunday!"

He pointed out that in the Bible, when Andrew met the amazing Jesus, he dropped everything to <u>first</u> go find his own brother to bring him to Jesus (John 1:40-42). That was a good thing to do!

Bro. Dave, then, posed the thought, "Why shouldn't we be willing to drop everything, and bring those dear to our heart to Jesus, as well. Instead, we make excuses why we cannot....or, will not!"

Bro. Dave had made a good point. One amazing lizard had energized a whole building of people to join together in the search, for the safety and well-being of others. Shouldn't that kind of care and concern be in our hearts every day?

I, still, don't know what happened to *Tippy*. It remains a mystery to this day! I just know he was an amazing creature that God had made; but, *you* are even more amazing than a *Tippy*! God did not send His Son to redeem lizards. *He* sent *His* Son to redeem <u>you</u>. That's how amazing you are to Him! Isn't that amazing!

THE KINDERGARTEN EXPERIENCE

In St. Marys, kindergarten was, mostly, for the elite. At least, it used to be. The main one in our small town was taught by Mrs. "K". She lived on the street behind my house, and taught her kindergarten from her home.

Some kids could afford to go to kindergarten, and some could not. I was in the "could not afford" camp. That was no big deal for me. I don't think it bothered my parents, too much. It was just the state of our affairs.

Some of the parents in the "could not afford" camp were hurt, and socially embarrassed. They responded to their economic inability by keeping their kids inside their homes, until after Mrs. "K" let her class out at noon. By letting their kids out at the same time, they thought it would be more difficult to tell if they were a "could' or a "could not" afford family!

Affordability was never a 'social issue' in our family. Mom and dad had earned the respect of our small town by being good, honest, hard-working people. Wealth, or the lack of it, did not define our character, nor our integrity.

Dad worked at a paper mill and, barely, earned enough to pay our bills. Yet, bills _were_ paid, sometimes creatively, but always on time. He just didn't make enough to send three kids to kindergarten. It was a simple fact that needed no explanations, nor apologies.

Thank Goodness, I was never a morning prisoner. I got to go outside to play anytime I wanted…after my chores were completed, of course. Using my imagination, I could play quite well without the presence of others. When I ran out of things to do by myself, I'd play with my imaginary friend, my companion of convenience, _Tommy_.

When that grew tiresome, I would drift through the woods behind my house, to the wooded area behind Mrs. "K's" house. There I would sit, and wait for the kids to come out for their recess time. While I waited, partially sheltered by the trees and bushes, I would pass some quality time playing with _Buckets_. He was Mrs. "K's" friendly basset hound.

Like most basset hounds, _Buckets_ looked a little out of proportion. He had the body of a full grown blue-tick hound dog, but the short legs of dachshund. He was a cute white dog covered with brown and black spots. His short front legs were slightly crooked, and his long ears, nearly, drug the ground. When he ran, his tongue would hang out and almost touch his paws.

He worked very hard at running. It was funny to watch him try. When he ran at high speed, he seemed to never reach the velocity he desired. He tried, so hard, to be fast! But, what can I say? He was slow! Yet, he did try hard!

When he got excited and cranked up, his huge paws thudded, loudly. They were even louder when ran at full throttle. If you didn't know better, you would have thought a 'herd' of wild animals was coming through! His oddities made him awkward, but…cute. We, instantly, became friends.

When the kids, finally, came out, everyone wanted to pet, or play, with _Buckets_. He was a very popular attraction. Before he would go play with anyone else, he would look up at me, as if to say, "Is it alright with you?" I'm not saying he favored me above the others. It was obvious, however, that he liked me.

One of the reasons for that, I guess, may have been the leftovers I brought for him to eat from my house. Most of whatever mom had laying around unwrapped, or was about to throw out in the trash, found its way to *Buckets*. I guess *Buckets* was being loyal to his food connection when he looked at me first. Of course, I really came to play with the others children; so, it didn't matter to me who *Buckets* played with. After all, I had other things to do.

Although my friends encouraged me to do so, <u>many</u> <u>times</u>, I never crossed over Mrs. "K's" backyard fence. I knew that the other kids had to pay to be there. I, also, knew that my fees had not been paid! Besides, I wasn't sure what they were doing inside Mrs. "K's" house. And, really, I didn't want to know!

For more reasons than that, I felt it was best to stay on the wooded side of the fence. From there I could play with *Buckets* and the kids. From my side of the fence, I could, easily, catch and throw the football, pitch baseballs, and talk with the other guys about 'girls'.

It was fun joking around, playing and sharing. When Mrs. "K" came to the door sounding her hand bell, everyone knew it was time to go back inside her house. When the kids returned to their class, I, mysteriously, disappeared back into the woods.

Now, I'll tell you, right now! It was no secret. Everyone in town could tell you that Mrs. "K" was a pretty smart lady. She had a couple of degrees…in something! She was an expert in math and spelling! With smarts like that she could have been teaching in real school. It didn't take her long to figure out what I was doing.

After one of my kindergarten 'stake outs', mom received a telephone call from Mrs. "K". After the call, everyone on our 'party line' knew where I had been that day! When I got home, Mom asked me, "Where did <u>you</u> go, today?"

Have you ever had the feeling that someone was asking you a trick question? Like they, already, knew the answer *before* they asked you the question? This was one of those questions that inspired that kind of feeling! I knew that Mrs. "K's" yard was on the border line of my permitted perimeter of play. Technically, it was on the same block, if you measured from Bailey Street to Margarate Street. Only the woods separated the two yards…and a couple of houses over. Not knowing which way this question may be leading, I figured honesty might be the best policy. I mean, this could be a test of some kind.

Parents, often, would throw out a test question, like that, just to see if you'll be honest with them. They already know the answer to the question. They just want to see if you will tell them the truth. I wasn't sure which way this was going; so, in order to help with my defense, I put on my 'innocent puppy' face. I gave it the full treatment, too. I even included the heart-stirring quivering lip.

Cautiously, I fessed up to the truth, which I revealed in degrees. I only wanted to fess up to what I had to! And, I, certainly, didn't want to fess up to things she didn't know about!

I was informed that Mrs. "K" had seen me behind her fence, playing with her kindergarten kids. I couldn't see anything wrong with that, so I fessed up to it! I mean, she didn't own the woods! I wasn't trespassing on her property. I hadn't disrupted her class; so, I couldn't see a problem. I knew, however, that if she had complained to my parents, my play time with my friends would be over…at least, until after her kindergarten let out.

Instead of complaining, Mrs. "K" had offered to let me attend her kindergarten…*at no charge*! Mom, cheerfully, asked, "What do you think about that?"

I've got to tell you, it sounded a little fishy to me! Even at this early age, I knew nothing came, totally, *free*. After a moment of awkward silence, she revealed the 'catch'. I had to be her class "*helper*".

A class "*helper*"….What was that!? I didn't even know what kindergarten was; and, now, I'm supposed to be a class "*helper*"! Was that a good thing, or a bad thing? Was I being rewarded, or punished?

I admitted to mom, up front, that I didn't know what all they did inside Mrs. K's house. I was, only, interested in the play time. What kind of "*helper*" could I be!

Mom was still looking cheerful wanting me to give her a positive answer; but, I didn't know how to answer mom. I didn't know *what* to think. To be honest, it sounded like a trap, to me!

Mom's obvious excitement, however, eventually, won me over. I agreed to give it a shot. I'm not, really, sure the choice was ever mine; but, for mom's sake, I decided to 'say' I would give it my best shot!

When dad got home and heard the news, he expressed mixed emotions. He felt this was something we 'ought' to pay for. He felt a little better, when mom told him I would be a "helper". To him that meant, in some small degree, that I was earning my way through kindergarten. With that in mind, he gave the final "all clear".

Dad loaded us up in the old <u>Ford</u> station wagon for a trip downtwon to <u>Moore's 5 & 10 Store</u>. He reasoned that kindergarten was kind of like school. If that be true, it would, without question, require <u>new</u> school clothes. The <u>5 & 10 Store</u>, customarily, stocked up with new clothes twice a year: Christmas and the start of a new school year. The school rush, however, was, officially, over. School classes had already begun. That meant the "*pickin's*" would be slim!

At any other time, or place, family hand-me-downs would have been just fine. The first day of school, however, was <u>*too*</u> special for hand-me-downs. It required new duds! Since dad had declared kindergarten to be like school, that meant I had to have new clothes before attending!

Throughout the years, I have noticed that most people seem to be able walk into a store, buy a new pair of pants and wear them home. Not so, for me! Manufacturers, across the globe, have <u>*never*</u> made a pair of pants the length of my short legs. This has <u>always</u> made buying a pair of pants a hassle!

The pre-school rush didn't leave much behind! Leftovers at the old <u>5 & 10</u> weren't much to speak of, and not much to choose from; but,

I tried on clothes. The lengths on some pants were so long, that when they were rolled up, the rolls bumped together when I tried to walk!

The jeans were worse! They were so stiff, I could hardly walk in them. When the pants' legs were rolled up, I couldn't walk at all! I felt like a stiff-legged toy robot that couldn't bend over! They made me feel foolish, not to mention being very uncomfortable. I, silently, suffered, while, mom and the store personnel giggled at my modeling. They thought it was *cute*!

Once the jeans issue was settled, we moved on to the shirts. I tried on dozens of shirts that mom picked out for me. None of the shirts that *I* liked made her list of possibilities. Mom made the choice. Her favorite one was a bright yellow shirt. Huh! Yellow shirt…I couldn't believe *how yellow* this shirt was! In fact, it was beyond yellow. It was…'yeller'! I pleaded for one of the other shirts. I looked to dad for support; but, I could tell he chose his battles, too carefully, to enter this one! The 'yeller' shirt ended up coming home with us.

Now that the shopping ordeal was over, mom, who wore many hats in the family, became a seamstress. She measured me…then she measured the jeans…then me….then the jeans, again. After her measuring frenzy, she went to work, cutting and hemming. She wanted to make sure the length was perfect before she cut off the leggings. The perfect length for her was leaving a little bit for rolling up. This was in case of a sudden spontaneous growth spurt! These jeans were intended to last a while. Sometimes, a growth spurt would happen spontaneously, and without warning, before the jeans wore out! In her thrifty way, she was planning ahead…just in case.

When she was through, they fit, just right! Of course, there was nothing that could be done for the stiffness. Only continual washings, over and over, could help that! Besides, continual prewashing would make all the new blue come out! While they were new, she wanted the blue to shine through!

The 'yeller' shirt needed no tailoring. For it to be ready, she only had to wash, starch and press it. When she was finished with the shirt, it could, just about, 'stand' in the closet on its own! And, it was still 'yeller'.

With her tailoring done, she insisted on getting a picture of me clothed in my new school garb: blue jeans, a 'yeller' shirt and new _Ked's_ tennis shoes. Standing stiff as a board, I felt like I was being laid out for one of those old western photos of dead people! I wondered, what was the use! All we had for picture taking was an old <u>Kodak</u> <u>640</u>, or <u>820</u>, or something like that! It was a camera that Uncle "D" had given mom, after he was through with it at his print shop. It only took <u>black</u> and <u>white</u> photos!

No one was going to be able to tell much about the colors in the photo. However, even now, when I see that old photograph, I am reminded of how 'yeller' that shirt was! Of course, it is my 'memory' that holds that image which is triggered by the photo. The actual _black and white_ photo in mom's <u>Memory</u> <u>Book</u> is still black and white! But, I don't think that even a color photo could ever have captured the true 'yellerness' of mom's choice shirt! But, she loved it!

After the photo session, it was off to bed. "Early to bed, early to rise makes a man healthy, wealthy and wise"…At least, that's what I was told. I'm not sure if it is true, or not. I've been doing it off and on over the years, and I still don't have much money…the wisdom part is debatable! That night, it didn't matter. It was off to bed. I obliged with no resistance. The affairs of the day had left me exhausted. All I can remember of that night is closing my eyes, then hearing mom shout, "Get out of bed!"

I don't remember sleeping! I don't think I even had time to get one good dream, or nightmare, going! Just like that…boom! It was morning. It was time to get up, and get ready for kindergarten!

While my brother and sister got ready for school, I had to bathe. Mom wanted me to be _squeaky_ clean! After the cleaning ritual, it was time for breakfast. Mom, always, believed we should eat a hardy breakfast; and, we did!

Upon completing the robust meal, I had to brush my teeth. I didn't mind dental care, too much. It was the rinse with that icky *Blisterine* mouthwash that I hated. It tasted terrible! It *undid* all the good flavorings of the delicious and hardy breakfast.

Hair care was a mystery to me. I could never understand why I had to wash my hair, only to grease it back up with <u>Vitalis</u>. It didn't make a lot of sense to me. My hair produced enough grease on its own. I didn't need any help in that department!

After re-greasing my hair, I had to present myself to mom in order to pass inspection. The inspection involved several routine questions like: "Did you wash *all over*?"; "Did you brush and gargle?"; and, "Did you put on clean underwear?". If the answer to any of these questions was, "No", or "Maybe", or followed by too long of silence, you had to go back and start over! It all *had* to be done, <u>before</u> you could leave the house for school or kindergarten.

On <u>that</u> day, I passed inspection with flying colors. Mom kissed me on my forehead, gave me a hug, handed me an apple for my snack; then, she looked square into my eyes. (That meant she was about to say something very serious.) With no expression on her face, she placed her hands on each of my cleaned facial cheeks and said those dreadful, horrible words any kid hates to hear: "Don't get these clothes dirty, *or else*!"

Why do parents insist on torturing their children this way!? Do they expect new clothes to, somehow, transform a preschool child into a responsible young adult? Don't they realize that clothes are made for the child, not the child for the clothes!

What a child *hears* a parent say <u>is</u>: "While you have these new school clothes on, you <u>cannot</u> play on the slide; you <u>cannot</u> play with the dog; you <u>cannot</u> play ball of any kind; you <u>cannot</u> 'rastle'; you <u>cannot</u> be a kid...*or else*!" Why not just go ahead and hog-tie me and shoot me! It would have been almost as humane!

Orders like that made me appreciate 'hand-me-downs' even more! All the newness had worn off of 'hand-me-downs'. All the restrictions had expired. No one expected them to last very long; so, you could do whatever you wanted to do in them. 'Hand-me-downs' were seen as transitional at best. You wore them a while, then passed them on, *if* they were still wearable. Usually, our house was a 'hand-me-down's' last stop! By the time it got to us, it had already been regenerated several times.

There was no question, 'hand-me-downs' were a lot more fun to wear! But, there I was, heading out to my first day at kindergarten. I was headed out to be some kind of class "helper"…in brand new clothes, under a mandate <u>not</u> <u>to</u> <u>play</u>…*or else*! Boy! I was really looking forward to this! What a fun day this was going to be!

The cleanliness mandate prohibited me from walking to kindergarten <u>*through*</u> the woods. I feared the morning dew might get them wet and muddy. I had to use the paved street. It was a bit longer that way; but, it *was* cleaner…less messy!

Even with the longer route, I was still able to arrive at Mrs. "K's" on time, and without an embarrassing incident, or accident. I was still clean. I wanted Mrs. "K" to document my cleanliness; but, she didn't have a clue what I was talking about.

Upon my arrival, I was welcomed by my friends, and, of course, Mrs. "K" was happy to see me. Once inside the actual classroom, I was surprised at what I saw. The room was filled with books for reading, and some to just look at. There were some interesting posters on the wall, a few learning toys scattered about, and cute little tables and chairs to sit at. There was even a restroom for little people. It had a midget toilet! It was the funniest thing I had ever seen…in toiletries.

Besides a few of the posters, pictures and books, nothing else was of much interest to me! Where were the hardcore toys? I could see <u>none</u> around! Even the *cards* on the tables were strange. They only had words and numbers for adding and subtracting on them. They were no good for 'slap-jack', 'go fish', nor 'crazy eights'!

After the ringing of the bell, things got very structured and serious inside Mrs. "K's" house. We had very little freedom in the classroom. We were told what to do; and, when to do it. Mrs. "K", also, talked a lot…and expected us to listen! She told us that she was telling us things that we would need to remember for _later_. I couldn't remember them _then_, much less later!

I kept asking about recess. She kept saying things like: "All in due time." I don't think it registered with her that the _only reason_ I hung out in her woods, in the first place, was recess. Recess was what brought me here; and, it was long overdue!

After several delays, and a lot of other learning stuff, Mrs. "K", finally, announced it was time for recess. Boy! Was I relieved! At long last, this was what I had been waiting for!

Don't worry! I didn't forget that I was under the 'no dirt…no play' rule. I knew my play for that day would have to be restricted. The 'no dirt….no play' rule, however, was, quickly, made mute. When Mrs. "K" opened her side door, you could see it was raining. There would be no playing, of any kind, in her yard that day. Instead, we were all instructed to stand under her carport for our break time. That's all. Just stand there for fifteen minutes. This day was not working out like I had hoped!

When we exited to her carport, we could see that her yard was, too, wet for any kind of serious play. The dark, sandy loam soil had been transformed into black, gushy mud. Unless you were cleared for "rain play", which meant the wearing of 'old' clothes, there was nothing that could be done in her yard. This made mom's rule a little easier to swallow. The next day I could were regular 'hand-me-down' clothes with the play ban lifted.

All of us kids were huddled under her carport trying to make the best of a bad play day. We stood around in groups telling jokes and making up stories. We shared some of our dark phantasies and adventurous day dreams. We laughed and giggled as each one tried to outdo the other.

From the backyard, we could hear _Buckets_ having a barking fit. I guess he heard us laughing, since we did get a little loud. I think he missed us not being in the back yard with him. He, no doubt, wanted to be us wherever we were. I'm sure he was lonely back there by himself. I'm sure he could not understand why we couldn't come out into the rain, and play with him. I'm sure he was just as miserable as we were. What made it worse, for him, was that he was fenced in the backyard…forced to be away from his kindergarten friends.

As we stood there, we got a little louder with each fantastic story; and, *Buckets* got louder with his barking. Eventually, *Buckets* couldn't take it anymore! He searched and dug and whimpered, until he found a way under the fence! Once freed from his fenced prison, he came charging around the corner of the house to be with his friends. He wanted to be with us; so, badly, his pounding flop could be heard over the light thunder! Once we came into his sight, he headed straight for the carport!

Several girls began shouting, "Stop! Stop, *Buckets*! Stop!" The more they yelled, the faster his little basset legs churned in the mud. Mrs. "K" tried to stop him by commanding him to halt, and go away! But, her commands went into one floppy ear and out the other! He was determined to charge ever onward!

He, evidently, had a "Ronnie radar" built into his system! It, soon, became obvious it was honed in on <u>me</u>. He ran around Mrs. "K", through some of the other kids and straight up to me. Just as you would expect any 'dog pal' to do, he jumped up on me, embracing me with his two front paws. Before I knew it, his large muddy paws were all over my mom-chosen, brand new 'yeller' first-day-of-school shirt. Mrs. "K", immediately, pulled him away; but, the damage had been done!

Muddy paw prints were everywhere! Instinctively, I tried to wipe them off, which, only, smeared it more, making it worse! Mrs. "K" applied a damp rag; but, it was no use. The stain was set. My fate was sealed!

Mom's "or else" was echoing in my head. I knew, all too well, what that meant. It was hard to hold back my tears. How could I have avoided this…What could I tell her that would make her understand…How could I make her see that I *wasn't* to blame!

Mrs. "K" tried to console me. I *tried* to explain the "or else" clause, and the "no dirt, no play" rule. I don't think she took mom's warning as seriously as I did. I knew what it meant! You see, I had been the victim of the "or else" clause, before.

Mrs. "K", however, assured me all would be well. She insisted that I not worry. *She* would telephone mom, and explain the whole thing to her. Her promise to call my mom did help me feel a little better. I, still, wondered, however, if it would be enough. I mean, mom *really* liked this 'yeller' shirt…I just wasn't sure that Mrs. "K's" phone call was going to be enough to remedy this situation!

When Mrs. "K's" class ended for the day, the rain had stopped. The dark clouds had been replaced by bright sunshine. Even with Mrs. "K's" offer to help, I was hesitant to leave the company of my friends, and the safety of the kindergarten yard. After a brief delay, I began my walk home. I walked slowly, in fear and trembling. I didn't rush. I wanted to give Mrs. "K" plenty of time to make her call. I wondered if mom and dad would, *really*, believe this was not my fault. I wondered if the 5 & 10 would have another 'yeller' shirt. I wondered if a preschooler needed a last will and testament…whatever that was!

I decided to go home through the woods. I figured, it wouldn't make any difference, now. The 'yeller' shirt couldn't get any nastier and the blue jeans were too dark to show much stain. Besides, it would afford me some cover as I scoped out my house for any activity before approaching it.

For a while, I just stood motionless in the edge of the woods. Eventually, mom came to the backdoor looking for me. I waited for her second call before stepping out of the woods. To wait for a third call would have made matter even more disastrous! After the third call, it wouldn't matter if Mrs. "K" had made the call, or not!

Mom always astounded me. She was an amazing woman of great intuition, and excellent eye sight! No matter how far away I stood from her, she could, always, see my stains, and my pains! Before I could take my second step out of the woods, she began to exclaim, "What have you done to your new shirt!?"

It was obvious! Mrs. "K" had _not_ made the call. My goose was cooked!

I started to dart back into the woods; but, that would have been a _bad_ move! Instead, I walked, slowly, towards mom. With each step, I tried to explain what had happened. The more I tried, the more I cried, making my explanations unintelligible and useless. It didn't seem to matter, anyway. She had, already, assumed the worse.

She felt compelled to, immediately, fulfill her promise of "or else". If there was one thing that mom, and dad, believed in, when it came to correction, it was _never make a promise that you don't intend to keep_!

In my day, correction rods took many forms. Some used switches from bushes. Others preferred paddles or belts. Mom's trusted our correction, primarily, to wooden yard sticks. Yard sticks were good to use; because, they were light, and had a good popping sound to them. Plus, she got them free from the local hardware store, as well as, the 5 & 10 store. If she got carried away in her correction, they broke, easily. The little sting, really, didn't hurt that much; but, it _sounded_ like it should have hurt more!

Also, did I mention, they were free! She would come home with a box of them at a time. I think it must have been considered as part of her compensation from the times she helped them out during the store's crunch seasons!

As effective as her correction rod was, and it was effective, I was more concerned about my dad's choice! If this turned into a "tag team" correction event, it could get nasty!

"Tag team" correction meant, she spanked me, now; then, dad would spank, again, when he got home from work. It, usually, had to be a very _bad_ thing, or an act of total rebellion, to warrant a "tag team" correction. Messing up that 'yeller' shirt might have just qualified!

If dad got a turn at correction, he would, most likely, use his old razor strap. Sometimes, he would change his tactics and through us a curve by using the "talk" method. When he did, we, usually, stopped him, and retrieved the razor strap. The talks were torture! The razor strap was swift, then it was over!

As I had feared, by the time she used up the rest of her yardsticks in her stash, this had turned into one of those "tag team" events! Of course, they only corrected me, because they "loved" me. They were afraid that I might turn into a terrible criminal, if I wasn't corrected, properly. Who knows! They may have been right!

I never liked correction; but, I knew that, when it was necessary, they *did* do it out of love for me. You know, God does the same thing. He chastens those whom He loves (Hebrews 12:6, and Revelation 3:19). That kind of love is a tough love. It's a love that is not appreciated during times of correction; but, it is a love that inspires respect appreciation, later. It was a love that led me to hate disappointing my earthly parents, and my Heavenly Father!

After my evening of correction, I was pretty upset with Mrs. "K", and her pretty little dog, too! My affections towards had *Buckets* changed! I believed that I was an 'innocent victim'…a pawn in the game of life…and, I didn't even know what a 'pawn' was, nor what game was being played!

Buckets was the real culprit. *He* was the one who deserved correction. I had paid a debt I did not owe; and, the thought of that was eating me up!

As a preschooler, I was just learning about how Jesus Christ had paid a debt He didn't owe. He willingly did this, proving the depth of His love for us, all. Maybe, I should have had that kind of love for *Buckets*; but, I didn't! My love for *Buckets* had been a conditional love, and the conditions had changed!

My selfish thoughts, at this point, were not driven by love, compassion, nor forgiveness. My thoughts were being driven by my hurt and sense of revenge. This dog *had* to be taught a lesson! "Grace" and "forgiveness" were not terms that I had, totally, grasped, nor understood, yet. I went to church every Sunday; but, preschoolers had not, yet, been taught that vengeance belonged to God (Romans 12:19). The way I was feeling, I'm not sure it would have mattered!

I found myself wanting to take personal charge of vengeance; and, it was not going to be a good thing! A plan of revenge took shape in my little head, with no measure of grace in it. In order to put it into play, however, I had to wait, until after mom made her last bed check. Then, I could make my move.

My plan of temporary evacuation called for me to leave the house, undetected, under the cover of night. This was rarely done; because, the consequences were severe. When it was done, my, usual, escape route was through my bedroom window, onto the above-ground propane gas tank, and out! My brother and I had only tried it a few times; but, it seemed to work well.

My plan of attack was simple. I was going to sneak over to Mrs. "K's" house and tie up the culprit, *Buckets*, with my trusted "wonder cord", (which was, actually, discarded clothesline; but, don't tell anyone!). After tying him up, I was going have a heart-to-heart talk with him, then let him go. It was never in my plan to hurt the dog. I just wanted to *teach him a lesson*. I planned to immobilize the dog, temporarily, for this serious talk, like one of dad's talks.

As I ponder about it, now, it does seem harsh to bind a critter that way. At the time, I felt that he had it coming; but, now, I have learned to be more compassionate than that! At that time, however, I was letting my anger and my desire for revenge run away with me!

When I arrived at Mrs. "K's" house, I could see that her car was not under her carport. The front drive seemed to be clear. Conditions were perfect for my plan to be enacted. I could get in, and out of her backyard, quickly, and without being seen.

I approached her backyard fence, a bit fearfully, yet stealthily. I felt like one of the characters in an episode of <u>Combat</u> which we watched quite often on our television. I, also, felt as though I was on a mission like <u>Sergeant Rock</u> of comic book fame.

At the fence, I was greeted by *Buckets*. He was glad to see me. He acted as if nothing had happened, earlier…like nothing was wrong! Without delay, I climbed the fence and took *Buckets* into custody! Then, he got out of custody…then back into custody, until I, finally, had him in custody…kind of!

I began to try to explain to him why I had to teach him a lesson. Nothing I said registered with him. He was just happy to see me! He moaned with joy, and licked my hands the whole time. He rolled over on the ground thinking I might scratch his tummy; but, when I tried to apply the "wonder cord", his rolling turned to squirming which hindered my task.

After many attempts, I, finally, got the "wonder cord" around his chest. Before I could make my next move, however, he took off running pulling me behind him! I had to 'rastle' *Buckets* to the ground to get the "wonder cord" around his feet. He turned out to be a strong little sucker! I figured the only way to get him to listen to me was to hoist him into mid-air. That way, I would have his undivided attention!

With much travail, I was able to get the "wonder cord" over the top of Mrs. K's clothes line pole. It took every muscle I could muster to hoist *Buckets* about six inches into the air, and tie the cord off at the fence pole. I was just about to start my very serious 'talk', when Mrs. "K's" car turned into her driveway.

I panicked! Dropping the cord and leaving *Buckets* stranded in mid-air, I scaled the fence, and ran for home.

I ran scared. My heart was pounding. I reached the house in record time. I jumped onto the propane tank, shimmied up the side of the house, and through my window into the safety and comfort of my bed.

As a child, I thought I was safe from ghosts and goblins when I was in my bed, with the covers pulled over my head. Hopefully, this made me safe from Mrs. "K", too. That's how I went to sleep! As far as I was concerned, the incident was closed. Boy! Was I wrong!

The next morning the physical evidence of my struggle with *Buckets* was evident. The trail of mud and my dirty pajamas were hard to explain. I had tried the idea of sleepwalking, already. Mom and Dad never bought it. I thought that since this was an act of corrective justice why not just tell the truth.

During my explanations of what I did, and why I did it, I began to sense that my concept, and interpretation, of justice was a bit cloudy to them. It all seemed clear to me; but, no one was buying it! Then, Mrs. "K" called. Mom and Mrs. "K" talked a long time on the phone. Afterwards, it was decided that I wasn't ready for kindergarten, and shouldn't go back to Mrs. "K's", any more…. ever!

Mom was hurt and embarrassed. I tried to make her feel better by continuing to explain my position; but, it wasn't helping. My sister and brother were moved to uncontrollable laughter. Mom was moved towards another box of yard sticks!

In their long conversation, Mrs. "K" *did* confirm my story about the dirty 'yeller' shirt, and proclaimed my innocence in that affair. She, even, apologized for not calling earlier. She confessed that she should have, at least, sent a note home with me.

Mom apologized to me for not believing my story, and for, automatically, jumping to conclusions. I had to apologize to Mrs. "K" for all the confusion I had caused and for stringing up her dog. Mrs. "K" made no apologies for why I couldn't come back. Mom, then, explained why I couldn't go <u>anywhere</u> for quite a while. Dad *explained* the rest!

This story would be even more tragic than it seems, if it were not for the valuable lessons learned. I learned what being "expelled" meant, and that it was *not* a good thing! I learned that pursuing vengeance had serious consequences. I learned that escape routes out of the house are <u>only</u> good for fires. I learned that being slow to anger and quick to forgive was better than those things in reverse!

I discovered some other jewels through this, as well. I found that the Lord knows us better than we know ourselves. He knew that, in seeking vengeance, we wouldn't stop at what is "just". The selfish nature of sin wants more -- much more -- than is needed, or required. Only God can *justly* repay.

Our duty is to love one another (John 13:34)…to forgive others as we desire God to forgive us (Matthew 6:14-15)…to forbear the weaknesses of one another (Ephesians 4:2; Colossians 3:13)… to encourage in times of despair (Galatians 6:2)…and, to leave vengeance in the hands of the Lord (Hebrews 10:30).

If we can do these things, we will live in peace with one another, with ourselves, and with God. May God bless us all as we learn to fulfill these responsibilities, and trust <u>Him</u> for <u>His</u>.

"Buckets couldn't resist!"

Miss Mae's Story

She was a loving and kind person…most of the time. She was a strong, healthy woman who walked every where she went…every day! She never owned a car, and never asked for a ride.

She was highly regarded by everyone who knew her. She was…a revered sage…or, as close to one as you can get in the swamp and marsh lands of Camden County.

She was one of the first to conquer the marsh. She proved that by building her unique house upon stilts, twelve feet off the ground, near the edge of the marsh. At eighty years old, the traverse up and down her long front stairs never seemed to tire her. Her pace was always swift, on the go, never slow. For many years only the marsh was her front yard. Her high position upon stilts gave her a commanding view of the North River.

Age meant nothing to Miss Mae Tutleybelle. She lived a much more active life than many younger persons I know. When asked what her secret to healthy living was, she always said that gardening and keeping children in her home kept her young and alive.

I was fortunate enough to be one of those children she kept. I would stay in her home, along with other children, whenever mom filled in for a worker at the 5 & 10 Store. It was always alright with me to stay with her, if one of my relatives couldn't keep me.

Miss Tutleybelle was strict in and about her home; yet, she was always fair. The reward for obedience was a feast of homemade cookies and fresh milk. Boy! Could she make some awesome cookies!

To a large degree, she had me wrapped around her little finger! Let's face it! Her cookies were great! She lived in one of most unique houses in St. Marys. And, the cookies were great! Oh! Sorry. Beyond the cookies, she was a nice lady who loved kids. The fact that her house was listed among some of the oldest in town didn't register with me. However, the fact that her house was built upon stilts fascinated me!

Her mannerisms intrigued me. Her 'sass' was honest. She, always, knew how to cut through all the 'bull' and get down to brass tacks! When I was in her home, I felt it was in my best interest to make every effort to please her. I *really* wanted to do everything she told me to do in order to gain her rewards; but, there were times when I missed the mark.

It was evident that Miss Mae loved to work in her yard. Nothing pleased her more than to see little hands helping her work in the dirt. She took great pride in her azaleas, tulips, begonias, and other colorful flowers. Her fruits trees, always, produced luscious fruit. She would horrify her neighbors during harvesting, as she hung from the limbs picking her pears and knocking pecans to the ground.

She was a straight talker. You, always, knew exactly how she felt about any issue, or careless action. She left little doubt where you stood with her, though she tried to remain polite when telling you.

Safety for "her" children was her main concern. Any frolicking that put any child in harm's way was lovingly, yet strictly, rebuked! And, believe me, her scolding took root in everyone who received it! She hardly ever lost her anger; but, when she did, you wanted to get out of her way!

Not even Mr. Seals, a man of constant complaints, could get under her skin. She was always prepared for his "wise cracks". She could come back with *cracks* of her own, without a blink, or any hesitation!

Her solid rejoinders would leave Mr. Seals, almost, speechless; and, he loved every minute of it!

It has been suggested, by some, that there may have been a few times that I might have come close to getting her dander up...that I might have caused her to come near her boiling point. Whereas that might have been true, I assure you, it was never on purpose. The cookies were, too, great!

She taught me many lessons: never mess foolishly with her flowers... never use her <u>Red Flyer</u> wagon as a race car, nor in a demolition derby...and <u>never</u> slide down the long wooden banister on her front steps (the splinters were embarrassingly placed and hard to get out!). Lastly, she taught me to never cross a woman who could bake heavenly tasting cookies.

While in her care, it was, always, important to remember to never do anything that would get you "the look"! Boy! She could give "the look"! It was a cold stare that sent chills up and down your spine. It was a frightening and unsettling "look" to encounter. Not to mention, it, usually, meant you ended up with <u>no</u> <u>cookies</u>!

One day, I got carried away with my playing. I ended up getting "the look"...twice! Without meaning to, I came, dangerously, close to losing my cookie privileges! Instead, I was restricted to just one cookie and half-a-glass of milk.

I figured I had better do something to make it up to her. I didn't have anything I could give her. So, I decided the best gift I could give her was to be really good all the next day. When I arrived the next day, I wasted no time in being good! I picked out a nice, comfortable rocking chair and started to rock. I planned to sit there all day, except for "nature" breaks. Until cookie time, I didn't want to mess up or make a mistake. Until mom returned to get me, I was going to be the perfect gentleman.

I knew it was going to be hard; but, I was determined to make a valiant effort. I started by being very careful not to over-rock. I knew that bothered some people. I didn't want to run the risk of it irritating

Miss Mae. I *really* was trying to be good. I rocked smooth and gentle on a thick rug in her living room. I was determined to stay out of trouble.

As I rocked in her chair, I noticed she had several old photographs placed all around the room. They were mounted on her walls, and in frames resting upon her aged furniture. Some of the pictures were, obviously, very old. They seemed to cover a long span of a history long past.

A particular picture caught my eye. It was of a young man in a military uniform. His warm smile drew my attention. His eyes seemed to be filled with joy. I felt as though he could be a very friendly person. The photo made me want to meet him!

The picture was old; but, it was well-kept. It was housed in an intricately, and carefully, crafted, hand-made wooden frame. I couldn't help, but to stare at it. In my imagination, I pondered about who it might be, and what war he might have fought in.

After a while, Miss Mae came to see if I was still alive. She seemed genuinely concerned. She knew I wasn't being my 'normal' self. She felt my forehead for a fever. Detecting none, she made me stick out my tongue. She wanted to see what color it was. Hey! She was the cookie commander. I wasn't about to question her tactics!

After the tongue viewing, to be sure about things, she stuck a thermometer in my mouth; then, asked how I was feeling. It was hard to answer her with a mouth full of thermometer; but, she seemed to understand every word I said!

I told her I was fine. I was just trying to be good, since I messed up the day before. She smiled...She had a tender smile. It was the kind that made you feel good, even when you did feel bad. It, even, made you feel better when you already felt good!

I told her I was just rocking and looking at her many pictures around her room. I hesitated for a moment, though I don't know why, then I asked, "Who is that man in the uniform?"

The question seemed to startle her. Her countenance suddenly changed. Her eyes went glassy. Her breathing pattern changed. She paused for a moment, as if she was drifting back through time. I thought I had, inadvertently, done something wrong, *again!*

She slowly walked over to the photograph and, gently, picked it up. She caressed and cradled it for a moment, like she was holding a precious baby. With an uncommonly raspy voice, and in a tone I had never heard from her before, she asked, "Do you, really, want to know?"

At that point, I wasn't sure if I *really* wanted to know, or not! She didn't appear angry. She just seemed to be drifting far, far away. The look on her face was no way near "the look"! Certainly, not "the look" I had received just the day before. This was something different.

Something had, definitely, changed about her. You could hear it in her voice. Her tones were softer, much more tender than before. Since I was the <u>only</u> child in her care for that day, I guess she felt more at ease to speak. I just wasn't sure I wanted to hear what she was going to say! I, definitely, didn't want anything to interfere with getting some of her cookies! So, I just sat there for a moment. I didn't how to answer her; but, out of respect for her, and my acute curiosity, I, finally, answered, "Yes, mam."

She pulled a padded chair close to my rocking chair. She slowly sat down still holding the picture close to her heart. She began by saying, "His name is Rhupert. We were engaged to be married."

Whoa! Don't go any further! I was ready to pull the plug right there! I wasn't sure I wanted to hear any more of *that* story. It sounded, to me, like it had the potential of being a mushy saga! As I am sure you are well aware, mushy stories are torture to a six year old! There is only so much mush that a boy of that age can handle!

I felt I should have stopped her; but, I couldn't. I don't know why! I guess it was the smell of her fresh home-made cookies baking in her oven that kept me silent. I remained seated, quiet and poised. I was afraid to say a word as she continued.

She shared that they had formally courted for over a year. When asked, both sets of parents, cheerfully, granted permission for their marriage. They made many wonderful plans in the months that followed. Before they could follow through with their detailed plans, the Spanish-American War of 1898 erupted.

Rhupert felt it was his duty to enlist. He was very young to be a soldier, she thought. His family tried to persuade him to wait a while; but, he felt it was his duty to volunteer. He felt he needed to go, even though he was, barely, old enough to enlist.

He was accepted as a special volunteer. In his training, some chose to pick on him; but, they, quickly, learned that he was a mighty force to be reckoned with. His wiry construction may have looked frail; but, he was far from it!

Though they wished he had waited, his whole family respected his choice. They were all very proud of him, and never stopped telling him so. They were concerned; but, tried not to show it. They were, somewhat, comforted when an old family friend, who was an officer in the new Volunteer Army, told Rhupert's father that he would look after the young lad. That assurance meant a lot to all of them, except for Miss Mae.

Miss Mae had mixed emotions about Rhupert's choice to enlist; but, she never let him know her true feelings. She, always, showed her support for him, and always told him how proud she was of him. She did not want to add to his woes; and, did not want him to worry about her. She did ask if they could be married before he was shipped out. Rhupert, however, insisted on waiting. He couldn't bear the thought of the possibility of making Miss Mae a widow at so young an age. It wasn't his plan to die; but, he felt it was best to wait. So, they did.

After his training was complete, Rhupert was allowed to come home for a few days. The time at home was a glorious time that passed all, too, quickly. They shared some great days together planning their marriage and future home. Time seemed to pass so fast in those few days…it almost seemed to be a blur in her memory! Before she knew it, his leave was over. The dreaded day of his departure was at hand. The time they had spent together, temporarily, faded. Nothing was real, except the present. Everything seemed to be in a fog! She felt she should panic, but held it back. The memories of that last day of leave seemed hidden in haze. What she could remember seemed to pass in fast motion, whenever she tried to recall it. Her emotions were, truly, in a "pitiful state".

In order for Rhupert to board his proper train, he would have to go to Jacksonville, Florida. Rhupert's father, Hadley, asked Miss Mae if she would like to go with them to the train depot where they would send Rhupert off. She, desperately, wanted to go; but, she hated the thought of him leaving.

Her parents granted permission for Miss Mae to partake in the send off. It was to be a two-day journey by mule-drawn cart. That didn't matter to her. She wouldn't have cared if the two days were two weeks! This meant she would have more time to spend with Rhupert before he had to go. The thought of "extra time" made her feel better.

The journey was filled with laughter and goodhearted pranks. Yet, for her, each joyful moment was filled with a sense of dread. She tried to put the journey's end out of her mind. She wanted to concentrate, solely, on their time together. It was difficult; but, she had to try.

Along the way, they had to spend one night under a "lean-to". Rhupert's father lined everyone up in their 'proper' sleeping arrangement. No one was allowed to lay down, until they *all* laid down. When they were ready, Hadley announced the order of alignment. Miss Mae was placed on one end, next to Rhupert's mother. Hadley was positioned next to his wife; then, Rhupert was placed at the other end of the line, next to Hadley. Their blood hound, *Fatso*, laid at their feet.

Fatso served as the movement alarm. Every time one of them moved, *Fatso* would grunt. When *Fatso* grunted, Hadley would mutter, "What do ya need?" No matter what their thoughts *may* have been, everything remained proper and decent. Each of the young lovers was obedient to the core; but, that didn't stop them from stealing glances at one another all through the night.

The next day they arrived at their dreaded destination. The train station in Jacksonville was a very busy place. It was filled with travelers of all kinds, from all over. Many were there for the same reason as Rhupert. All of the soldiers were accompanied by family and friends. Preachers of all sorts roamed the station and platform area ready to offer a prayer if permitted.

When they entered deep into the heart of the station, they could see it was filled with young men sporting their fresh new uniforms... looking 'smart' and ready for action. As they crossed under the big arch way at the entrance of the depot's platform, a big lump swelled up and tightened in Miss Mae's throat. She could hardly speak above a whisper. When she tried, she squeaked!

Miss Mae's cheeks had a hint of *rose* rouge. She had used it that day just for Rhupert. As they neared the train, trails of tears trickled down rosy cheeks leaving small streaks. She tried, so hard, to be brave. She wanted to hold her tears of concern back; but, it was useless. Rhupert, sensing her struggle, smiled and squeezed her hand. He, gently, whispered, "Each tear is one more reason for my return."

The family entourage stood on the platform, almost numb. Everyone was very silent. Hadley tried to break the silence by engaging in some lighthearted conversation concerning a woman's strange looking hat; but, no one was interested.

When the first call to board was sounded, they ignored it. They flinched at the second call. Then, the last call came! "All, too, soon!... All, too, soon!", Miss Mae recalled. Rhupert's mother cried, then she kissed him, promising her constant love and prayers. His father reminded Rhupert of an earlier war in which he had participated, and that he had returned home safely. "Just as God protected me, I am sure He will protect you...That shall be our prayer...I love ya, son."

With that, they all knelt on the platform and prayed. They needed no assistance in voicing their sincere prayer. Several others around the platform, spontaneously, joined in. A couple of the preachers standing nearby, knelt with the crowd. After Hadley ended his prayer, a muffled round of "amens" could be heard. Others continued in prayer for a few moments longer.

Miss Mae and Rhupert were left alone for a few moments as Hadley drew his wife away. Miss Mae stared deep into Rhupert's eyes trying to find the proper words. What is the proper thing to say at a time like that? What would you, later, have *wished* you had said?

They ended up saying it all with their eyes, with the touch of their foreheads, and with a parting tender kiss. What more needed to be said!

The boarding whistle blew, once again, then the train jolted. It seemed to move in slow motion. They embraced and kissed, once more, as they said their heartfelt, "I love you's".

Rhupert, hesitantly, mounted the train. With all the noise and clamoring of the 'iron horse', Miss Mae, clearly, heard Rhupert say, "Count each tear while I am gone. I will give you a kiss for each one, when I return."

Miss Mae was rejoined by Rhupert's parents. They stood on the platform waving and blowing kisses, until the train was completely out of sight. Hadley embraced the two women; then, softly said, "Let's head for home."

Miss Mae said she didn't remember the ride home. She did remember her promise to write Rhupert. She started writing letters that day, and continued each and every day. Sometimes, they wrote more than once in a day!

Rhupert shared in one of his letters that the family's old friend, the Army officer, had Rhupert transferred to his unit. That was very comforting, and seemed to make everyone feel a little better.

The letters continued daily, until one day they stopped! Miss Mae knew in her heart what that might mean; but, she insisted on believing it was for some other reason. Days past, still no letter came!

She was in her room praying for Rhupert's safety, when Hadley came to her house. He spoke first to her parents. Miss Mae could hear their whispers through her bedroom door. She kept on praying on her knees, harder and harder, then prostrate on the floor she prayed! When they knocked on her door, she refused to open it. She hoped, somehow, it might change the message. If she didn't hear it, then it couldn't be true!

Her mother had to opened the door with a pass key. With puffy cheeks and a stern resolve, Miss Mae stood to face them. Without speaking a word, they all fell together, and cried. Rhupert had been killed in action. Shot down while charging up some hill with their family friend, Colonel Teddy Roosevelt. The Colonel had written a very nice letter to Rhupert's parents with a few heroic details. These details meant nothing to Miss Mae. Not then...not now. He ended the letter with, "Tell Miss Mae that the last words of Private Hawkins were of her."

Her only response was, "Who will kiss away my tears, now?"

After a brief pause in her story, she admitted, "Mae Tutleybelle died that day, too!"

Her voice hardened as she spoke of being angry and hurt. She wanted to blame someone...anyone! She blamed the Colonel who had failed to do what he had promised. She remained angry at him for a long time. Later, she would not vote for him when he ran for the Presidency of the United States.

Blaming the Colonel wasn't enough; so, she blamed God, too. She had prayed, so faithfully, several times a day, for Rhupert's safe return. Sometimes, her prayers had lasted all night! Why hadn't God heard her prayers? Was she being punished for some sin? Where was God in all this?

She admitted that in the midst of her hurt, anger and anguishing pain, she wanted nothing to do with God! But, God wouldn't leave her alone! He never stopped loving her. He never stopped trying to offer some sense of comfort. But, she had hardened her heart. When she felt compelled to pray, again, it was in a spirit of bitterness. Her prayers changed from delivering Rhupert, to "What's wrong with you, God!" She was hurt and in anguish. She, finally, asked the Lord to deliver _her_ through this nightmare, "God, if You are _really_ there, help me!"

For a while, she had put her Bible aside, refusing to read from it. She wouldn't even pick it up! After several restless, lonely nights, and depressing, despairing days, she made herself pick up her Bible, once again. When she did, she slammed the Bible hard into her lap, letting the pages fall where they may. The Bible came to rest, opened at the _Book of Daniel_.

She didn't know why; but, she felt compelled to read where it lay opened. The Scriptures revealed the story of Shadrach, Meshach, and Abednego. She had read this story before and was very familiar with it. In this reading, however, she saw something she had never seen before, not before that very moment.

She had never realized that God did not take away the ordeal of fire from these faithful biblical servants. Instead, _He_ had been with them _through_ it! The rest of the night, she pondered upon that Scripture. Though she had many questions, she came to realize that her faith and trust was, still, firmly vested in God.

She became convinced that she would have been consumed in the fires of her desperate rage, savage disappointment and complete broken-heartedness, _if_ the Lord had not been there, with her! _He_ was with her through the blaze of her tempered spirit! _He_ had sat with her in the vengeful fire of her despair.

I was spellbound…speechless…and a little scared! She cried a bit. I cried a bit. By her own admission, she said, "Ronnie. I've never told anyone the whole story, before."

I wasn't sure _why_ she had told me! My shocked expression must have given her a clue that it was time for milk and cookies! She was right!

It took several doses of delicious cookies and quite a few glasses of milk, before I was back to my normal self. She smiled and patted me on my head. We never spoke of Rhupert, again.

Miss Mae never married. The children she boasted of were her nieces and nephews…and *some* of those she had kept in her home.

Eventually, she purchased the piece of land she and Rhupert had picked out for themselves. She built her house just like Rhupert had designed it -- on stilts. Once built, she lived there all of her life believing that, one day, she would see Rhupert, again. On that day, he could kiss all her tears away.

Twelve years later, I accepted God's call into <u>His</u> ministry. Miss Mae, then ninety-two years old, came to my licensing service. It was great to see her there.

She hugged me, and kissed me…giving me her warm smile of approval. She weakly pulled me close to her, and said, "Now, I know why I could tell you about Rhupert…God gave you a heart to listen. You may not always know what to say, but always listen, like you did with me…and trust the Lord…Of course, crying with them may be all you can do…It may be all that is needed."

When Miss Mae got sick and couldn't traverse her long stairs, there was no shortage of caretakers for her. Her nieces and nephews, those she had helped, and several of the kids she had cared for, took turns caring for her every need.

She had plenty of food. Her bills were paid. Her house was cleaned. Her flowers were tended. And, she had cookies galore delivered to her bedside (none of which tasted like her own!). But, we all knew that!

She never left her house, again…not until she went to be with the Lord…and, of course, Rhupert!

Only the Lord knows why I was made privy to her story. Maybe, *I* needed to hear it. I, certainly, have never forgotten it! Nor, have I forgotten her advice.

From that day forward, I have always believed that the Lord would be with me *through* the fires of adversity! Just like <u>He</u> was there with Shadrach, Meshach and Abednego…just like <u>He</u> was with Miss Mae <u>He</u> would be with me. Hasn't <u>He</u> been there with you?

POCKETS

In my early years, my major mode of transportation was by putting leather to the pavement...walking. During the daylight hours, I could ride my bicycle. After dark, my parents preferred that I walk, since riding a bike at night could be *dangerous*. In those days we weren't concerned about muggings, murders, kidnappings and such. In our small town, those things were alien to us.

We didn't have a "Neighborhood Watch". We had a "Whole Town Watch"! Most all adults, especially church folk, were expected to watch out for all kids. I always felt that <u>any</u> adult was ready to assist me in times of trouble. It was a good feeling! We, rarely, called upon them; but, it was good to know that they were there.

In St. Marys, Friday and Saturday nights were movie nights. We, only, had one walk-in movie house and one drive-in movie theater. The walk-in movie house was used, mainly, by the preteens. After you got your driver's license, you graduated up to the drive-in theater. The drive-in was a bit rustic. It was, originally, started out as someone's backyard. Eventually, it took up a whole field. It became the adult and family movie place; but, on any given weekend night, it was, mainly, filled with driving teens.

As preteens, we felt the walk-in movie house 'belonged' to us! That's just the way it was...and, that's the way it, mostly, turned out.

Our parents *may* drop us off at the theater; but, if it wasn't raining, we were expected to walk home. If you didn't have anything broken, you walked home. Even if you were scared of the graveyard after a scary movie, you walked home! Of course, there were exceptions. If you lived out of the city limits, or if you were injured, sick or had birth defects that prevented you from walking, you were given special riding privileges. Otherwise, you walked home.

Walking wasn't so bad. We really preferred it that way. It gave us some adventure time after the movies. We got to socialize a little at the *Greasy Spoon* diner, where we picked up an ice cream, or a soda, for the journey home.

We, often, walked in groups, preferring the company of friends and increasing the fun. Groups, also, gave us a sense of security, especially, after a *really* scary movie. In a group, we were more able to face the spooky stuff and scary places encountered on the way home. Groups made the journey a lot easier.

This weekend routine was practiced for years. Only once was it, nearly, interrupted. It was, fiercely, threatened when the price of a movie ticket went up from 35 cents to 50 cents! It was scandalous! The whole town was thrown into a tizzy! The rumor mills jawed on it for months. There was talk of a boycott on the movie theater; but, we were, too, addicted to movies, popcorn and coke to follow through!

Finally, the theater owner had enough of the jawing, rumors and disenchanted people calling him at home. He threatened to shut down the movie house, if he was accosted about the increase any further! We bit our tongues, and paid the 50 cents for a ticket!

No matter how much the ticket cost, we still had to walk home after the movie. At times, this could get a little frightening for my group. The way home, for us, meant walking by the Oak Grove Cemetery. The cemetery was, most likely, the second oldest graveyard in the United States...or, so we were told! It had a long history of haunting spirits!

Horror nights at the movies were, especially, difficult. When the moon peers through those majestic oaks, filled with Spanish moss, your imagination can run wild! In the day time, it was beautiful. Many sightseers walked through it, daily. At night, however, it took on a mysterious and forbidden nature. The town's street lights were of little help. The town could only afford a few; and, they were far in-between.

Facing the graveyard and shadows were enough to make any child nervous; but, there was another issue which made matters even worse! We, often, had to contend with the town 'character', as well. He was nicknamed *Pockets*. He was dubbed with this name; because, whenever he saw anyone approaching, he would pull out his empty pockets to show that he needed money.

He was a sad figure, who could, rarely, work due to his drunkenness. He was, always, needing things. You had to be careful how you helped him, however; because, whatever he was given he used to buy another drink. He, evidently, had some success at begging! He stayed drunk most all the time!

This made encounters with *Pockets* a bit eerie, and uneasy. Just running into him during the day was tough. When you ran into him at night, it was enough to send a person into the *heebie-jeebies*!

When he tried to talk, it got worse! His words would come out slurred and unintelligible. He mumbled a lot. He would mutter something; then, get frustrated when he had to repeat himself, which he did, over and over.

I don't believe I can remember a time, when I ever saw *Pockets* able to walk a straight line. He tried. He tried, often; but, he couldn't! He was always stumbling over…anything…sometimes, nothing! When he stumbled, he would reach out for something, or someone, to steady himself. Who, what and where he grabbed provoked some concern, and a lot of gossip!

He was deemed, by most, to be harmless. We kids couldn't be sure about that. His drunken actions and instability frightened us. Older teens ridiculed him, and taunted him. They made fun of his inabilities. My solution was to stay clear of him, whenever and wherever possible.

One Friday night, Lamar and I had to walk home after a horror movie. Lamar was a good walking buddy. We talked about many things we had in common: girls, school, girls, church, girls, *etc.*

He was tall and slender, and I was short and stubby. To others, we may have seemed like the swamp version of the "Odd Couple", or "Mutt and Jeff"! That didn't matter to us. We were friends. It didn't matter that he was a year, or two, older. It didn't matter that I was a bit stronger. His two year seniority lent me confidence; and, my brute physical strength offered him a bit of self-reliance. We were a good match, as friends.

Our regular group was not at the movies this particular night. Just the two of us showed up. That meant we had to go it alone! We dreaded the thought of walking by the graveyard alone! We, both, knew that just getting home through the dark was going to be tough, enough. Walking by the graveyard made matters worse!

The horror movie we had just seen was a tough one. It compounded our concerns! We just knew that "things" would be coming alive in the shadows! We needed more strength. We, definitely, needed to make a stop by the *Greasy Spoon*. We *had* to have a double scoop our favorite ice cream to help calm our frizzied nerves. The strongest drink we were allowed, at our age, was an original <u>Dr. Pepper</u>, which I gulped down.

The stiff soda, and the *brain freeze* from our ice cream, seemed to settle us for our journey home. The ice cream was, especially, good that night. It acted as a cool sedative on a warm night. I'm sure it must have been the sugar rush; but, it seemed to give us a bit more confidence for our dash into the darkness. Having walked as slow as we could, we could delay no longer. We gripped our ice cream cone, firmly, as we made our usual turn at <u>Sterling's</u> <u>Grocery</u>. This way home gave us the shortest pass by the graveyard. With no group to boost our confidence, that's what we wanted…the fastest way home.

We paused for a moment to collect our thoughts, and our courage. We took a deep breath; then, proceeded, cautiously.

There was only <u>one</u> street light between <u>Sterling's Grocery</u> and the graveyard. The darkness in between them was very dark. There was no thick fog to contend with; but, as we approached the darkness in-between the street lights, it seemed to be growing darker and darker!

We paused, again. We took two good licks of our double-decker ice cream cones; then, began our graveyard run with earnest. Well, actually, we didn't really run. That would be, too, cowardly! We walked fast…with fear and trembling! But, we were ready to run at any instant!

We, nervously, talked and giggled as we approached the safety zone of the *one* street light between us and the graveyard. Under the light, no ghost or goblin would dare approach us…at least that's what we had heard!

Within a short block of our safety destination, we thought we saw *something* move near the street light! We couldn't tell what it was; but, it was moving in the edge of dark shadows of the lighted area. We could tell *something* was definitely there; but, it was, too, dark to tell what, or who, it may have been! The not knowing for sure gave us chills!

At first, we hoped it might be another walking group on their way home from the movie. If that were true, then they had chosen a way that was even darker and longer, with fewer street lights. If *that* were true, that meant they were a braver, stronger group than Lamar and I. And, if <u>*that*</u> were true, then we, definitely, wanted to link up with them!

The street light was at the intersection of the two roads. To get to the street light on our road, we had to cross a bridge over a tidal creek. The bridge was very close to the street light, so the likelihood of trolls getting us was, nearly, nil! Besides, trolls rarely attacked groups of people. We were happy to see another group approaching the light safety zone. We hoped the group was favorable to our merging with them. I, for one, have, always, believed that there was strength in numbers.

After a few more hurried steps, our hopes were dashed! It was clear to see that the *something,* or *someone,* in the shadows was <u>not</u> another friendly group! It was, instead, *Pockets*!

We froze in our tracks! Our heart sank as we witnessed the drunken performance going on before us. He was making several attempts to cross over the bridge, without falling into the water. He was all over the road! He staggered from one side of the bridge to the other; then, he would retreat back into the shadows to re-focus in order to try another crossing.

We thought about turning back; but, there was, now, more darkness behind us, than in front of us. Also, it was getting late. We had spent a little more time at the <u>*Greasy Spoon,*</u> than we had to spare. We were all out of 'after-movie' time! Soon, our parents would get worried and come looking for us. If they came looking, we *needed* to be suffering, or nearly dead! Or, else, we *would be* suffering <u>and</u> nearly dead! We were not sure that being afraid of *Pockets,* and the graveyard, was enough to warrant a parental rescue pardon.

Besides, turning back was <u>never</u> a good option. It was a well-known movie fact that retracing your steps, often, led to <u>*certain*</u> disaster! Counting the cost, we decided to press on. In order to do this, we had to alter our plans a little. Now, with *Pockets* at the light, we felt it was best to hurry through the intersection without stopping. We would miss our re-strengthening moment; but, we might avoid an unwanted encounter with the town character.

We tried to time our walk giving him time to get off the bridge. That way we could scoot by without saying much, if anything. This would allow us to slingshot through the intersection, and hurry homeward. It sounded like a good plan to us.

We reached our vantage point and stood still. We waited for our opportunity to make our slingshot pass. The street light revealed the drunken activity going on. After several tries, *Pockets,* finally, reached the other side of the bridge. He stumbled, without falling, off the bridge and onto a grassy area beside the road. This was our chance! We, hastily, made our move! As we approached the bridge, it became apparent that *Pockets* was crying as he teetered, then tottered!

This worried Lamar. You see, among the many things that I was known for, be it good or bad, being cruel to someone that was hurting was <u>not</u> among them. I admit I *was* a bit mischievous; but, I was, also, the defender of a girl's honor and safety; an encourager of the underdog; and, a caregiver to the broken hearted. When I noticed *Pockets* was crying, something inside of me had to offer assistance.

Lamar, who knew me all, too well, could see it coming. He begged me to leave things alone. He warned me not to say anything! Still, I had to ask: "What's wrong?"

Pockets tried to answer; but, he mumbled and slurred his words. We couldn't understand anything he was saying. I asked him, again. He just kept pointing to the ground, as he mumbled and cried. At first, I thought he must have dropped something…maybe something important, like his keys. Lamar didn't care. He kept pushing me towards the bridge. He was ready to go! It was easy to see that Lamar had rather take on a dreadful Dracula, or a psycho-slasher ghost, than deal with *Pockets*.

I tried to move on; but I just *could not* leave *Pockets* crying. I mean, he could have been in serious need of help. He might have *really* needed assistance this time, and not a hand out. At this point, Lamar didn't care! He was, *definitely,* ready to move on; but, he was not brave enough to go it alone! So, when I stopped, he stopped.

Together we tried to figure out what had *Pockets* in such a tizzy. I kept looking on the ground, while Lamar kept watching *Pockets*. With his constant pointing to the ground, Lamar, finally, noticed that *Pockets'* shoes were untied. In his drunken state, he couldn't bend down to tie his shoes without falling over. He was crying, evidently; because, he couldn't help himself on such a simple matter.

Lamar still refused to go near him. On that, I whole-heartedly agreed!

Instead, we decided to coach him down to the ground. We thought if he was sitting on the ground, he could reach his shoes easier. Without touching him, or getting, too, close to him, we tried to tell him to sit on the grass beside the road. We, certainly, didn't want him to sit down in the middle of the road! The grassy area was a much better place. It was out of traffic, and was softer in case he fell over.

He, finally, began to understand what we were instructing him to do. He tried to sit down, several times. Each time he tried, he stumbled closer and closer to the creek. We told him to back up before trying, again. We were afraid he might stumble; then, go tumbling into the creek.

I think he wanted to prove, to us, or himself, that he *could* do it! So, he gave a giant effort to accomplish the simple task of sitting down on the ground. Stumbling and tripping, stumbling and tripping, he treaded right across the grass, and into the creek!

Panic was all over his face! He splashed and bobbed! He wildly, waved his hands yelling for help! He gasped for air; then, swallowed a bunch of creek water! He was in need of help!

Lamar took off towards Deacon Lowe's house. He lived in the corner house at the creek. Without thinking, this twelve year old sub-super hero jumped into the creek to lend a hand to a drowning drunken man! I felt as though I could help. I had taken a 'junior' life guard course that summer, and felt I could offer the drowning victim some assistance. I was wrong! It never occurred to me that *Pockets* was bigger and stronger than I. My only concern was to render assistance. His only concern was to stay alive, no matter what!

I attempted to assist him; but, *Pockets*, repeatedly, sank beneath surface of the water, kicking his feet wildly into the air. I tried to grab hold to him; but, he fought me all the way! After struggling with him for a while, I realized something very significant. I could touch bottom!

I stood still to measure the depth. It was only chest deep on me! That meant it would be just above waist deep on him! I tried to tell *Pockets* this profound discovery; but, he was beyond listening.

Just behind the floundering victim was a water pipe that crossed the creek. It crossed just above the surface of the water. I tried to move *Pockets* towards that pipe. He resisted my every effort; but, I kept pushing him! I pushed, and pushed, until he hit the water pipe. Once he knew it was there, he grabbed hold to it, hanging on for dear life!

When Lamar and Deacon Lowe arrived, *Pockets* and I, both, were hanging onto the pipe, and were, completely, out of breath! I could tell by Lamar's expression, he wanted to ask, "How did you get in the water?" But, he didn't ask; and, I didn't tell!

Deacon Lowe was a tall and slender elderly man. He was a physically hardened man by a life of hard work. He was a well-meaning deacon in our church who, often, felt inclined to 'shush' noisy children, and pray very lengthy prayers. I never pictured him as a rescuing type of person; but, he was there to help! And, we needed his help!

Pockets and I were exhausted. He was clinging to the water pipe, mumbling. I was leaning against the water pipe, barely, able to raise my arms. Deacon Lowe eased himself down into the creek from the steep bank to offer his assistance. He tried to get *Pockets* to walk to the creek bank; but, he wouldn't let go of the pipe. Deacon Lowe had to pry his fingers loose from the water pipe. Once loosened, he was able to move *Pockets* to the creek's edge; but, that's as far as he got. *Pockets* would not attempt to climb the high bank. He wouldn't offer any efforts to help himself. We were stuck at the creek bank with a 175 pound lump of lifeless meat. He was, too, heavy for us to push, or pull, out.

Deacon Lowe was just about to start preaching to the drunken man and me, when Chief Watts arrived. Boy! Was I glad to see him! He was the chief of police, and the director of the school boy patrol program, of which I was a member.

Chief Watts took command of the situation. Having every confidence in his leadership, we, gladly, followed his directions. He decided to use the hoist that was affixed to his police car to lift the victim out of the creek. The hoist was strong enough to pull cars out of ditches, so, certainly, it should be able pull *Pockets* to safety!

Deacon Lowe put the hoist wire around *Pockets'* waist. We, both, assisted as he was hoisted up to dry ground. By this time, *Pockets* was spent! The advanced stages of drunkenness had set in. He went limp as he passed out.

Deacon Lowe assisted me out of the creek. He was mumbling something he didn't care to repeat! The old Deacon Lowe asked for no assistance and required no assistance, as he climbed the high creek bank on his own. Mrs. Lowe arrived on the scene by this time. She brought dry towels with her that felt *really* good around our shoulders. We, all, thanked her for the towels, and for calling Chief Watts.

The events of that evening have had a lasting impact upon me. It made me see that drunkenness was <u>not</u> something to be proud of. It made me aware of the Scripture that says: "*...do not be drunk with wine...but be filled with the Spirit*" (Ephesians 5:18, NKJV).

I could see that drunkenness makes people loose mental and physical control. Communication becomes unclear, and unreliable. It makes our message confusing to others. The importance of the meaning of our words we try to convey, while drunk, are compromised by the condition of the messenger.

Drunkenness may have some kind of a "rush" to it; but, the "crash" seems, hardly, worth it. And, the respect we lose is hard to restore.

Pockets continued to stay drunk. When he died of liver disease, it was said that he "lived drunk and died sober". What that meant to me was that he had wasted his life living in the delusions of drunkenness. In the end, he had to face the sobering eternal realities of his choices. What kind of choices are you making?

I Did Not Goose Granny!

I, readily, take my pen in hand to declare my complete…well, almost complete, innocence. I did not goose Granny!

There has never been any doubt that I loved my Granny with all my heart. I have always had the upmost respect for her as a woman of integrity and my beloved Granny. I would have never done anything to harm her, nor to put her into harm's way…At least, not on purpose!

I do admit that my actions that day may have seemed a bit questionable. To some, these actions may have seemed a little suspicious. But, I can *assure* you, with no reservation, whatsoever, that there was no malice, nor evil intent in my heart. Though the events of that day may have appeared, to an unknowing witness, as an overt act of goosing an old lady, I can, and do, attest that it was something altogether different!

It started out as a typical "family gathering". It was to be a weekend of fun and frolic. It was planned as a time for all of mom's brothers and sisters to bring their families together for bonding and relaxation. It was, as always, to be a joyful time of eating, playing games, catching up on family gossip and affairs…but, mostly, eating and fun!

Most of our family gatherings, usually, took place at Granny's house. There were times, however, such as this particular time, when we went on the road with our family frolicking.

Everyone, who was able to do so, rented log cabin cottages at this picturesque Georgia State Park. The park was located in the beautiful north Georgia mountains. The park's cabins surrounded a beautiful, spring-fed lake. The lake was filled with fresh, clear ice-cold water. The enchanting cabins resembled little cottages and were old, but neat and clean. Each cabin had a fire place and windows with no screens. The rustic cabins were comfortable, even without air conditioning or central heat.

The family response to this outing was so great that all of the cabins were taken by family members, except for two. Those who couldn't get a cabin, or couldn't stay with someone who did, took tents and pop-up campers.

The scenic countrified setting was beautiful. It was like a painting, or a picture, that caught all the natural beauty of a moment on canvas, or in a print. The trees seemed to move in synchronized rhythm as the breeze danced them ever-so softly. In the early morning the air was cool, which prompted an occasional fire in the stone fire place. The midday was the hottest time of day, which passed quickly by. This may have caused a brief warm moment inside the cabins; but, the opened windows were fine.

The wonderfully created surroundings added to the joyful spirit of getting reacquainted with family members. I got to play with cousins, rarely, seen. Having them in the play crowd added to the fun of playing with those I saw all the time. And, play we did! We played hard, challenging "kid" games...games that were fun and physical. Our directory of family recreation included games like "Cutthroat Croquet", "Barnyard Bad-minton" and "Woofle Ball". After dark, we played "Kick-the-Can" and "Monster Tag", which could get a little loud. When the other cabin dwellers complained, we came indoors to play our favorite board games.

The older family members played adult games, like "Canasta", "Rook" or "Setback". Late at night, adult men and older boys gathered in secret places to play "Five Card Draw" or "Blackjack" using toothpicks and matches as currency. These games were hidden away; because, they were games that could lead to delinquency...or so we were told.

While the official indoor games were going on, we snacked; and, we snacked well. We feasted on homemade cakes, pies, cookies, turnovers, as well as other goodies. Everyone shared the food that they had brought with other family members. Drinks, however, were a different issue all together. This was, strictly, a BYOB gathering, which did <u>not</u> include liquor, of any kind. Tea and coffee were constantly on the brew, and were shared openly; but, <u>Coca Cola</u>, <u>Pepsi</u>, <u>Frostie Rootbeer</u>, <u>NuGrape</u> or other sodas were restricted for the use of the family who brought them!

If your tribe ran out of sodas, you went out and bought more; or, you got special permission to take a soda from someone else, with the promise to replace it _ASAP_! Anger erupted if this procedure wasn't followed to the "t". If you asked, you were never turned away, unless it was the last soda. I guess every family has it limits on sharing. I know ours did!

Meats were combined and, primarily, grilled out. Boy! Was the food good! We grilled hamburgers, hotdogs, pork chops, hams, ribs, chicken, country sausage, goat and deer. Whatever someone brought, it got grilled!

Family vegetables were mixed together and consumed by all. The only exception to this consummation rule was the baked beans. Someone, always, brought them; and, we were, <u>always</u>, sad they did!

Granny would make two large pots of chicken and dumplings, which, rarely, made it through the first night! _Tons_ of fried chicken, prepared in a variety of ways, were brought as back up meats. You could, usually, tell whose fried chicken it was by the crust, and how well-done it came out.

On this festive outing, the beautiful lake, also, afforded us with a variety of activities. You could fish in the lake, ride paddle boats, canoe, or picnic along the shore on wooden picnic tables. If you got stranded on the lake, the Park Rangers would ride out to offer assistance and a tow to the docks.

There were several ducks and swans on the lake, especially at the picnic areas. We could not get over how friendly and tame they were. The whole duck herd would come right up to you for food, or steal it from your stash!

The lake had a nice sand beach with an area roped off for swimming. You could wade out into the water from the beach, or dive into the water from the dock. Midday was about the only time you could stand to swim. It was too cool any other time. The water was spring-fed, and ice cold! It was so cold that if you stayed in the water, too, long, you would turn purple and go numb. It was great!

On Sunday, no matter where our family circle was, it was our custom to worship with Granny. Not everyone was happy with this custom. Some tried to sneak out of it. Those who chose to break the tradition were later nabbed by Granny. They, rarely, did it again!

The friendly Park Ranger gladly gave Granny a list of Baptist churches, and wrote down directions to each. Not knowing, exactly, how long it would take to get to one of the churches, we decided to dress out early. It was *always* better to be early to church rather than late. If you were early, resident church folk were glad to see you. If came in late, resident church folk would look at you funny!

On that Sunday morning some family members dressed early enough to take a morning stroll by the scenic lake. Granny and Uncle G. headed down to the docks for such an early morning stroll. A few others followed. Not to be left out, mom decided that we should all go down to the docks and stroll, too. That way we could all enjoy the scenery together, and we could all leave together.

The lake, in the still of the early morning, was awesome! Part of it resembled a huge mirror reflecting a perfect image of the woods on the opposite bank. It was so picture perfect! You couldn't tell where the lake ended, and where the reflection began.

Other parts of the lake appeared to be steaming, almost to a boil, as a layer of fog formed on its surface. The morning surface fog only stayed for a little while; then, it was gone! It was a momentous sight that I shall, always, remember.

Everyone seemed to be gathering at the docks after their morning strolls. They came in groups of two's, three's and more. As the ensemble assembled we looked more like a group headed for a funeral than to church worship service! Some acted like it, too. They acted somber and sad; but, I really think they were just half asleep!

We stood there on the docks tugging at our collars, straightening pants and dresses, leg-shining our shoes and complaining about getting up so early. No matter what our desires may have been, you couldn't deny that we were a well dressed group gathered upon the docks.

Granny had bought a new dress for the occasion. She looked great in it! She even had on stockings! That was a rare sight. Ever since Grandpa died, she stopped shaving her legs. When she didn't want anyone to notice, she would were a pair of thick, pull-up stockings to hide her unshaven legs. As she aged, the natural firmness of her legs dwindled. The stockings had very little leg muscle to cling to; so, they kept falling down. She was, constantly, bending over and pulling them up, to keep them from noticeably sagging.

Her morning walk must have caused them to slip down, again. By the time she reached the dock, her stockings were in a bad need of adjustment. As she bent over to pull her stockings back into position, I noticed that a red wasp had landed on her *rear end*! Anyone knows that red wasps are mean critters. They pack a "wallop" when they sting; and, they attack for no apparent reason. They just liked to sting you for the fun of it!

I knew if Granny was stung, she would *really* be in for an awful hurting! In an attempt to protect my beloved Granny from a painful red wasp attack on her rear end, I decided to take rescue measures into my own hands. Without a second thought, and with no malice intent, I, strategically, positioned myself behind Granny. Taking careful aim, I gave the huge red wasp a big thump!

In order to insure a direct hit on the red wasp, I had to get close to that part of Granny's body that was sticking up. I guess, I got, too, close! I ended up thumping her, too!

Events accelerated from that point on! I thumped. Granny yelped. Her arms spread open wide as she sprang up and, involuntarily, vaulted forward into the icy lake!

It all happened so fast! Everyone was stunned! No one knew, exactly, what had just taken place. Had Granny slipped? Had she suffered a heart attack? Had she been sipping on her cough remedy, and lost her balance? No one knew for sure!

After a stunned pause, dad and few uncles jumped into the lake to assist Granny. Aunt 'L' started crying as she screamed, "More help! More help! Get more help!"

Mom was directing the lake rescue issuing forceful commands from the dock. Everyone who wasn't, directly, involved in the rescue attempt gathered about to see what they could see, whispering, "What's going on? What's happening?"

I stood motionless. Frozen in amazement! How could a simple rescue mission go so wrong! I stared at my thumping fingers as I pondered, "Did I do that!?"

The Park Rangers rushed out to make sure that Granny was rescued properly, and without injury. They wrapped her, and her rescuers, in towels and blankets. They offered to take her to a hospital, or have the emergency unit to come out to examine her; but, she wouldn't hear of it! She *insisted* that she was alright.

Shivering from the cold, and, possibly, a little from the shock, Granny was escorted back to her cabin. Everyone followed. Her cabin wasn't big enough for everyone to fit into it. Those who couldn't fit into her cabin gathered out-side her front entrance. It was obvious that this matter was not over, yet!

Mom and her sisters helped Granny get dried off and presentable. Some were still crying over the thought of, almost, losing Granny. Others were snickering, silently of course.

Granny kept insisting that she was alright, which gave us all a great sense of relief. After things got settled down, and most of the crying dried up, the official tribal investigation began! Granny was asked what she remembered happening. All she could remember was bending over to pull up her stockings, when *something* "popped" her on her derriere. I'm not sure that any of us had ever realized, until that moment, that Granny was so *gooseable*! How could I have known that she was so sensitive…back there!

It never occurred to me that she might think someone would, actually, 'goose' her, while she was in such an embarrassing position. The thought of someone, purposely, doing that outraged everyone, even me! I would have, definitely, jumped on anyone who purposely goosed Granny.

With each passing moment the investigation got more complicated. After a while, it turned ugly! Each adult was questioned about where they were and what they saw. After getting little to go on, the inquisitors turned towards the children. Now, I don't know why, exactly; but, it always seemed that when children were to be questioned, I was among the first. In this case, however, I was ready to give my eyewitness account of what had *actually* happened. I was anxious to clear this matter up. I was convinced that everyone would understand. Certainly, the true intentions of my heart would vindicate me!

Uncle 'G' was the 'bailiff' sent out to summon the children witnesses. When I volunteered to go first, his response was, "Why am I *not* surprised?"

Though his attitude was puzzling to me, his response seemed to sum up the adult consensus. I, immediately, sensed that I was headed for trouble! No one wanted to listen to what I had to say; but, I offered my account anyway. I was convinced that _truth_ would prevail.

When Uncle 'G' suggested to the family tribunal to hear what I had to say, he was, almost, "booed" out of court! Still, he insisted that if I had some information on the matter they should all hear it.

Aunt 'L' didn't have to hear my information. She convicted me of the crime on the spot! She wanted my head on a platter! She, angrily, accused me of all kinds of unrelated bad stuff. In her mind, I was guilty of mistreating her son, the disappearance of a cat named "Puffy", the disappearance of some guy named, Jimmy Hauffa, and the malicious, devious action of 'goosing' Granny into the lake!

Mom got more angry at her sister than at me! In her motherly fashion, she asked me, "Do you know what happened to Granny?"

My willing acknowledgement of knowing what happened seemed to shock them! I attempted no cover up, nor did I try to blame anyone else. Some thought no further information was needed. One aunt went out in search of a good "switch"! My fate seemed to be sealed! No one seemed willing to embrace the full picture. Their angered, violent response surprised me. I _wanted_ them to know what had happened. I was convinced that I had done nothing wrong! At least, I intended to do nothing wrong!

I knew what a red wasp could do. I had been stung by the red menace before. I would have, willingly, taken the accidental icy plunge into the lake over the painful sting of the dreaded red wasp! Anyone who had been stung by one might would have agreed with me. I had wanted to save Granny that painful agony. What happened beyond saving Granny the misery of such a terrible sting was, merely, coincidentally accidental!

I explained it to them as, carefully, as I could. As I laid it out for them, I could see many doubting nods and head shakes. They refused to see it as a rescue operation gone wrong. I had to tell the story several times. Each version was _exactly_ the same. I never wavered from the truth.

A few of the relatives took the opportunity to point to some other times, when I might *not* have been so innocent. They doubted my sincerity. They challenged my intent. They questioned the accuracy of the events as I had stated them. They wanted to pin stuff on me that I hadn't, even, thought about doing! _Then_, it got nasty!

Through it all, my story stayed the same. I held true to my good intentions. I stood as firm as a ten year old could stand before an angry mob. When the truth failed to exonerate me, I cried! These tears were genuine. These were not false tears offered to gain pity, or to soften hardened hearts. These were true tears shed for the sake of truth.

While mom and dad were keeping the others at bay, Uncle 'G' made sure no one could get hold of a rope, or any tar and feathers! After watching me carefully throughout the inquisition, Aunt 'ML', finally, saw the genuineness of my heart in my words. She, boldly, proclaimed, "I believe Ronnie!"

Her words were heaven sent to my ears. The majority, however, was not convinced. The only _one_ who really mattered to me, was Granny. I wanted her to believe me most of all. I didn't want her to think that I would, purposely, do something to hurt her, or cause her to nearly have a heart attack. Also, as the matriarch of the clan, what *she* believed would settle the matter.

The debate seemed endless. Finally, it was put to Granny. She thought for a moment; then, she motioned for me to come to her. We stepped into the kitchen area to speak privately. Knowing me, and my past experiences, made her a bit cautious. She had some genuine doubts, especially, since the 'fact-finding' team, that had been commissioned to search the docks, found no trace of red wasps...not a single critter, nor a nest of any kind!

Bombarded with unsubstantiated accusations, and a lack of physical evidence for my defense, Granny wasn't sure what to think! She stooped down and got nose to nose with me. Eyeball to eyeball, she demanded the truth! Nose to nose, eyeball to eyeball, I said, "Granny,

I ain't never told the truth like I'm telling you, now! And, the truth is…a red wasp was on your butt!"

Her frown turned into a half-smile. She smooched her lips, and nodded her head. In that moment she had made her decision. With her arm around my shoulders, we returned to the courtroom area. She announced to the family tribunal that I was innocent of ill intent. All family charges were dropped. All punishment suggestions were suspended. Granny did insist on one thing. She put both of her hands on my face like blinders on a horse. With my undivided attention, she said, "Next time, warn me <u>before</u> you attempt to rescue me!"

Though the official family ruling that day was "innocent", I was branded as the <u>one</u> who 'goosed' Granny! To this day, I have to declare my innocence at family gatherings. My complete vindication may never come, until I stand before the <u>Judgment Seat of Christ</u>! That's where the secrets of all hearts will be revealed; and, the works of all Christians will be tested.

Even then, it may take the Lord, <u>Himself</u>, to declare, "Ronnie did not 'goose' his Granny!" Even if He was to proclaim it to be so, some relatives, still, would still not accept my innocence. That won't matter at that point, for the Lord will <u>know</u> that my motivations were pure. To Him, motivation matters (Proverbs 14:14; Luke 6:45). He will know then, as He knows now, that my intent, my motivations were for good…not for goosing!

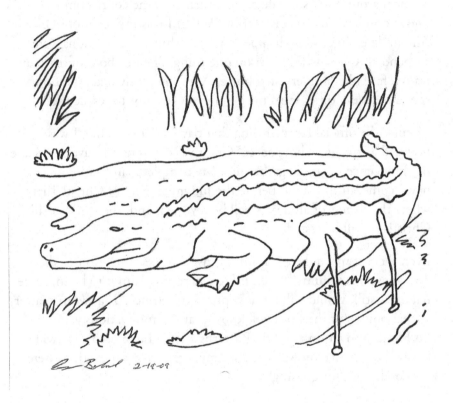

THAT'S ALL...FOR NOW!

A self-compiled GLOSSARY
of
SWAMP terms,
COASTAL expressions
And
Unique sayings
from other REGIONS OF GEORGIA

By the

Swamp ponderer

(it may help!)

Agape - Undeserved love, unmerited love. God's love.

Ain't - "Am not", sometimes, "is not"; "are not"; "have not"; or, "has not".

Airhead - A not-so-smart person; one who acts as if they have "air" in the space where their brain should be. A blond woman's answer to being referred to as a "*blond*".

Alligator snapper - A snapping turtle with an elongated snout that may reach 150 pounds, and up to 5 feet in length. A nasty-looking critter that won't turn loose after he has "snapped", like some folks you know.

Armadillo - A burrowing critter with a hard exterior shell, and armored head to tail, with long nail-like paws. Believed to have migrated from Texas, along the Gulf States to the Okefenokee Swamp areas in the 1950's. Some people eat them and call them "possum on the half-shell".

Average class - A class in grade school made up of students who were considered to be "average", or nearly average, in ability.

Barf - To through up…vomit!

Befuddle - To confuse, or perplex.

Bested - To be gotten the best of; or, outdone by another.

Betwixt - Between, in-between.

Black wood bee - A black bee resembling the bumble bee in size, but completely black in color, who bores holes into soft wood to   make its home. It, often, will invade fresh-cut lumber used in construction. A very aggressive bee.

Blade grass - A wiry grass with thin leaves sharp as razor blades that will slice through skin easily if brushed against.

Bobcat - A common North American lynx with a short, stubby tail which is natural for the breed, and hangs out in the woods and swampy areas.

Bogus - 1.) Something fake, not real or genuine. 2.) Bad news, tough luck.

Braino class - A class in grade school made up of students who were considered smart, or who had gone to kindergarten and proven that they were smart.

Boondoggle - 1.) A large amount. 2.) A lot of trivial, useless, or wasteful material or activity.

Border grass - Any of different, distinctive grasses that are used to outline, or define, a grassy area, or a portion of a yard. It is not desirable for the whole yard; because, it usually grows in clumps or patches. If left unattended, or uncontrolled, it could invade other areas of the yard in spots or patches.

Britches - 1.) A pair of pants. 2.) "stringing britches" refers to stringing large pole beans to hang them out to dry into hard beans for cooking.

Brittled - Made brittle, or the act of making brittle.

Brush arbor - An outside covered area with open walls and a thatched covering for a roof, used for church meetings, public meetings or community gatherings.

B.S.U. - The Baptist Student Union, a college club of Christian-minded students sponsored by the Georgia Baptist Convention and the Southern Baptist Convention.

Bunch - Several items you might could hold in your hand, or both hands.

Buzzard (turkey buzzard) - Any of several types of large North American vultures.

Caniption fit - Close to a "hissy fit". (Sometimes, confused as the same thing.) An emotional outburst that could include screaming, stomping, crying and hissing.

Cherry bomb - A large, red, ball-shaped firecracker, about the size of a large marble.

Critter - Any animal, usually, the size of a dog, or smaller.

Crud - 1.) Bad, nasty, ugly stuff. 2.) Sickness that includes runny nose, clogged throat   and excessive drainage.

Cruddy - 1.) Of bad, nasty, ugly quality. 2.) Worse than bad.

Cabbage palmetto - A fan-shaped cabbage palm native to coastal regions of the southern United States.

Caboodle - A significant collection…the whole lot!

Cahoot(s) - In partnership with; in league with a sinister plan, person or entity.

Caldron - A large iron kettle, or boiling pot, often heated by fire wood stoked around its bottom. Used for cooking food and cleaning clothes and objects.

Carp - A large fresh water fish that eats anything and everything! Often used in man-made and natural ponds to keep water clear of debris and dead stuff. A scavenger fish.

Catboat - A sailboat having a single mast, far forward, carrying a single large sail extended by a boom, and light drafted.

Chatterbox - One who talks idly, all the time and doesn't seem to stop, nor know when   to shut up!

Chicken-livered - A fainthearted, cowardly person.

Chigger - A six-legged mite that sucks blood from critters, and people, causing intense irritation.

Cock-and-bull story - An extravagant, extremely hard to believe, story told as absolute truth.

Conch - A large, spiral-shaped shelled sea snail. The meat is eaten in stews or fried in strips. The shell is used for collecting and jewelry.

Coon - A raccoon -- nothing more!

Coot - A harmless, simple, sometimes cute, often old, person. A colorful personality.

Cootie - A body louse (bug). Also, used to refer to the "creepy crawlies".

Corny - Something that is stupid, doesn't make a lot of sense; but, could be cute.

Cotter pin (carter pin) - A half-round metal strip bent into a pin whose ends can be flared after insertion through a slot, or hole.

Cowlick - A tuft of hair growing in a different direction from the rest and, often, turned up and hard to manage or blend in.

Crawdads (crawfish, crayfish) - A freshwater smaller version of a spiny lobster used for fish bait and for eating.

Croaker - A fish (salt water or fresh water) that makes a croaking, or grunting, sound. Good for eating!

Crud, the - A bad cold with a lot of congestion, nagging cough, running nose, watering eyes and a lot leakage that makes you feel like "crud"!

Cut-and-dried - Results according to a perfect plan, set procedure or a certain formula.

Daddy longlegs - A non-poisonous, friendly spider with a small body and very long legs, which give you the "creepies" when it crawls on you.

De____ - Denotes *the* as in: Denote = the note. Despair = the spare tire. Despot = the spot. Depot = the pot. Design = the sign. Detour = the tour; *ect.*

Diddlysquat - 1.) Useless matter or material. 2.) When someone has a nature call and squats to poo poo!

Dixie - Name for the southern states of the United States made famous in a song, *Dixie*, by Daniel D. Emmett, 1859.

"Does a fish have a water-tight butt?" - Used to state an obvious, or more than obvious, fact.

"Don't count your eggs before breakfast!" - Has the same meaning as: "Don't count your chickens before they hatch!"

"Don't dismount a gator until you are through with the ride!" - A little more severe in meaning than: "Don't change horses in the middle of the stream."

Doofus - A really stupid person; or, someone who says a really stupid thing.

Doornail - A large-headed nail use to mount doors. (NOTE: The phrase: **"deader than a doornail"** meant that something or someone was *really* dead!)

Doubting Thomas - 1.) Thomas, the Apostle of   Jesus, doubted the resurrection of Jesus until he had proof of it (John 20:24-29). 2.) A habitually doubting, or doubtful, person.

Dummo class - A class in grade school made up of students who were considered to be less than average, and not smart at all!

Dutch oven - A cast iron kettle with a tight, sometimes flat, cover that is used for baking in an open fire, or using hot coals.

Dyed-in-the-wool - 1.) Uncompromising. 2.) An exact replica, or reproduction.

'em - Them.

Fantasy (phantasy) - The free play of creative imagination.

"fess(ed) up" - 1.) To confess. 2.) To make known a truth that may carry unfavorable consequences with its revelation.

Fit as a fiddle (fit as a fritter) - 1.) Ready and prepared. 2.) Practiced and ready to go.

Fit to be tied! - Angry, or irritated...a lot!

Five-and-ten (five-and-dime; 5 & 10) - A variety store selling articles priced at five and ten cents, or as low as possible.

Five-finger discount - To steal something.

"fixer upper" - A person who "fixes" you up with a remedy, a cure or a date.

Flapdoodle - Something that is nonsense!

Flapjack - A pancake.

Funnies (funny paper) - The comic strip in the daily newspaper, and the comic section of the Sunday paper.

Gator - Alligator.

Gator-bait - 1.) Usually, a pretty girl much younger than you, and whose family is very protective...militantly protective! 2.) You, once someone angry with you catches up to you!

"Gave up the ghost" - 1.) To die. 2.) To give out, completely.

"gee and haw" - "gee" = turn to the right

"haw" = turn to the left

"gee and haw" = getting both sides of an issue.

Georgia cracker - 1.) First coined by a northern newspaper writer who wrote about the men harvesting the trees from the Okefenokee Swamp in the latte 1800's. They "cracked" their whips to drive the oxen as they pulled giant cypress trees from the swamp. 2.) Someone who is quick-witted, able to snap back with a verbal whip. 3.) A native of Georgia.

Gewgaw - A trinket, or a showy but inexpensive object, especially an ornament.

Gofer - 1.) Someone who goes for (goes-fer) this and that. 2.) A person who retrieves items.

Gonna - "going to".

Gooey - 1.) Something that is real sticky and may ooze a bit. 2.) A messy substance.

Goose - To poke, or pinch, between the buttocks, un-expectantly!

Gruffy - 1.) Hoarse; rough and hoarse in sound. 2.) Rough and stern in manner, speech or aspect.

Grunters - People who grunt their answers and/or comments, expecting you to know what they mean.

Hankering - A yearning for, or desire for.

"hard as pulling hen's teeth" - Referring to something that is very difficult, or next to impossible.

Heads up! - A call to instant awareness, like, "Watch out!"

Heebie-jeebies - 1.) Shaking, skin crawling effect. 2.) Extreme nervousness; or, the nervous jitters!

Hex - 1.) To cause something to happen as if by an evil spell or spirit. 2.) To jinx someone.

"hissy fit" - Closely related to a "caniption fit". An emotional outburst of disapproval and condemnation. Close to a nervous break-down with explosive emotional outbursts. Often, includes laying down and squirming on the floor.

Holy mackerel! (Holy moley!) - A phrase that means much the same as: "Oh, my gosh!", revealing surprise and shock.

Hoodoo - Something, or someone, who brings bad luck, or puts bad luck on you!

Hootch (shine, swamp water, moonshine) - 1.) An intoxicating liquor that is home-   brewed. 2.) Home-distilled whiskey.

Hose pipe   1.) A flexible tube for conveying fluids, like water, from a faucet. 2.) A garden hose.

"Hot dog!" - An expression of complete joy! (When said without quotation marks it means food.)

Humongous - Larger than large, and beyond huge; and, enormous doesn't touch it!

hunky-dory (hunky-dorie) - 1.) Conveying that everything is OK, alright. 2.) An endorsement of approval, being quite satisfied. 3.) Fine.

Hussy - A lewd, brazen woman.

Icky - 1.) Dirty, messy. 2.) Messy/sticky with sweat. 3.) Not a good situation.

Idee - Idea.

Ilk (y) - 1.) Rotten stuff. 2.) Smelly stuff. 3.) Rotten and smelly stuff!

Imagona - "I am going to _____"

Indian pudding - An old Indian pudding mix of cornmeal, milk and molasses, or honey.

Infighting - Fighting (physical or verbal) within a family, or group. Often, vicious, but stays within the family, or group.

Insight - 1.) In the field of vision. 2.) Ability to see intuitively; to discern; to rightly divide.

Iotta - "I ought to___"

"I've a mind to____" - Means the same as: "I ought to_____".

"I've got a bone to pick with you!" - Means: "I've got something to seriously discuss with you that you may not like."

Jalopy - A rundown, old automobile or truck.

Jawbreaker - 1.) A round, ball-like hard candy. 2.) A word too difficult to pronounce.

Jenney - A female donkey or mule.

Jezebel - 1.) A ruthless, shameless woman. 2.) A hussy!

Johnboy boat (johnboat) - A narrow flat-bottomed, square ended, light boat propelled by pole, paddle or light motor. Mostly, used in shallow, inland waters.

Johnny-on-the-spot - A person who is present and ready to perform duties, to do tasks, or to respond to an emergency.

Joint grass - A coarse creeping grass used a fodder and as a soil binder...<u>NOT</u> for smoking!

Jug player - A person who blows into a jug to get a musical note, or tone, that changes with the various volumes of liquid substance within the jug. (Some say that the substance in the jug itself makes a difference in the quality of the musical sound. Those that say that, say that moonshine makes the best music!)

Juice harp - A small lyre-shaped instrument that, when placed between the teeth, gives off strange tones from a metal tongue struck by the finger. The tones are affected by the amount of spit that accumulates on the device while being played. It is often accompanied by a jug player. (NOTE: This device is also called a *Jew's harp*.)

Juke joint - A small, inexpensive, hole-in-the-wall eating place that allows alcoholic drinks, and dancing to music from a jukebox.

Julep (mint julep) - A drink consisting of bourbon (or moonshine whiskey), molasses and mint served over crushed ice in a tumbler.

June bug (June beetle) - A rather large leaf-eating beetle that flies, chiefly, in late spring, and has white grub larvae that live in the soil and feed off of roots of grasses and other plants. Some say the beetle makes a distinctive sound in late evenings conveying various meanings. Some use them to predict weather patterns and/or future events.

Kakapoo - Same as manure, or something smelly like manure.

Keelhaul - 1.) To rebuke severely. 2.) To punish harshly. 3.) To smack, up side of the   head!

Kickapoo joy juice – A refreshing drink that is sometimes mixed with moonshine; but, not necessarily alcoholic at all.

Kinfolk - 1.) Relatives. 2.) People who are kin to you in   *some* way.

'Know how' – Knowing how to do something with special skills.

Ladybug - A small, hemispherical, colored beetle that feeds on larvae and adult insects. Many states imported them to help control aphids and mosquitoes, and are protected in many states by law.

Lame duck - A wounded duck that needs to be put out of its misery (and on my plate for supper!).

"Layover to catch meddlers!" - 1.) Concealed bait put out to catch people, or critters, that meddle in your affairs, or stuff. 2.) Can be used as an evasive answer to a question you don't want to answer.

Lean-to - A one-sloped frame made of cut sticks and covered with canvas, branches, palmetto fans, or some other covering.

Libation - A drink containing alcohol.

Love bug - A black bug with orange on its wings that mates in September-October in south Georgia and north Florida by linking together with its mate. They travel in huge swarms when linked together which   makes them very slow and easily smashed onto an automobiles' windshield, clogged into radiators and splattered upon hoods. The smashed residue is hard to clean off and can stop up radiators and dissolve paint finishes.

Low-country boil - A mixture of clams, oysters, shrimp, crawdads, sausage and corn-on-the-cob cooked in a spiced bouillabaisse.

M-80 - A firecracker larger than a cherry bomb with louder bang and more destructive power.

Make-believe - To pretend.

Mason-Dixon Line - The boundary line between the Northern and Southern states, defining North and South during the *Civil War*.

Matriarch - 1.) A woman who rules, or has influence over, her family. 2.) A venerable old woman.

Mayfly - A slender, fragile-winged, light-colored, short-lived flying insect which is drawn to a light in the evening, and can be used as bait for fishing.

Monkey grass - A long, thin leafed grass with two shades of green, often used as border grass, but is a very aggressive grass invading other grassy areas if left unattended or uncontrolled.

Monkey wrench - 1.) A wrench with one fixed and one adjustable jaw at right angles to a straight handle. 2.) Something that disrupts a flow of action or motion.

"More than one way to skin a cat" – It originally came from stating that there was more than one way to skin a catfish. It became to mean that there is more than one solution to a problem, more than just one course of action, or more than one way to attain a desired goal.

Mrs. (Mr.) Grundy - One marked by prudish conventionality in personal conduct.

Muck - 1.) Soft barnyard manure. 2.) Slimy dirt or filth. 3.) To dress with, or be dirty with, manure or some foul, smelly substance.

Murky - 1.) Intense darkness, or gloominess. 2.) Thickness and heaviness of air, fog or mist.

Nanny - 1.) A female mother goat. 2.) A woman who mothers other's kids.

Nickenpoop A silly-minded person.

Nicknack, Knickknack - 1.) A small item of food. 2.) A small trivial item intended as an ornament, or whatnot.

Night crawler - A large worm found on the soil surface at night and used as fishing bait.

Nimkenpoop – Same as "Nickenpoop".

Nitpicky - 1.) To criticize something for some petty reason. 2.) To complain about insignificant details.

Noggin - A person's head.

"no how" - "Not at all".

Noreaster - A storm, strong wind, or gusty gale coming from the northeast and, probably, cold and bad.

Nuff - 1.) Enough. 2.) A degree or quantity that satisfies. 3.) A tolerable degree or amount.

Numskull - 1.) A dull-witted, or stupid person. 2.) A thick-headed, or muddle-headed person.

Oblige - To bind to, by a favor, act of kindness or service rendered.

Oftly – Often or often enough.

Old cuss(es) - Old, onerous, critical people that may, or may not, cuss.

Omagosh - "Oh! My gosh!"

Oodles, oodlins - A great quantity; a lot!

Oomph – 1.) An utterance, usually, by a man at the sight of an attractive woman. 2.) A grunt made for communication purposes.

Ooze - 1.) A soft, moist deposit, like mud, slime, marsh or bog, that flows slowly in a gooey mass. 2.) To move slowly like an ooze.

Organic - Someone who works on, or who can play an organ.

Over against - As opposed to, or in contrast with.

Palmetto - A low-growing, fan-shaped palm bush.

Panther - A leopard type of fierce cat. (NOTE: In our area, they were brown.)

Pastoring - The act of being the pastor, spiritual leader and head administrator of a church.

Patriarch - 1.) A man who rules, or has influence over, his family. 2.) A venerable old man.

Piles - The condition of one afflicted with hemorrhoids.

Pompano - A salt water fish, good for eating, that is bluish, or greenish, with a yellow tail.

Poo poo - Human, or animal, waste material.

Pooh-pooh - An expression of contempt, scorn or disapproval.

Poot - The relieving of body gases with no smell.

Ponder - 1.) To weigh heavily in the mind. 2.) To think about, or consider at great length, quietly, soberly and deeply.

Ponderance - 1.) That which is being pondered. 2.) The result of pondering.

Possum - Opossum.

Privy – 1.)Originally, an outhouse toilet. Later, a bathroom toilet. 2.)

Privileged information that was revealed while setting in an outhouse, or alone in contemplation.

Pucker brush - A brush to shield you when you had need of a restroom in the wild.

Pulpwood - A wood, like pine or spruce, used in making pulp for paper production.

Push-plow - A hand-held plowing device that uses no animals to pull it. Its plowing effect only results from the power of the person pushing the plow.

Push-pull - An object/person being pushed at one end and pulled at the other end.

Pussy foot - 1.) To refrain from committing oneself. 2.) To tread, or move, warily and/or stealthily. 3.) Stalking like a cat.

Put about - To change course or direction.

Rastle (wrastle) - 1.) To contend with another by grappling with, striving to trip and/or throw down an opponent. 2.) A perverted form of wrestling with little, or no rules, and could include biting and spitting in the opponent's eye. (NOTE: This kind of "rastling" could be done for fun, or entertainment, or to settle a matter between two, or more, people.) 3.) To contend with making a decision in an agonizing manner.

Reckon - 1.) To count, estimate or compute. 2.) To regard, or consider as being the fact. 3.) To make an appraisal and settle the account, or matter. 4.) To make a judgment based upon revealed facts.

Red breast - A red-breasted bream, or a reddish bellied sunfish pretty to look at and good for eating.

Ringworm - A fungi characterized by it ring-shaped patches on the skin. Common in our area for a long time. Originally, thought to be caused by a worm under the skin.

"run by" - The act of running by someone you are afraid of, or by a scary place, and not stopping. In the "run by" you might throw something, or say something, but do not stop, pause or wait for a response.

Salve - A healing ointment, sometimes homemade, sometimes store-bought.

Sandy loam - A soil mixture low in clay and high in sand and silt.

Sassafras tea - A tea made from boiling the roots of the sassafras tree or bush, then sweetened to taste. The natural flavoring for root beer that comes from the same sassafras root.

Saved - 1.) Life has been spared by someone. 2.) Eternal Life has been received thus *saving* one from hell.

Scum - 1.) A gooey layer of slimy, foul covering as in *pond scum*. 2.) Someone who relishes in living in a low-class, filthy manner.

Seine - A large net with sinkers on one edge and floats on the other used vertically to enclose fish when its ends are brought together, or drawn ashore.

Self-tackle-ization - Tripping over oneself, or over nothing apparent, or nothing at all. (NOTE: The phrase was made popular by an early entertainer and adapted for swamp and coastal use.)

Shotgun marriage - A forced marriage, or one required due to pregnancy. (Also called a "Swamp Military Wedding"; because, guns were usually present.)

Shotgun seat - 1.) <u>The</u> most prized seat, usually, next to the window in an automobile. 2.) The seat next to the driver for observation and danger detection.

Slaphappy - 1.) Punch-drunk. 2.) Recklessly happy with delirium.

slapsilly - Reckless silliness with no regard for the consequences.

"Slap the snot out of you!" - A derogatory phrase that means: "I will slap you so hard that it will knock the non-dripping snot out of your nose!" It can, also, be used in ridicule or taunting or kidding around.

"Slap you silly!" - Means that a person will slap all the sense out of another...A derogatory statement.

Slush(ed) - To make one's way through soft, semi-liquid mud, or mire.

Smirk - To smile in a quirky way, almost as if you didn't mean to, or you didn't want anyone else to know.

Smith - A blacksmith, or someone who works with a blacksmith.

Smores - A delicacy of roasted marshmallows smashed around a piece of soft chocolate, stuffed between two graham cracker wafers...m-m-m-good!

Snickering(s) - To laugh, snort or sneer in a light, covert or partly suppressed manner.

Snipe hunting - 1.) A game that includes a croker sack, flashlight, a stick and a person placed alone in a scary place. The flashlight is placed within the croker sack while the person holds the sack open holding the stick. He is told that the snipe will run into the sack seeking the light, then he/she is to beat the snipe to death with the stick. Usually, it is used as an act of initiation. 2.) Hunting in the march for a real snipe: a small game bird found in marshy areas resembling a woodcock.

Snooker - 1.) One who say persnickety, harsh things and often ending in a gesture of derision consisting of thumbing of the nose. 2.) To beguile someone.   **Snookered** - To be the object of beguilement; being '*had*' in an embarrassing way.

Snuffer - Someone who uses snuff (a pulverized, powdered tobacco) inhaled through the nostrils, or placed between the tongue and cheek.

Souwester - A storm, or gale, from the southwest, usually wet, and destructive.

Specter - A visible disembodied haunting spirit, meaner and madder than a ghost, most of the time.

Sploshing - To walk through thick mud or mire splashing residue everywhere.

Spoof - A light humorous parody.

Spook - An accidental and colorful ghost that has a tendency to startle people...if you believe in that sort of thing.

Still - Equipment put together in order to distill liquors, moonshine, hootch, swamp water, *etc.* illegally, or for personal use.

Stinkbug - A greenish bug that looks fearsome and emit's a disagreeable order.

Stumped - 1.) Puzzled over something. 2.) Perplexed.

Sunerlater - "Sooner or later".

Sugarcane - A large stalked, fibrous grass whose sweet juice is squeezed out and used for a drinking beverage, making sugar and making syrup.

Swamp smart - 1.) Someone who lives life reading between the lines. 2.) The same meaning as being "street smart", except in swamp terms and ways.

Tabby - A concrete substance that early settlers along the coast used in building structures and foundations that would last. Called "coastal concrete", tabby is made of equal proportions of oyster shells, sand, lime and water.

Tenders - People who attend something, anything.

Thwack - A hard blow to the body, or some part of the body, like the head.

Thwart - To block or defeat a sinister plan, or another's actions or purpose.

Toadfish - An ugly salt water fish with large pelvic fins, a large thick head, a wide mouth, scaleless, slimy skin and ugly as all get out!

Tongue-lashing - 1.) To chide or reprove harshly. 2.) A very strong reprimand; a good talking to; or, a strong telling off!

Tuffed - 1.) To be tough, strong through an ordeal. 2.) To outlast the adversity.

Twerp - A silly, obstinate, contemptible person.

"Ugly as all get out" - Very ugly.

"Ugly as home-made sin" - Very, very...very ugly, physically or socially.

Unchurched - Those who do not attend a church of any kind...ever.

Upchuck - To throw up; vomit.

"Up to snuff" - In good shape.

Vamp - 1.) A woman who uses her charm to seduce and exploit men. 2.) A Jezebel with an agenda!

Vex - 1.) To bring trouble, distress and/or agitation to another. 2.) To puzzle, baffle   or confound.

Visquane - A plastic covering used in wrapping large products to help weather-proof it. It, also, can be used in gardening as a   grass shield.

Wallop - 1.) A powerful blow, or to thrash soundly. 2.) To beat by a wide margin. 3.) An emotional, or psychological 'gut punch'. A sucker punch.

Walking cactus - A small ball-shaped, or oblong-shaped cactus with long, thick, barbed spines that latch on, or prick very easily. Often unseen until they attached themselves to a person, critter or thing, which makes it appear as though it snuck up on you, or walked over to you.

"Well, butter my butt and call me a biscuit!" - A statement of surprise at a fact previously unknown.

Whimp - 1.) Someone with no backbone. A spineless person. 2.) A person who gives in then complains and/or protests in an irritating manner.

Widow's perch (widow's walk, widow's watch) - A railed observation platform, or deck, atop a coastal house where a woman watched for the return of her husband from the sea.

Willy-nilly - 1.) A weak person. 2.) Driven by compulsion with no course, or choice, in direction.

Whatnot - A small item, or collection of items, for display as a conversation piece.

W.M.U. - The Women's Missionary Union, a Southern Baptist missionary support organization started by Annie Armstrong and made up of ladies involved in missionary support and belonging to a Southern Baptist Convention church.

Woofle ball – (Sometimes called "whiffle ball") A plastic ball with holes cut into it to help it make a woofling sound and change directions when thrown. The object is to hit the ball with a plastic bat when it is pitched. Regular baseball rules apply during play, except when the *"stingray rule"* is applied. (NOTE: The *"stingray rule"* allows a player to through the plastic ball directly at a runner making him out if it hits him before the runner makes it to a base.)

Yeller - 1.) Several times brighter than yellow. 2,) Beyond yellow; and/or, yellow in a wilder dimension!

Yonder - 1.) *At that* place; *to that* place; or, *over there at that* place. 2.) A farther, more distant place that is barely in view, or just out of view.

Yo-yo - 1.) A rounded spindle device made to fall and rise by the winding and unwinding of an attached string. It is used as a device for fun and recreation. 2.) A person who goes back and forth in trying to make a decision.

Yummy - 1.) Very delicious. 2.) Highly attractive, or very pleasing to the sight.

Zillion - 1.) More than a centillion (the largest of numbers in the American and British systems). 2.) A large indeterminate amount. 3.) More than you can handle. 4.) More than I want to count!